From Kathmandu
to Kilimanjaro

From Kathmandu to Kilimanjaro

A Mother-Daughter Memoir

MARGARET ELIZABETH LOVETT WILSON
and SYLVIE WILSON EMMANUEL

Edited by Patricia D. Beaver

Patricia D. Beaver, 2020

McFarland & Company, Inc., Publishers
Jefferson, North Carolina

Library of Congress Cataloguing-in-Publication Data

Names: Wilson, Margaret Elizabeth Lovett, 1897–1985, author. | Emmanuel, Sylvie Wilson, 1935– author. | Beaver, Patricia D., editor.
Title: From Kathmandu to Kilimanjaro : a mother-daughter memoir / Margaret Elizabeth Lovett Wilson and Sylvie Wilson Emmanuel ; edited by Patricia D. Beaver.
Description: Jefferson, North Carolina : McFarland & Company, Inc., Publishers, 2020 | Includes bibliographical references and index.
Identifiers: LCCN 2020031916 | ISBN 9781476683003 (paperback) | ♾ ISBN 9781476640945 (ebook)
Subjects: LCSH: Wilson, Margaret Elizabeth Lovett, 1897–1985. | Wilson, Margaret Elizabeth Lovett, 1897–1985—Travel. | Emmanuel, Sylvie Wilson, 1935 | Tanzania—History—To 1964. | Great Britain. Colonial Service—Biography. | Great Britain. Colonial Medical Service—Biography. | Moshi (Tanzania)—Biography. | Physicians—Tanzania—Biography. | Teachers—Tanzania—Biography. | Wilson family.
Classification: LCC DT443.5.W55 A2 2020 | DDC 967.8/0309252 [B]—dc23
LC record available at https://lccn.loc.gov/2020031916

British Library cataloguing data are available

ISBN (print) 978-1-4766-8300-3
ISBN (ebook)978-1-4766-4094-5

On the cover: *insets* The authors with their Ford V8 and on Mount Meru; *background* Snow covered Mount Kilimanjaro (© 2020 Shutterstock)

Printed in the United States of America

McFarland & Company, Inc., Publishers
Box 611, Jefferson, North Carolina 28640
www.mcfarlandpub.com

Contents

Acknowledgments

This project would not have come to fruition without Patricia Bartlett's persistence and diligence in the details—helping develop interview questions for Sylvie, arranging for tape recorders, scanning and sending documents from Tanzania to the editor in the U.S. She spent many hours devotedly with Sylvie, taping letters and conducting interviews, and with the editor, proofreading and searching place names, archaic terms, and medical terminology. Christina Dideriksen then carefully transcribed interviews with Sylvie from Tanzania and North Carolina that provided primary texts for this work. Sandra Ballard provided wise counsel at the very beginning of this project and read and edited the manuscript as we neared completion. Gillian Berchowitz provided valuable consultation and encouragement. Margaret McFadden provided resources on turn of the century women in higher education in England. Michael Moore suggested historical sources on Nepal. Eric Karshmer pointed the way to global malaria scholarship and John Bartlett provided critical reading of our interpretation of Peggy's medical terminology and the experiences of Peggy and Donald Wilson in Tanzania. Richard Watson provided African history sources, as did Michael McGinnis for Tanzania. Nic's nephew Gregory Emmanuel provided Emmanuel family history, genealogy, and family naming patterns. Chris Drakeley aided the search for Wilson and Wilson bibliography. Dear friends and family, especially my husband Bob White, encouraged this project and listened to my tales of wonder.—*Patricia D. Beaver*

A Note to Readers

by Sylvia Wilson Emmanuel

My mother wrote a memoir after she retired. I have always regretted that I didn't help her have it published, as she had such an interesting life. But when I met Patricia Beaver, I knew that having her involved as editor of this project would make it happen. My friend Patricia Bartlett has helped so much with recording and organizing and printing letters. None of it has been made easy by the fact that both my parents and their families kept all their letters, including my grandfather's letter to his grandmother in 1867 when he was eight years old!

I often sit on our verandah looking at our wonderful view of Kilimanjaro. So much of my life and my husband Nic's has been lived here. We have had good times and very difficult years, but we are thankful for so much.

Machame, Tanzania

Preface

by Patricia D. Beaver

This memoir resulted from a series of invitations. A college friend, Patricia Bartlett, and her husband John invited my husband and me to visit them in Moshi, Tanzania. John Bartlett is professor of medicine, global health, and nursing at Duke University Medical Center in Durham, North Carolina; he serves in the same capacity at Kilimanjaro Christian Medical Centre (KCMC) in Moshi, Tanzania. Patricia Bartlett, a social worker at Duke and KCMC, works with community groups on issues related to children and families disrupted by HIV/AIDs. John invited my husband Bob White to join a marlin fishing expedition in the Indian Ocean. Arriving in Moshi, Bob and I set off with the Bartletts, John's brother Tom, and their friend Bob Kasworm across Tanzania, into Kenya, and on to the village of Shimoni, where we were joined by Greg Emmanuel and his family, including Greg's parents, Nic and Sylvie Emmanuel. We met the Emmanuels on January 18, 2015.

We boarded fishing boats trolling the Pemba Channel, and several marlin strikes (tag and release) enlivened the expedition. The fishermen caught shimmering dorados, vibrant yellow and luminescent green in the sunlight. In the evening under the stars, Nic and Greg Emmanuel grilled the day's catch for dinner on long tables overlooking the bay. Bob and I talked with Sylvie, Nic, and son Greg about Greek migration and settlement in Tanzania.

Back in Moshi, we were invited to visit Nic and Sylvie at their home at Machame. On their porch, the lunch conversation flowed with Nic's stories of Tanzania after independence, of living in the house the Emmanuels bought from Germans and now lease long-term. Nic told stories of growing beans, with crops destroyed by buffalo, by rats, by floods. We were enchanted by Nic and Sylvie—their life stories, their home, books, and view of Mount Kilimanjaro.

At home in North Carolina, I received an email from Sylvie on December 15, 2015, asking for my help on her memoir project and inviting me to work with her in Tanzania. "I realise I am just never going to put together the story of my parents' lives and Nic's and mine. I have all these letters and my notes. I also have the autobiography that my mother wrote.... I am asking you as you have experience and I felt that we 'clicked.' So many of these books about African reminiscences are awful and I wouldn't want that!"

I welcomed the opportunity to collaborate with Sylvie long distance. Patricia Bartlett and I developed interview questions for Sylvie. My intent was to guide Sylvie to complete her own project. Yet I gradually became more involved. Patricia Bartlett faxed to me Sylvie's mother's memoir, and I was stunned by her spirit of adventure. I was amazed by her travels and the boundaries she broke as an English woman in the early twentieth century.

In June 2016 Sylvie arrived in the North Carolina mountains to work with Patricia Bartlett and me in recording her life history. Sylvie, Patricia, and I recorded stories and letters and sorted through documents. In Tanzania, Sylvie and Patricia spent many more hours together at Sylvie's home, reading letters into a tape recorder.

In August 2017, we interviewed Nic Emmanuel in Naxos, Greece, where Sylvie and Nic maintain a home. There we met Sylvie and Nic's daughter Sophia Karavias, her husband Thanasi and son Costa. I learned about Nic's family and their twentieth-century history in East Africa as his father, Gregory Emmanuel, began farming sisal.

Sophia shared her extensive knowledge of Greek history. She had been reading Peter Frankopan's (2015) interpretation of the intricate trade routes from the East—spreading goods, ideas, religions, conquest, and disease. These patterns of trade foreground the nineteenth- and twentieth-century colonial contexts that took Sylvie's grandfather Henry Lovett to South Africa and to Egypt, her mother Peggy Lovett to Nepal and to East Africa, her father Donald Wilson to Tanganyika, and her father-in-law Gregory Emmanuel from the island of Tenedos (then part of the Ottoman Empire) to Egypt and on to East Africa. Sylvie and Nic Emmanuel, children of colonial path breakers, were both raised in Tanganyika.

Introduction: Considering Time from Mount Kilimanjaro

by Patricia D. Beaver

Sylvie Wilson Emmanuel lives with her husband Nic in Machame, Tanzania, on the slopes of Mount Kilimanjaro. For the past two centuries, Britain's colonial expansion led her family members to spread out and write home about travelling, war, disease, loss, wonder, love, and the complexity of humanity as they were soldiers, tourists, messengers, and healers. Sylvie has continued her mother's tradition of keeping the family letters, diaries, and photographs. They shape and inform the narratives to follow. Sylvie's stories and those of her mother, Margaret ("Peggy") Lovett Wilson—who wrote an unpublished memoir—lead us through the twentieth century from England, east to Nepal and south into Tanganyika in East Africa.

Peggy was born in 1897 into a prosperous family and spent her childhood in Shrewsbury, England. She worked in a Voluntary Aid Detachment (VAD), performing nursing services during World War I. Then she studied medicine at Birmingham University and accepted a position in Nepal as physician in charge of the Maharajah's granddaughter. After nearly four years of work and travel between Nepal and England, India, and other destinations in the East, she boarded a ship for Tanganyika to meet Donald Wilson, whom she had met and courted when they were both medical students at Birmingham.

Donald went to Tanganyika in 1929. Peggy arrived in 1930, married Donald, and spent the next thirty years conducting malaria research alongside her husband. After Donald's death in England in 1960, Peggy returned to Africa and worked in The Gambia until her retirement.

Donald's death was traumatic for his family, yet it allowed Peggy to return to Africa and accomplish new research independent of collaborations with her husband. Both Donald and Peggy were awarded the Order of the British Empire (OBE), Donald Bagster Wilson in 1950 for his work on malaria in East Africa, Margaret Lovett Wilson in 1973 for her malaria research in The Gambia. Peggy also received the Royal African Society's bronze medal "For Dedicated Service to Africa."

Peggy's decisions to attend medical school and travel to Nepal had the enthusiastic support of her father, Henry Lovett, a compelling character in this family saga. Henry Lovett's letters provide a firsthand account of the Zulu War (1879), and of buying camels in Egypt in support of the military attempt to rescue General Gordon in Khartoum, Sudan (1884–1885).

Sylvie's father's father, Donald Bagster Wilson, was a descendant of the Samuel Bagster family, well known for publication of Christian Bibles and texts. "The Daily Light on the Daily Path" was prepared by Jonathan Bagster and other members of his family, descendants of Samuel Bagster (1772–1851), founder of the publishing firm Samuel Bagster & Sons Ltd. in 1794 (Wholesome Words, 2017). Their ancestor Rachel Wilson was a Quaker minister who journeyed to America from Kendal, England, in 1768, then travelled on horseback from Philadelphia to the Carolinas, eight years before the American Revolution. Rachel spoke against slavery. Her stories are documented in *Isaac and Rachel Wilson, Quakers, of Kendal, 1714–85*.

Early twentieth century racial and colonial mentality shaped the worldview of Donald and Peggy Wilson (Fanon 1961, 1967; Said 1978; Tilley 2011). In turn, their work influenced the medical field, and Donald and Peggy are significant figures in the development of tropical medicine and malariology. "[Donald] Bagster Wilson was hugely influential as a malariologist in Tanzania and wrote seminal papers ... on basic epidemiology and clinical manifestations" (Chris Drakeley, email to John Bartlett, April 28, 2019). The firsthand account of their work at the Amani Research Station in the 1950s adds to the body of research focused on that important institution in the research and treatment of malaria (see Geissler 2017; Geissler and Kelly 2016; Ghyselen et al., 2017).

Donald Wilson was appointed to Tanganyika as a British Colonial Medical Officer (MO). The London and Liverpool Schools of Tropical Medicine opened in 1899 to provide specialist training for MOs in Colonial Service throughout the British colonies. In 1929, prior to going to Tanganyika, Donald completed the course in tropical medicine and hygiene that MOs were required to take. Peggy had taken the course in 1927 in hope of an appointment to Kashmir. Tropical medicine was growing in importance in response to the perceived needs in the colonies. In 1921 a unified East African Medical Service (EAMS) was created, then in 1930, a single Colonial Service was established with different vocational branches, including Colonial Medicine. The Colonial Administrative Service was formalized in 1932, and the Colonial Medical Service in 1934, offering "one of the first practical opportunities for those medical personnel who did not want to be missionaries to work [in Africa]" (Crozier 2007). In 1932 Donald and Peggy spent two months at Horton Hospital in Epsom, England, for additional malaria training.

MOs were united by specialized, progressive training in colonial medicine and their common purpose of promoting British medicine abroad. MOs were also united by shared British colonial culture, including social events such as sporting matches, sundowners, clubs, and dinner dances requiring strict attention to appropriate dress—as Peggy reminds us—and guest lists, detailed menus, cooks, and servers (Crozier 2007). Even hunting safaris were part of this culture, and Peggy had adequate training from her youthful experiences in foxhunting.

The Colonial Medical Service employed few women, but colonial wives were another matter. Many worked alongside their husbands or went into private practice.

Peggy began doing medical work in Tabora hospital soon after arriving in Tanganyika, and she worked closely with Donald on medical safaris. According to Crozier, Peggy received her first official appointment as part-time entomologist in 1933, as Health Officer in 1939, and as full MO in 1948.

This mother-daughter memoir echoes and honors decades of feminist narratives, as women define the terms of their own lives. Peggy's journal defies the norms of twentieth-century womanhood in England, Nepal, and Tanganyika. Sylvie defies her parents in whom she chooses to marry, and throws herself completely into the Greek community in Tanganyika. She celebrates Tanganyika's independence from Britain and the creation of the new nation, Tanzania, and she endures the loss of property through nationalization. Both Peggy and Sylvie were shaped by cultures into which they were born and raised, and they helped shape the worlds in which they lived and worked. Now they are writing that culture (Behar and Gordon 1995). Their lives reflect the history of the twentieth century, as they narrate their experiences of coming of age, working, travelling, finding love, forming families, bearing and raising children, living in communities, experiencing the wonders of the natural world, and living through revolution.

Women in England, 1900–1926

Peggy Lovett grew up near Shrewsbury in the west of England, during the Edwardian era, the *belle époque*. Born into a well-off family, she knew garden parties, archery, dancing lessons, foxhunting, and summer holidays at the Welsh seaside.

Peggy's parents met at Bath, where her mother was "taking the waters" for her health. Peggy's mother, Jeannie Campbell Connell, was raised on the family estate of Craigallian House, north of Glasgow. At 30, her health problems may have limited her marriage prospects. In Bath she met the very attractive Lieutenant Henry Lovett. On her honeymoon she was diagnosed with multiple sclerosis. Jeannie later visited Lourdes in France; accompanied by her daughters, she sought healing from the sacred waters of the Sanctuaires Notre-Dame de Lourdes.

For Peggy's father, Henry Lovett, this was clearly a good marriage. Henry grew up with wealth at Henlle Hall, but did not inherit the estate, which went to the first-born son, Hubert. Henry's marriage to the daughter of a wealthy Scottish shipbuilding family allowed him to leave active military duty for a life of foxhunting, bird shoots, archery, and garden parties, and being a popular, attractive guest (with a frequently absent wife). They bought and established the family home at Dunstone, which included a trout stream. Henry wrote longingly of "trout and the cool water of the Ceiriog River in Wales," close to the family home, from his desolate outpost on the Nile in 1884. Trout fishing was a recurring theme in several of his letters.

Jeannie and Henry had three children: Peggy, Rosie, and Dicky. Like well-off families of the period, the Lovett family had a large staff of nine servants. Their treatment of the servants was probably common for the era and their class, providing housing, food, clothing, and probably a small wage.

Peggy laments that she and her sister Rosie "never had any pretty clothes." Peggy's experiences before and during the war paralleled those of noted author Vera Brittain, whose *Testament of Youth* was published in 1933. Brittain writes, "...all girls clothing of the period appeared to be designed by their elders on the assumption that decency consisted in leaving exposed to the sun and air no part of the human body that could possibly be covered with flannel" (1978, 34). Both Peggy and her daughter Sylvie read Brittain's *Testament of Youth*, a story that mirrors Peggy's privileged upbringing and wartime experiences as a VAD.

By the time Peggy was born, the suffrage movement was thriving in Europe and America. Peggy came of age as the "new woman" was altering European society. The "new woman" proved her "physical endurance on long bicycle rides and walking tours," and defiantly smoked cigarettes (Smith 1989, 317). Peggy describes a 14-mile bicycle ride during the war years. Later, as she prepared for medical school, she rode her brother's motorcycle to and from her tutor's home. Peggy was also accustomed to taking long hikes for the pleasure of the journey, especially in Nepal. She apparently smoked for much of her life.

Returning from a year in Paris, Peggy Lovett confessed that the 1914 assassination of Archduke Ferdinand meant nothing to her, as she was most interested in what to wear and what do with her hair. As war began, Peggy Lovett was foxhunting twice a week and, like Vera Brittain, knitting socks for soldiers.

When war came, both Vera and Peggy joined the thousands of trained and untrained women in the war effort. "Trained women enrolled as nurses, and the unskilled joined the Voluntary Aid Detachments" (Grayzel 2002, 39). Peggy worked at Sister Hunt's Orthopaedic Hospital at Baschurch for the duration of World War I.

Nursing, seen as a feminine occupation, subservient to the male doctors, "gave women an opportunity to get close to the battlefields to supply vital aid while still enabling them to be seen as fulfilling a caregiving and therefore feminine role" (Smith 1989: 38). Many of the VADs, like Peggy Lovett and Vera Brittain, were from a higher social status than the professional nurses, and "saw themselves primarily as performing a war service" (Grayzel 2002, 40). At the end of the war, Peggy Lovett turned to medical school. Vera Brittain, having lost her fiancé, brother, and other friends, returned to Oxford University to pursue a writing career as a pacifist.

Under pressure from activists, higher education gradually opened to women before World War I. In the 1870s, women's colleges were established in England: "Girton and Newnham at Cambridge, followed by Somerville College, and Lady Margaret Hall at Oxford." A photo caption of a riot by male students at Cambridge reads, "Women in universities democratized the pursuit of knowledge, while they simultaneously threatened male privilege and their monopoly in higher education ... men across Europe rioted, especially as more and more women took first place in exams" (Smith 1989, 323). Going to medical school was difficult, yet more women were enrolled in universities, medical schools and law schools in the 1920s and 1930s, than after World War II (Solomon 1985; Margaret McFadden, email message to this editor, January 27, 2019).

A note on formatting: Unless otherwise indicated, Peggy Wilson's voice appears in regular roman font, and *Sylvie Wilson Emmanuel's voice is in italics.* (Their comments appear in parentheses.) [The editor's comments and additions are in brackets.] The two INTRODUCTIONS, to Nepal and Tanganyika, are by the editor.

Chapter 1

Beginnings

by Peggy Lovett Wilson

My father, Henry Wilson Lovett, was born on July 31, 1858. He was quite mature at 38 when he married my mother, Jeannie Campbell Connell. She was 30, born on December 8, 1866. Craigallian House, north of Scotland, was her family home. Father was Adjutant to the Depot of the Somerset Light Infantry, then stationed in Taunton (Somerset). My parents met in Bath where my mother was "taking the waters." My mother came from a shipbuilding family with money, which must have made her attractive to my father, who wasn't going to inherit any land as he had an older brother. They were married in 1896.

My father was very handsome, with dark brown hair and dark blue eyes. My mother had glorious pure gold hair, pink cheeks and rather small green eyes. She was very shy and not strong, and had already begun to suffer from multiple sclerosis, diagnosed soon after their marriage. Because of her illness my father decided to retire from the Army, as his wife could not possibly go with him if he were to be posted abroad.

I was born July 21, 1897. My parents left Taunton and went to Shropshire when I was two years old and rented a house called The Elms on the outskirts of Shrewsbury. My father's eldest brother Hubert inherited the family home, Henlle Hall in Gobowen. Hubert and my father Henry were both Major H. Lovett, so my father decided to become Lt. Colonel since that was his rank in the Shropshire Volunteers. We stayed at The Elms for five years.

Our family doctor was awe-inspiring. Dressed in frock coat, black and grey striped trousers, and carrying that frightening black bag, I didn't like him to touch me or to look at my chickenpox or my tongue. He was tall and strong with protuberant blue eyes, a hooked nose, and a cleft chin. He came to vaccinate my baby sister and although I didn't like her much then, I didn't want him to hurt her, so I took hold of his coat tails and tugged as hard as I could. I was jealous of her, though, and didn't like her to sit on my mother's lap. One evening I was playing with my blocks and with one in each hand I clapped her fat cheeks as hard as I could. I had a good and well-deserved smack.

My father and mother were both keen on archery and in summer had a big painted oilcloth-covered straw target set up on the lawn. I loved the feel of the bows with their smooth, polished wood, and the handgrip of green velvet. I was allowed to retrieve any arrows that missed the target and went into the lawn, and was shown how to pull them out carefully, straight towards me by the feathered end.

I remember the rejoicing at the end of the Boer War [1902]. I recall Nanny, who looked after us children, singing Lord Roberts and Kitchener, Baden Powell, and the long red, white, and blue cotton fringed decoration put up in the garden.

One summer my parents gave a big garden party. Children were supposed to keep out of the way and I was lying on the grass with my book well away from the guests when a waiter with a tray of ice creams stopped and offered me one. I took it joyfully because we never had ice cream, but oh dear, it turned out to be a water ice. A bitter disappointment. We gave one other big party about that time, a winter children's party in the Music Hall in Shrewsbury—a splendid tea, games, and little competitions like who made the prettiest picture looking through a horse collar.

In 1908 we bought a fair-sized, red brick house that Father named Dunstone, which means a little stone fort. There were three fields, a little beech spinney in which there was a piped spring of ice cold, delicious water, and at last he had his much desired bit of trout stream where he spent many happy summer evenings. Lots of rabbits had burrows in the hillside of our bottom field. The top field had a duck pond and the new vegetable garden.

Father gave each of us, Rosie, Dicky and me, an apple tree to celebrate the making of the "New Garden." My tree was a "Peasgood Nonesuch," and it bore fine apples, but alas, they were cooking apples.

Henry Lovett in uniform, Oswestry.

Our first pony was an obstinate hard-mouthed little roan named Charlie. We were all three rather frightened of him and Dicky, my little brother, didn't want to ride him at all. Morgan, our coachman, used to make us jump him over small obstacles, and when Charlie objected and set off fast in another direction, Morgan would shout, "Puul at him, puul at him, dar let him get away from yer."

It was important to learn to ride, because in the grown-up world, everything revolved round foxhunting between September, when cubbing started, and April, when the crops were coming up, which put an end to hunting. Then too the vixens had their litters and must not be disturbed so that they could rear healthy cubs for the coming season.

In the country everyone hunted, if possible at least two days a week. Some farmers objected to the hunt galloping over their land, and some, regarded as being shockingly unsporting, even wired their fences. But by and large everyone who could, went out hunting. If not mounted, then if the meet was near enough, on foot. Some followed in traps or pony carts or on bicycles.

It was very important to be properly turned out. A few men wore hunting pink, but most wore dark coats, top hats, white breeches, and of course top boots with pinkish tops to them. There was such a bustle in the stables on hunting mornings. Horses' coats shone like satin, their hoofs were blacked, the pigskin saddles and the leathers all shone from polishing, and the bits and stirrups and snaffle and curb chains fairly glittered. And the horses were so excited—they loved hunting mornings.

Cubbing mornings in late September and early October did have a sort of glamour. One got up at six and had tea and eggs and bread and butter. The scent of the woods, the shining cobwebs on every bush and shrub, the crashing of galloping horses up and down the grassy rides, the thrilling sound of the horn, the waiting outside a culvert to see a fox stealing out into the open and the waiting to give him a chance to get a start before yelling, "Gone away."

We lived very well in the winter. My father was so good looking and amusing and such a good shot that he was asked to all the big shoots in the country. Not the least of his advantages as a guest, I sometimes think, was that his wife could not go with him. He never came back from a shoot without at least a brace of partridges or pheasants. As they were always hung for the correct length of time, I didn't like the bitter taste and would have enjoyed them far more not hung at all. After a big shoot father used to say that he fired so many cartridges that his gun barrels got red hot. I used to have a confused idea about it all. I thought it must be necessary to shoot and kill so many birds and necessary to hunt and kill as many foxes as possible.

When I was six I had my first governess and from then on, we had a succession of daily governesses, all kindly nice women, for the next 10 years. It really was lovely doing lessons at home, and our schoolroom at Dunstone had a window opening on to the verandah, so it was very easy to get out into the garden.

Our household staff in my childhood days consisted of Nanny, who came to us when I was a small baby, a nursery maid, cook, parlour maid, and nursemaid. Outside there was a coachman, gardener, and a garden boy, who also cleaned the knives and shoes and pumped water up from the well near the back door. This last chore only happened at Dunstone, but such a weary chore it was that Father made a rule that anyone who wanted more than three inches of water in their bath must pump it next morning. In the winter such a small bath got cold so quickly that quite often one or other of us would have a good big hot bath (the water heated from the big kitchen range) and conscientiously pump it after breakfast.

There were coal fires in the day nursery and in the smoking room and in my parents' bedroom, but never in the drawing room, except on Sunday evenings unless, as rarely happened, an aunt was staying with us. I had to practice the piano in the drawing room after breakfast and my fingers were so cold in winter that I couldn't play my scales, but I did my best.

We treated our servants with very little consideration, I grieve to say. Their small bedrooms faced north and were very cold. Their bedclothes were inadequate, they could never have a bath; the parlour maid had to carry terribly heavy trays along the passage from kitchen to dining room. The cook had to wrestle with the huge coal range. And they had no really comfortable chairs to sit in when off duty. Mrs. Morgan, the coachman's wife, was sadly anemic and very overworked. She did all our family washing for a pittance.

We always went to church on Sunday mornings, and on Sunday evenings, when a fire was lit in the drawing room, Mother would play hymns that we sang, like "Shall We Gather at the River" (gather what, I always wondered) and "Onward Christian Soldiers," and the like. Our nursery supper was always scrambled eggs. When we were much older, dining room Sunday supper was always corned beef and honeycomb mold.

I never drank any milk. Not everyone realized the desperate importance of it for children's bones and teeth. Old Nanny certainly didn't, and as I disliked it, I never had any at all and drank water or tea. And so my teeth were weak and decayed rapidly. I had to go to the dentist for painful fillings and fairly often extractions of my first teeth. I had an unsuspected slight spinal curvature and an (equally unsuspected) deformed pelvis, which was responsible in later life for the deaths of my first two babies. As our clothes kept out all sunshine with hats, stockings, and long sleeves, we got no Vitamin D from that source, or very little.

Every week we went to Shrewsbury in the carriage. Mother would tell Morgan to put up at The Raven, or later on, at The Unicorn. Then we went shopping first to Lee's in the square where Mother bought our groceries and where they sold the most delectable biscuits—long, finger-shaped, coated with plain chocolate and with pink sugar inside—then to Della Porta which had the date 1567 over the door and the salerooms were incredibly small and dark. It was here that my father, rather unkindly but entirely in fun, told me to go in and ask for a pint of pigeon's milk and a tin of elbow grease. And sometimes up Pride Hill to Liberty's where we occasionally had tea, brown bread and butter, and fruitcake in a kind of little alcove smelling of carpets and materials.

Every week in the winter we went to a dancing class in Shrewsbury for which Rosie and I wore our accordion pleated white silk dresses and small brother Dicky his sailor suit. Occasionally we went to a children's party where there would usually be games, dancing "Sir Roger de Coverley," the "Swedish Dance" and the "Lancers," and a wonderful tea. Or if it was a later party with perhaps a conjurer, or if at Christmas time, a splendid glittering tree and a marvelous supper with turkey and tongue, trifle and meringues with lots of whipped cream. We usually had to go home inside the closed wagonette, and I was always sick out of the window at the back.

If, however, it was not too bitterly cold, Nanny might allow me to go on the box beside Morgan. That drive along the lanes after dark with only the carriage candle lamps for light, and the air so keen and cold, was very heaven. We never, or hardly ever, met any other vehicle on the road.

Sometimes we children had friends to tea, Jackie and Bobby Howe, or the Clease girls, or the little Corbetts. Always after tea, winter or summer, I suggested we play hide and seek in the garden. If it was in the dark of winter there were a lot of grazed knees and bruises, but it was great fun. We seldom had anything the matter with us except for colds, but when I was about 12, we all had measles. My temperature went up to 105. Mother read to me when my eyes were sore, and we all felt very important as invalids. When recovering we had huge appetites and between the three of us, we

Lovett family (left–right) coachman, Rosie in carriage, Morgan with Peggy on horseback, Nanny, Dickie on horseback, Henry Lovett, Jeannie Lovett.

ate 12 chickens! Then we had tonics and a change of air to the seaside, as was the custom then for the fairly well to do.

In 1907, when I was 10, my father hired a car and took us all to his old home, Henlle Hall, for the day. I fell violently in love with my cousin Tom, who was 14. It was a great experience. We went the 20 miles each way with no mishaps at all.

Every year we went to the seaside in the summer, usually to North Wales, and stayed in lodgings. My father generally went somewhere else to fish, but Mother and Nanny took us. One year at Llandudno, the seaside resort in North Wales, I made friends with a boy of about my age. One evening he came into my little room to ask about some arrangement next day. Nanny, of course, vetoed our going together to Conway Castle. I was in bed and he bent over and kissed me goodnight. The lovely smells of Harris Tweed and milk chocolate stayed in my memory for years. I never met him again.

Often we went to Aberdovey [West Wales] for our annual holiday. Once we went at the same time as friends who had a son of my age and a girl a little younger. Gordon and I were very fond of one another. I was envious of Rena who had a different pretty frock for each day we were there. Rosie and I never had any pretty clothes, only the same butcher blue smocks with white feather stitching at the yoke, day in day out, except for best [clothes for special events]. They were high to the neck and had long sleeves. In hot weather we left off our stockings and our Liberty bodice, but Father did not approve.

I was confirmed when I was 15. Old Mr. Wayne who prepared me for Confirmation, took a great deal of trouble and when I thanked him, said, "And now may I have my reward?" This was nothing more than a chaste kiss on my cheek. Later, when I was away at school and had told Mother something about experimenting with a little mild makeup, Mr. Wayne wrote to me saying, "Never paint your face. It would be as absurd as to paint a rose." As I had then a really lovely complexion, I mostly had the sense to take Mr. Wayne's advice.

Paris: Finishing School

In 1913, when I was 16, it was decided to send me to a finishing school in Paris. A small school in Auteuil, it was run by two maiden ladies, Miss Metherell and Mlle. Guibert. It was not a large school. There was only one French girl, named Germaine de Chambure, whose father was a count. The rest of us were English but we were supposed to speak French all the time.

I disliked the hard rolls we had for *petit dejeuner*, and in the winter I hated having no fires, only *rez-de-chaussée* [floor grates], but you could get nice and warm if you stood over them. I learned to speak French fairly well thanks to Germaine. My piano playing improved, and I learned to make a chocolate mousse at the cookery classes. Our expeditions I really loved. We were taken to all the famous *musées* and churches and to very many places of historic interest. The impressive size and gloom of Notre Dame filled me with awe.

We went to Versailles and to St. Cloud and by train to Fontainebleau where we spent a night. How magical on a hot summer's evening having *le diner* in the forest, even if it was only a number of gauche schoolgirls sitting at a long table. So many poppies were growing in the cornfields, those fields so soon to be red with blood.

We were taken to concerts and I heard [Belgian violinist Eugene] Ysaye play. We went to *Phedre* and *La Dame aux Camellias* and *Parsifal* (oh, how long it was), and *Carmen*. Sarah Bernhardt was Phedre. As this was 1913, it was after her leg had been amputated [Bernhardt, injured during her performance of *La Tosca* in Rio de Janeiro in 1906, suffered this amputation in 1915]. Her golden voice struck me as being raucous and grating and her face was snow white with powder, but anyhow I saw her.

Each afternoon expedition ended with tea at a *patisserie* and the cakes, after our plain sultana and ginger cakes at home, seemed right out of this world. The shops in the Rue de Rivoli at Christmastime were brilliant and so thrilling. I bought a white ostrich feather fan for Mother, and a silver letter rack for Father.

Towards the end of my last term we were taken to the Paris Salon. We found the pictures, especially the lovely nudes, entrancing, and I and three or four nice-looking friends thought we might make a modest attempt at reproducing a group and photographing ourselves. We were only bare to the waist and we all had long hair and the result, as I remember it, was really rather charming! We grouped and posed on a fur rug. Unfortunately one of the mistresses found the photos while they were being printed and then there was a terrible to-do. If we had not been leaving in any case, we should have been expelled. Our parents were very shocked and pained, but I couldn't feel that we had done anything so very awful. All the prints were confiscated, unfortunately.

And so home again, finished save the mark—hair up—and what a job to keep it up, long skirts, veils, young ladyhood.

1914: Coming Out and War

That glorious hot summer of 1914. In June, the very month in which I left France, the assassination of the Serbian Archduke Franz Ferdinand in Sarajevo meant nothing to me. I was only occupied with thinking about how I should "come out." I had gone to France wearing my hair in a ponytail or a door knocker [bun] and in each case with a great big black ribbon bow behind. Now my long heavy hair had somehow to be dressed to stay up pinned to the back of my head.

My Aunt Lina solved the coming out problem by inviting me to go with her and my cousins to a dance in the Drill Hall in Oswestry. My dress for this, to me quite important, occasion was a rather pathetic and skimpy affair of crushed strawberry tulle and silk. My stockings were silk halfway up the leg. My poor mother had no idea at all how to dress me.

The young officers said a good deal about its being the eve of Waterloo, and it was not long after this that we declared war on Germany. In that summer of 1914 I had my first proposal of marriage. He was just back from the battlefront in France and had been wounded. I was far too immature to think of marriage at that time, but I couldn't help being very touched by the way his blue eyes burned when he looked at me, and when he said in a letter, "I would rather call myself your slave as the thought of the bondage will be very sweet to me." But alas for poor Ernest Holliday, I was then violently attracted to my cousin Tom, an attraction that lasted on both sides for 13 years.

War VAD [Voluntary Aid Detachment]

The first autumn of the war, when everyone thought it would be over so soon, was for me a time of hunting twice a week on the lovely little chestnut mare Tango, which my father bought me that summer, and knitting socks for soldiers. I attended First Aid and Home Nursing classes in Shrewsbury and rather proudly passed the exams, the first exams I had ever passed. In the spring I went with my cousin Cis to work for a month at Sister Hunt's Orthopaedic Hospital at Baschurch. I learnt quite a lot in that month and was sorry to go home at the end of it. I then joined the St. John's Ambulance Corps as a VAD and went daily to a Soldier's Convalescent Hospital, Oakley Manor, on the outskirts of Shrewsbury. It was about six miles from home and nowhere near the station, so I went in the pony cart.

I learned to sweep, dust and polish and to wash up plates and dishes. There were about 50 patients so there was an awful lot of washing up and I thankfully accepted the help of one or two of the men. I would get home in the early evening and as my poor pony was longing for his supper, we careened down the last hill at a great pace. It was a narrow road and to my dismay one evening I saw a motorcar coming towards us. I managed to get the left-hand wheel up onto the bank where we rocked perilously for a minute, came down onto the road with a great bump, just missed the car and cantered on.

My hospital duties included little that could be called nursing, although I learned to take temperatures and put on an occasional hot fomentation. But in spite of all the washing up, I could not feel that I was doing a worthwhile job, so I decided to leave. I was very brave and very tactless when I told the Matron. She asked what I was going to do, and I said I was going back to Baschurch, so she naturally wanted to know why.

I told her that when there I had learned the supreme importance of asepsis in surgery and from what I had seen, I didn't consider that the standards of surgical cleanliness at Oakley were at all comparable. I think now that it was a frightful cheek on my part, although true.

So back to Baschurch I went and promised Sister Hunt that I would work there as an orthopaedic student for the duration. Sister Hunt was a most wonderful woman. She came of a Shropshire County family. Her father had built a magnificent house in a lovely park, Boreatton, but could not afford to live in it, and sold it to a Dr. Sankey whose son Hugh ran it as a mental hospital. His daughter Kathleen and I became great friends.

Sister Hunt had a tuberculous hip that lamed her for life, but in spite of this, she did a nursing training at the Salop Infirmary. She was a patient of Sir Robert Jones, the famous Liverpool orthopaedic surgeon.

Mrs. Hunt had a smallish house in Baschurch and her daughter Agnes, together with her great friend Miss Goodford, also a trained nurse, decided to take a few crippled children selected by Sir Robert Jones and look after them in one or two open air sheds just outside Mrs. Hunt's house; their number increased and so did the number of sheds. When war broke out there were, perhaps, 100 civilian patients, mostly children. The War Office asked Sister Hunt whether she would take wounded soldiers, which she agreed to do, and to begin with, a few lightly wounded men arrived.

I began my duties in the Babies Shed. There were many cases of poliomyelitis. Many of the cases were deformities from contractures resulting from lack of interest or improper treatment elsewhere. There was much bovine tuberculosis chiefly affecting the hips and spines. In those days treatment consisted of immobilization for long periods on back frames, in Thomas splints, calipers, back supports, and so forth. There were congenital deformities such as hip dislocations, clubfeet and others, and there were a number of spastics.

Sunday was the operating day. There was only one resident doctor; a Dr. Urwick would come out from Shrewsbury if sent for. A team of famous surgeons—Girdlestone, Dunn, McCrae, and Aitken—took turns coming on Sunday and would operate all day with a break for lunch. A very good lunch it was too, I believe, and my word! They had earned it. Open ether was the only anesthetic used. Strong men needed a great deal to get them under, and sometimes it took four of us to hold down a struggling, shouting patient, as he was sure he was being asphyxiated, as of course he was. Every patient had an injection of morphia and atropine beforehand, and the sister-in-charge used me to do this and also decide on the amount to give. I knew the rule about dosage and never made a mistake, but Sister Hunt found out that I was doing it and the sister-in-charge was thoroughly reprimanded, as she was responsible.

Once a man coming round from his anesthetic and still very dopey said to me, "I'll tell the Sister on you I will, you've bit my tongue something cruel." If he had had his tongue held forward by the sharp spiked forceps that prevented swallowing it, it would indeed have been very sore for some time.

I did not much like [operating] theater duty. The theater was kept at such a high temperature, and it reeked of ether. The first operation I ever saw was a trans-trochanteric

Peggy as VAD (left) at Baschurch with patients and nursing staff during World War I.

osteotomy [repairing a broken hip]. I really feared that the patient was being cut in half, and it was fearfully bloody. One dreadful day, I dropped a pair of forceps into a dressing drum that I was holding, just out of sheer nerves. It had to be re-sterilized. Sister Goodford hurt my feelings very much when she said my wits must have been woolgathering. It never happened again.

I made great friends with some of my fellow students. For some reason we were all called "Sister." The real hospital-trained sisters didn't like this, and no wonder. Most of us at the beginning of my training were from Shropshire County families. Sister Hunt gave me a warning when I first began to have anything to do with men patients after leaving the children's wards: "Now just remember, Peggy," she said, "there is to be no familiarity or goings-on. These men are of the same class as your father's gardener, although they are now soldiers." However, we were also told that keeping the patients happy was a most important part of the treatment.

There was a Recreation Room and a piano that I played for dancing. We also rehearsed songs in costume, and some of us nurses and convalescents gave concerts in the villages roundabout. We went in a brake [horse-drawn carriage]. I was the accompanist and the songs were such as "When Irish Eyes," and "The Pipe of Peace," dressed up as Red Indians round a campfire, and "Keep the Home Fires Burning." We all loved the concerts.

Our bedrooms were horseboxes that Sister Hunt had ordered by mistake, and in the winter they were bitterly cold. I often left the top half of the door open and sometimes in the morning would find the floor and my bed covered with snow. At times the hours for the night duty nurse seemed very long and she felt lonely, so she would wake up a special friend with tea and toast for a chat.

A kind donor presented a fine bath for the nurses' use. However the bathroom was a long way from our bedrooms, about 100 yards, and it took much resolution to go to it on a cold or wet evening, but the water was splendidly hot and it was worth it.

In time I was promoted to work in the Soldiers' Shed. One felt so sorry for the wounded when the ambulances drew up and they asked where the hospital was, and we said this was it. "What, these sheds, all open like this!" they said in disgust. But they soon got used to the idea and we kept them as warm as possible with extra blankets and hot water bottles and hot drinks. Their appetites were huge in the open air, and if the nurses fared badly as the war went on, we saw to it that the patients didn't.

The strictest economy was necessary as funds were pretty low and we were always being lectured about waste. An unpopular economy was to cut out afternoon tea for the nurses, but finally it was decided that we might be given ships biscuits (hard as iron they were), and either black treacle or margarine. The treacle was bitter, and the margarine was often rancid.

Our uniform was blue fitted overalls and caps, and our pay was £10 the first year, £16 the second and £20 the third, but our expenses were almost nil.

When I was 20 years old, I became a Staff Nurse, and was responsible for medicines and for doing operation dressings, some of which were horribly painful in spite of being as careful and gentle as possible. The men used to beg me to do their first dressings, although it was really the Ward Sister's job.

In one case with a bad septic wound of the arm, Sister Hunt ordered the drainage tube to be taken out, which I did. Next time she came round with a visiting VIP Medical Officer, the tube was back in the wound again. She was, of course, very angry. "I am sorry Sister," I said. "I found that the wound was healing over on the surface only so I opened it up again and put back the tube." Mollified, she said, "Very well, Miss Lovett, as you did it considering it to be better treatment, and not because you were forgetful or careless, you can leave the tube in, but take it out as soon as possible," which I naturally did.

Due to supreme care, to antiseptics, to fresh air day and night, and plenty of good food, added to the natural strength and resilience of youth, wounds did heal. It says much for the strict asepsis in the operating theater when Aitken, Dunn and Girdlestone took their operating day in weekly turn, that the long difficult bone grafts, or nerve sutures, or tendon transplantations, some of which operations might take up to three hours, all healed by first intentions. At the end of the list came reduction of congenital hip dislocations and wrenching of clubfeet and re-fracture of ill-set bones and so forth.

No one was left at my home, Dunstone, in Dorrington. My father was then Commandant at the Hospital for Artificial Limbs at Roehampton, my mother and sister were living at Bournemouth, and my brother was at school.

One glorious weekend in 1916, I bicycled the 14 miles home with my friend Vi Learoyd. Mrs. Morgan, our coachman's wife, had made up beds for us with the best linen sheets, lavender fragrant, and cooked us a splendid dinner of roast chicken, green peas, new potatoes, all home produced! We enjoyed everything as if we had never seen a garden before, the crimson rambler roses making a background for the row of Madonna lilies and the green lawns still kept mown, but that was the last summer until the family returned that anything much was done in the garden.

We set off on our return bicycle ride; I carried a paper bag of superb peaches intended for our friends at the hospital. Alas, when it was getting dark and we were still several miles away, the bag broke and all the lovely peaches fell onto the road. Having nothing else to put them in, we had to sit down on the bank and eat them.

I had one or two proposals of marriage, one was long and closely written, telling me that I was the only girl he would ever love and that when we married and went to live in his country of Canada, we could live in town or country, whichever I preferred. He ended by telling me that his Wasserman test [for syphilis] was negative. His fractured pelvis was uniting satisfactorily but he had shortening of one leg and he would always be lame. I hope he found a nice wife when he went home.

About then I went to live at Boreatton with my friend Kathleen Sankey in a big house set in a splendid park, the property of Roland Hunt, Sister Hunt's brother. In 1917 some of us student nurses began to work for the ISTM, the exam of the Incorporated Society of Trained Masseuses. We studied anatomy to second MBA [bachelor of medicine] standards and were taught electrical treatment and testing of nerves. It was a stiff course, carried out in addition to our daily work in the wards. We learned our anatomy in an unheated room over a butcher shop in Baschurch, from 5 to 7:30 a.m. After taking the examination, which we all passed, we worked in the massage and electricity department. We used Galvanism for mild contractions and Faradism for stronger ones. It was a standard treatment.

At the beginning of 1918, I was sent to Stoke-on-Trent to be given instruction in plasterwork. I was found to be too useful in the Massage Room, however, so I got little or no instruction in plasterwork.

I was in the Potteries when the Armistice happened in November. We did nothing special to celebrate the ending to the gigantic slaughter of the best of our male youth. I returned to my home at Dorrington Salop armed with my Certificate of Orthopaedic training. It said that my conduct throughout had been good and my work excellent.

I preferred it that way round.

Studying Medicine

Then what should I do next? Carry on at Baschurch as an After Care Sister, which meant visiting patients in their homes all over the country, or what? A lodging housekeeper in Colwyn Bay, where Rosie and I had gone for a week, said, "Why don't you study medicine?" I half seriously put the idea to my father, who initially said, "Oh dearie, I don't think you could manage to do that." Then after a good deal of thought, he said that he was prepared to pay for me if I would really like to try and do it. There were no grants in those days. Father took the advice of a Shrewsbury doctor who told him that Birmingham was a good medical school and near home. So I gratefully accepted. I would rather have gone to London or Edinburgh, rather for snob reasons I fear.

We did not really know how to set about going there. My father went with me to

Birmingham to see Dean Haslam of the Medical School by appointment. He said that I might take the ex-serviceman's matriculation and that I ought to work for the degree.

I had heard of the conjoint examination and that it was easier to pass than the degree examination, and also, which rather weighed on me in my ignorance, it had more letters to it than the degree. That point was shelved for the moment, however. I sat, a lone female, for the ex-servicemen's examination. It was a written exam and there were no Vivas [oral exams]. I remember one or two of the questions:

"What do you know of Darwin's Theory of Evolution?"

"State what you know of the flora and fauna of East Africa."

"Describe the plot of any novel by Scott or Dickens."

I passed this examination; I cannot imagine how or why, except that my grammar and spelling were unexceptionable.

Then the question arose as to how to get a little general knowledge into my head before starting at the university and embarking on the 1st MBA [bachelor of medicine] course of physics, chemistry and biology. My father had the bright idea that I should go for coaching to a clergyman who lived about four miles away. It was too far for me to walk and we had no horses left, so as Dick had been promised a motorbike when he was 17, it was agreed that he should choose one and I should ride it through the summer of 1919. He chose a 3 hp Racing Rover with TT handlebars, no kick-starter and no gears, only a Philipson pulley instead of gears. It was a big heavy machine and I had to run with it to get it started and then jump on to the saddle, which, with a rather long skirt—for breeches or trousers would have been considered most unladylike—was quite a feat.

My tutor did his best, but I am afraid he found me a pretty dim pupil. At age 22, I would much rather have been thinking of marriage. However, there was no one for me to marry then.

So I arrived in Birmingham for the October term and took up residence in the Women's Hostel, University House. I had a fine big room with a coal fire. I quite liked my room but it was very cold. Miss Orange was the Warden and Miss Burt the Assistant Warden. The food was simply dreadful as Miss Orange's mind was permanently set on higher things, and I lost half a stone [ca. 7 pounds] every term I was in residence. I was very healthy and nearly always hungry. I was really grateful to anyone who asked me out to tea at a cafe and gave me a buttered egg and a cake.

Father gave me 10 shillings a week but he did not realize that I bought my lunches out of that, as well as stamps, tram fares and oddments. I was so sensible of his generosity in paying for me to be a student that I never liked to ask him for more, although he could easily have doubled it. He would have immediately.

I found the biology easy and most interesting. Chemistry was interesting but very difficult. Physics I couldn't manage at all. Arithmetic was always difficult for me. At the end of the year, I passed biology, failed chemistry and got 12 percent in physics. Unhappy, but not surprised, I did the year's work again with coaching from various people, paid and unpaid.

As recreation, I had some very pleasant times, such as going to the theater, Barry Jackson's Repertory, where I made acquaintance with Ibsen's plays. I attended quite a number of operas at the Prince of Wales theater. The "Immortal Hour" [an opera by

Rutland Boughton] was being talked about then with Gwen Ffrangcon Davies and the haunting melody of "How beautiful they are the Lordly ones" stayed with me.

I was tried for the 1st XI in hockey but I really did not enjoy hockey very much. As "back," I had to tear up and down the field until I was tired and completely winded. I am afraid that too much smoking had not improved matters. I was thrilled with steeple chasing and would go off alone to any reasonably near meetings and stand on the course. I never bet and could not have afforded to, but I much enjoyed watching the jumping.

In the winter of 1922 our generous Scottish uncles paid for Dick and me to go to Switzerland for a fortnight with Aunt Edith and Uncle Cyril (Admiral Sir Cyril and Lady Fuller) and our cousins. We stayed at the Palace Hotel. It was a glorious holiday. We all hired skis and skates and the snow was perfect and the sun shone brilliantly. We were out all day, often taking our chicken and hard-boiled eggs up to the Scheidegg and hurtling down on our skis or partly on our behinds.

I became skiing and dancing partners with one Capt. Mansel Shewen, who was ADC [aide-de-camp] to the Governor of Bombay. He wore a monocle and was very smart and skied very well. One day we missed our train to go up to Wengern-Alp. "Oh that doesn't matter," he said, "we'll hire a special," which he did. There were glorious sunlit slopes and lunch outdoors in the glittering snow, then skiing home in the early dusk through the pinewoods, and dancing and fun every evening at the hotel. I entered a ski race before I left but I can only say that I didn't come in last—almost last, though.

One day I was luging down the railway line when a workman shouted what sounded like "Zug kommt!" [train is coming!] very urgently. It penetrated just in time and I hastily got myself and my luge [toboggan] off the railway track.

My skiing get-up wouldn't be thought much of these days. I wore Dick's riding breeches and puttees [leggings], a woolen sweater, felt hat, and woolen gloves—hopelessly wrong and the wool got so soggy with wet snow, but who cared?

It was a hard transition back to the world of medical school. At least I had the goal of passing my studies. Somehow I managed to satisfy the examiners at the end of this second year of 1st MB work, thanks to the help of a good many kind friends, and went on to the study of anatomy and physiology. About then I was asked to live at Cathedral Rectory by my friend and fellow-student, St. Clair Hamilton Baynes. I spent a very happy year or so there.

I had no serious love affairs during all this time, but one platonic episode (on my side at least) seems worth telling. I was quite friendly with a young man named Norman Kirby and invited him home for a brief visit. He behaved very peculiarly, to my surprise, for I had thought him a normal rather nice, if dull, young man. When he was to leave I rashly agreed to go for a walk with him near Shrewsbury before seeing him off at the station. His behavior was very odd, so much so that I feared he was starting a mental breakdown. We sat down to rest and a thunderstorm came on which affected him most curiously.

I tried to calm him in a matter-of-fact way, when he produced a little tin or zinc crucifixion that he began bending to and fro. The lightning flashed, the thunder roared, and Norman said, "When this crucifix breaks I shall kill you."

"Norman," I said, "You'll do nothing of the sort. Now try and pull yourself together. You are not at all well and I am going to take you to a doctor."

I went to a nearby farm and hired a horse and trap to take him the three miles to Shrewsbury. I took him to a doctor who agreed to keep him overnight, give him a sedative, and contact his father at Wolverhampton. Well, he turned up at our house next morning far from sane. My father told me to go upstairs and stay there. It seems he said to my father, "If a man ruined your daughter, would you let him marry her?"

"Marry her," roared my father, "I'd break his bloody neck." So then he was taken to the local police station in the bread van, the only available means of transport. His father was sent for to take him home and he was driven off, to everyone's relief.

Lourdes

In the summer of 1923 Mother wanted Rosie and me to take her on a visit to Lourdes. She was getting more and more crippled with multiple sclerosis, and although she was not a Catholic, still she hoped for some benefit, or best of all, for a miraculous cure.

We went by train to Dover, crossed the Channel by steamer and went by train to the south of France. Mother felt it was too extravagant to book sleepers for the long journey for three of us, so we sat up all night in our railway carriage. Our dinner was brought to us in the compartment.

We finally arrived in Lourdes and were driven to our hotel in a cab. Rosie and I went for a walk in the crowded streets of the town after supper. It was a hot summer evening. The crowds were most orderly; there was no shouting or rowdyism. At that time I was more or less an agnostic, and what impressed me tremendously was the strong atmosphere of prayer. One could really feel it.

In the morning we first took Mother to see the Grotto, a kind of cave in the rock, in view of the hill on which had stood the figure of the Madonna who appeared to and spoke to Bernadette. The roof of the Grotto was covered with bundles of crutches. Then we went to the *piscines*, the baths. Nuns were in attendance and gabbled prayers in Latin continuously. Each person who had come for the rite of immersion undressed in a cubicle, and wearing only one garment, descended a few steps into the long trough of water, walked along it, and came out up the few steps at the other end. People with all kinds of sores, deformities, skin diseases and dear knows what else, succeeded one another in walking in the water. One wondered how often the water was changed.

In the afternoon we took Mother in a wheelchair to join a crowd of people sitting in a great circle. Soon a priest came and blessed the people and held up the Host so that all could see it. There were prayers and chants and everyone hoped for a miracle, but on the days we were there, no apparent miracle occurred. When we left Lourdes, Mother had received no physical benefit, but neither did she catch any complaint from bathing in the incredibly dirty water. It seems that nobody does.

Meeting Donald

In the October term of 1924, several young men came to start doing their Clinicals in Birmingham. Among them was one Donald Bagster Wilson. He was strong looking, thick set, very pale, extremely fair, and he came to the first lecture carrying the latest number of the *London Mercury* that he read throughout the lecture. Afterwards, my friend Maurice Millard introduced us. We were attracted to one another and Donald asked me to go to the theater with him. Later I asked him to go for a ride with me. Donald helped me very much with my work. He had a good brain and was a good teacher.

Some weekends I hired a horse. Donald had been through the Cavalry, jumping at Tidworth when his father was a major in the RAMC [Royal Army Medical Corps]. I boarded with Dr. Mary Stone who had a house and a practice at Alecester Lane's End. It was four miles from the city of Birmingham and quite country. I went to and fro by tram, although if I felt very energetic, I sometimes walked back in the evening.

In 1925 Donald wrote to his parents, clearly exploring his feelings about his work and his relationship with me: "strange to say, I'm going to ask your advice, not of course that I'm going to take it. You know Peggy is not at all the sort of person to have missionary ideas. Now supposing that she loved me truly and I her, should one go on with the idea that her attitude may change? And if that should fail, should one be prepared to modify one's own programme? Or should one stop? I don't regard human affection as entirely possible to be recoverable from any trauma, but there is the other confusing side, which is the possibility of any missionary society I should care to work for refusing to have me. Also the knowledge that there is an urgent need for Christian men in government medical service in Africa."

I got German measles just before my finals in June 1925, and I like to think that was why I failed the examination. I wrote to Donald, "Please don't disown me when you hear that I have crashed completely my midder fiver [midwifery exam] but the kindest examiner in the world couldn't pass me in the clinical. Of course my patient was stone deaf, but that doesn't excuse me from diagnosing the man with a distended bladder as an ovarian cyst. I distinguished myself in the large and important subject of Ophthalmology. The best I can hope for is to be excused from Eyes in November."

I finally qualified in December, having taken six years to do so. I was then 28.

Introduction to Nepal, 1926–1930

Nepal of the 1920s was shaped by two centuries of British engagement in India as the East India Company and government of England expanded trade into Bombay, Calcutta, and Bengal (Frankopan 2017). Nepal had became a unified kingdom in 1768, but conflict with the British East India Company over bordering territories with India resulted in the Anglo-Nepalese War of 1814–1816 and the defeat of Nepal. The resulting Treaty of Sugauli of 1816 ceded border territories to the East India Company while ensuring the independence of Nepal.

The British crown officially assumed direct control of India in 1858; Britain was well served by an independent Nepal as a buffer zone between India and Tibet. They also benefited from the large numbers of Gurkhas, soldiers famous for their loyalty and military ability. Nepal was governed by a *maharaja* [prime minister], a member of the Rana family who were British allies (Miele 2017, 91). The British representative to Nepal was called the resident. "The resident is rather an ambassador than a supervisor" (Campbell cited in Lee-Warner 1910, in Miele 2017, 94).

During World War I more than 200,000 Gurkhas served in the British Army while military supplies were provided for Nepal. In 1923, Nepal and Britain signed a treaty negotiated by Peggy's employer, Maharajah Chandra Shamsher, in the palace in Kathmandu, Singha Durbar, superseding the terms of the 1816 Treaty of Sugauli. The new treaty guaranteed Nepal's independence and ability to conduct its own foreign policy. As Peggy arrived in Kathmandu, the British resident was in transition to the status of envoy. Peggy was welcomed by the Maharaja's sons, each called general, and especially the father of her patient Nani, who was called General Krishna.—*Editor.*

Chapter 2

Nepal, 1926–1927

by Peggy Lovett Wilson

Job Offer

As I completed my medical studies, the next step should have been to do my "House Jobs" [internships]. But then I had a letter from Dame Agnes Hunt. Sir Robert Jones asked her to choose someone medically qualified who had worked in orthopaedics at Baschurch to go to Nepal and replace an orthopedist, Miss Jessie Brown, in having charge of a granddaughter of the Maharaja who was sadly crippled by poliomyelitis. I was in a great quandary.

I am sure that all newly qualified doctors will appreciate what a difficult decision I had to make. House Jobs are tremendously important, and nothing can replace the training and experience they give in medicine, surgery, and midwifery.

Yet I was so tempted to accept! I rushed to get a map and see where Nepal was. I thought of tigers and rubies. I also thought of Kipling's "And the Wildest Dreams of Kew are the facts of Khatmandhu" [from Rudyard Kipling's poem "In the Neolithic Age," 1892]. I put it all to my father and asked him to decide. He said I must go. It would be "crazy to refuse," "wonderful country it must be," "chance of a lifetime," and so on. My father's experience as a traveller and adventurer was legendary. He saw no reason why his eldest daughter shouldn't attend medical school and travel the world.

I accepted the post in Nepal. The London Agent for the Nepalese arranged everything and booked my passage in the P&O ship, the Rawalpindi, at the beginning of March 1926. I only had a few thin dresses and a not very grand riding outfit consisting of breeches, a light Holland jacket and high boots. But I had a number of medical books and instruments, including midwifery ones, which I hoped I would never have to use.

Just before I was to sail, Donald's mother sent me a copy of the *Daily Light.* I wrote to Donald that I am "well supplied with devotional works and your mother will have a little devotional service every Sunday for me. I wonder what will happen when I come back. I wonder whether either of us will have recovered from our love. I expect it will be a tug of war with your family. I still feel wrapped in a warm glow from your love. I hope it will last a long time."

Travelling to Nepal

Father and Ellison, our gardener, carried my very heavy uniform case of books down the stairs and out to the car. My father went with me to Tilbury [port of London], and saw me onto the large magnificent ship. He seemed to think that my tiny cabin on D deck was the height of luxury, and perhaps to him it was, in comparison with the one he occupied when travelling to South Africa in the Zulu war.

I enjoyed myself until we got into the bay and then, oh dear, I didn't leave that little cabin for three days and nearly poisoned myself with chlorodyne. The stewardess was scathing and certainly when I did what she told me and dressed and went up on deck, I soon recovered.

Coming south of Spain to Gibraltar, the scent of a thousand flowers came through my porthole. I went on shore after breakfast with an eager escort and I was entranced by the warm sunshine, the masses of flowers for sale, the gaily woven cloths, and the attractive basketwork. Later I had a lovely day with my aunt and my Uncle Cyril, who was commanding the Mediterranean Fleet.

Next port of call was Marseilles, in the south of France, and I was fascinated by the Chateau d'If [prison fortress in the Bay of Marseille, setting of Alexandre Dumas' *Count of Monte Cristo*]. We got to Port Said, in the north of Egypt, and saw the statue of de Lesseps [Ferdinand Marie, Vicomte de Lesseps, French diplomat and developer of the Suez Canal] through the dining saloon porthole. The glorious sunshine was brilliant yet dazzling. I have had such an orgy of new impressions, and seen such a riot of color and changing scenery. The harbor at Port Said was filled with little rowing boats full of wares: rugs and shoes and beads and shawls. Men in turbans and fezzes, mostly in long blue smocks, and nearly all barefooted.

All afternoon we went slowly down the Suez Canal; mud banks on each side were very dull and ugly. It was extraordinary at night, gliding along so quietly. I put my head out of my porthole about midnight and we were just passing another big ship, so close that one could look right into their portholes.

We were between the Arabian and Egyptian coasts all day. No green anywhere, nothing but rugged mountains and sand. I saw Mt. Sinai in what looked to be the thirstiest land imaginable. The mountain ranges in the sunshine were like stage scenery, so unreal.

I have been promoted to the Captain's table. I like the little Captain, known as Twinkles, immensely. He is great fun.

It is much hotter today. We are well into the Red Sea and everyone is in white. The Deck Games tournament has started. Major Fitzgerald and I are a very hot combination but unluckily you have to draw for partners. However, he has also been asked to the Captain's table, which is nice. I was inoculated yesterday evening against typhoid, and my arm was pretty sore when we were dancing, but it isn't at all bad.

There is a certain Lieutenant Hall of the Indian Marines whose dancing is absolutely second to none. Otherwise the men are fairly average to bad. This is a warm, attractive, lazy life; I shall be really sorry to get to Bombay.

I didn't think there would be much fun in going ashore at Aden, Yemen, but I was invited to have tea at the Club. It was cool and shady with shelters down. Then we went in two open taxis to see the Tanks [Tawila Tanks, historic cisterns built to collect rain and prevent flooding].

We had a Fancy Dress Ball. I borrowed a sarong from the Chief Officer, a scarf or two and a basket with two herrings in it from the kitchen and went as a fishwife. The dance was fine as I successfully evaded my *bête noir*, a rich little Calcutta merchant, and had five dances with Major Fitzgerald. We have started a little romance but it got no further last night as after the dance, I was at a little party in the Captain's cabin when I tasted my first "Green Light."

It's impossible to do any work on board. As soon as one starts to read, some man comes and sits down and wants to talk and you can't be anywhere but on deck, everywhere is so hot. I have seen lots of flying fish and the water is all phosphorescent when it is dark. I don't feel a bit like a staid lady doctor.

Bombay [Mumbai], February 27–March 1, 1926. Colonel Hutchinson, who was asked by the Maharaja's family to meet me, came on board early and is arranging everything for me splendidly. I am staying with him in his large, delightful bungalow on Malabar Hill. I have a great big bedroom and a dressing and bathroom, and a little verandah, and everything is lovely.

I visited two hospitals yesterday morning, then shopped, rested in the afternoon and then picked up one of my swains at the Yacht Club and did more shopping. I returned to the Club for a dance, met Colonel Hutchinson and motored back to his bungalow, changed, dined at the Majestic with Twinkles and his cousin and her husband. Then we danced at the Yacht Club. Finally the captain took me for a midnight, moonlight motor picnic with a bottle of champagne and a packet of sandwiches. Alas for him, he hoped so much but his hopes went unfulfilled!

Colonel Hutchinson brought a tea basket and we took our bathing things and motored to Juhu, about eight miles out. Hot yellow sands fronted a belt of palm trees. The water was almost hot and I was floating about peacefully when we found we were over rocks that were under the water.

Then came about the most unpleasant hour of my life. We couldn't get away from the big jagged rocks just under the water and every wave flung us against them. I found a ledge and hung on like a leech, with waves breaking over my head until I was shivering with cold and got a cramp. Colonel Hutchinson, very bravely, maneuvered his way out to sea and eventually found a sandy way back to shore and then came and fetched me. I was glad to be on dry land again. We got off very lightly with only small cuts and bruises.

I had dinner with a party at the Yacht Club and was 40 minutes late, but I explained that I was lucky not to be a mangled wreck. We went to dance at the Majestic. Major Fitzgerald managed to wangle the P&O launch yesterday and in the afternoon, we went to Elephanta Island [in Mumbai Harbor, cave temples housing Hindu rock carvings]. It was a glorious evening for our voyage back. A huge yellow moon rose out of the sea but Desmond [Fitzgerald] wouldn't look. "No," he said, "it's quite hard enough to be good as it is."

Next morning he took me on board the Rawalpindi to say goodbye to Captain Redhead (Twinkles) who was dancing about on the bridge waving his topee [pith helmet]. Later I had the awful business of re-sorting and stowing away my new buys. My servant was extremely helpful, but I can't get used to seeing him handle my clothes.

Today Colonel Hutchinson is taking me to the place where they make plague vaccines for all India, the Haffkine Institute, and also antivenine [antivenom] for snakebites. At 9 p.m. I start the great journey. I am going via Patna and have to cross the Ganges and arrive at Peeprah Factory on Wednesday, where I am staying with people called Norman. Jessie Brown, whose place I am taking in Nepal, is meeting me there and we are to do the journey together. That is splendid.

I felt very alone and desolate when the train started. That night and the next day I saw no one but Indians, was desperately hot and smothered in dust. The next night was cold and I had to change at Gaya at 6:30 a.m., where I was met by a cheery English stationmaster with a note from a Mrs. Foley saying that she would meet me at Patna. This she very kindly did, and I spent the night very comfortably.

In the morning at 5:30, I was motored to the ghat [steps down to the river] where I boarded the steamer and went down the Ganges for three quarters of an hour. It was extremely interesting watching the natives washing themselves and their clothes and rubbing their teeth with a bit of stick, the women and children filling their pots with water and carrying them up the steep bank on their heads, two or three at a time, one on top of another. Then I got into another train.

My travelling servant is invaluable, arranges and remembers everything. He always comes to my carriage door to see if I want anything at every stop. I got to Muzuffarpur about 11:30 a.m. and had a large tuck-in in the Refreshment Room served by a stately polite old chap in a turban and spotless white clothes.

I got to Jindhara at 3:00 p.m. where Mr. Norman met me and motored me home for the night. They have a divine bungalow and the garden an absolute blaze of color, pink and scarlet bougainvillea, blue azalea trees, and creepers of all colors besides every imaginable English flower. They are charming people and so kind. We played bridge all evening. Jessie Brown arrived in the middle of the night, and next day she and I set off in a train. We made tea with my new spirit lamp and got to Raxaul at 6 p.m.

We started from Raxaul in a car in pouring rain, and the first stop was at Birunji, where we were able to ask the Burra Hakim, Governor of that province in Nepal, if we could have a covered lorry for our luggage, which was rapidly getting soaked.

Nobody hurries here and we sat for hours on his verandah watching the rain. At last the lorry came, luggage was stowed inside, and three extra coolies were discovered stowing away inside. The fat Burra Hakim stood and roared and grunted at them but they took no notice, so they came too. Then we had a 50-mile drive through pouring rain over a new road, only just finished. I missed the elephant journey by three weeks.

We held on for dear life because if you let go for a second the bumps threw you up so high that you banged your head on the top of the car. This was going at a maximum of 10 mph!

In the middle of the jungle part (the Terai), we burst a tire so we went on in the luggage van to the Churia rest house. There were three cars standing outside belonging to one of the Generals (all the Maharaja's sons are generals from birth) and his ladies, so the havildar [sergeant] was sent in to ask if we could have a room.

We went in with our tiffin [lunch] basket up some loft-like stairs into a big room with a wooden table and an old bedstead. There we had our lunch and changed into boots and breeches. It went on raining, and it never stopped until we reached Kathmandu.

We got to a rest house at the foot of the hill called Sisagarhi at 4 p.m. and there the van deposited our luggage and departed. There was no furniture at all, so we decided to walk up the Sisagarhi Pass to the rest house at the top and stay the night there, a climb of over 2,000 feet. We got started and mighty steep it was. Then we met Miss Brown's syce [groom] and pony coming down the hill, so we took turns on the pony. I got on first, and remembering what Father said about their liking to walk on the extreme edge of the khud [precipice], determined to be brave and let his mouth alone. What was my horror when the little brute walked straight over the edge and began to go down sideways, wanting to get to the village below. I thought my last hour had come as it was getting dark and I shouted to know what to do next. One of the men sprang down and caught the bridle, I grabbed the mane, and in two bounds we were on the path again.

It was a fearful climb over loose rocks and shale and desperately steep, and we were very tired when at last we reached the top. Then there was a long wait for our luggage and bedding, but finally it arrived. A servant made us a roaring wood fire and heated water for our tin tub and made us hot soup and buttered eggs.

We got up about 7 a.m. and finally got packed and saw the coolies loaded up with the baggage. My tin uniform case, which made Father and our gardener Ellison pant to carry downstairs, was strapped onto a small man, together with several other things to carry 20 miles! We chartered another pony but a mile or two on we met the dandy that had been ordered for me. It was the only time that I ever travelled in a dandy. It wasn't bad, just a steady shaking, like a perambulator with a canoe bottom, carried by eight coolies by poles, fore and aft, on their shoulders. The scenery was glorious with strange and wonderful greenery, streams, waterfalls, and always hills.

There was a landslip on one part of the road and rocks tumbling down the mountainside, so we made a detour over large boulders. On top of a grassy hill we lunched on cold chicken, biscuits, cakes and chocolates, with the watchful havildar, a dear, cheery little Gurkha, always smiling, ready to light my cigarette when I wanted it.

It became more and more hilly until we reached the famous Chandragiri Pass, which was terrible. The climb up was as steep as the side of a house in places, and all rocks. The coolies panted and sweated up it somehow. I kept reminding myself that it was the main road into Nepal. On Jessie's last journey she saw three motorcars being carried up, complete, not in pieces. There was no view at the top, nothing but an immense cloud below us. We walked down most of the descent, desperately steep and slippery after the rain, stepping from rock to rock. My riding boots were most uncomfortable.

It must be nerve racking to be carried down. I was so tired I was carried down the last bit, which was not very steep, in my dandy. On the flat at the bottom was a perfectly English brougham with a pair of horses for the last seven miles to Kathmandu.

Everywhere cheery little people smiled at us, and some played horns and flutes, as it is lucky to arrive to music.

In Service to the Maharaja

I arrived at last in March and settled down as if I had been here for ages, the great journey over and all my luggage present and correct. We drove straight to what is to be my bungalow when Jessie leaves at the end of the month: two bedrooms, a nice big sitting room and kitchen places. There is a garden with nothing much in it so far. Everything is paid for by His Highness the Maharaja, Sri Teen Chandra Shumsher Junga Bahadur Rana, servants and eatables and all.

I have a nice English-speaking ayah [maid or nursemaid] named Mohany, who was ayah to the children of the former Envoy and who actually had been to England with them. There was a nice tea all ready for us and a blazing wood fire, but my word, it did seem cold after Bombay.

Our neighbors the Brufords asked us to dinner that night. He is an electrical engineer. They are the kindest and most hospitable people imaginable. Just as we were finishing dinner three of the generals came to call to meet us. General Krishna, the father of my new little patient, and two of his brothers were all very nice and most anxious to make us welcome and be friendly. As a family they are on the short side and many of the men have to wear spectacles. The Brufords have just put in wireless and the Rana family appears in twos and threes to listen in.

Next morning we were fetched in a carriage and pair to the palace, the Singha Durbar, an enormous white plastered mansion. My small charge called Nani (which means something like "dear little one") is a most adorable child. She is very pretty with large brown eyes, beautifully shaped nose and chin, perfect teeth and delicately colored cheeks and with a very sweet expression that at times can be gay or roguish, and a pretty wit. She is better in some ways that I expected to find her, and she can walk in an unsteady sort of fashion holding on to one's hand. But she is extensively paralyzed and has a bad spinal curvature.

I have also one of General Baber's sons (General Baber is Krishna's elder brother) as patient with a fractured elbow. I hope to Heaven I make a success of it. There are several other royal patients; General Krishna, Nani's father, is worried about his wife who is very thin and has a cough. He has asked me to examine her. She is the most beautiful little lady I have ever seen. She is only 24 although Nani is eight. I did examine her and was not quite happy about the apex of her left lung, but there was nothing definitely wrong. She is of royal blood, being a sister of the king.

The days are much alike. I have tea and fruit at 8 a.m. and breakfast at 9 a.m. At about 10 a.m. a carriage and pair arrives and takes us to the Singha Durbar. We go up on to the roof where Nani has her breakfast and we compose her menu for the day. Then General Krishna arrives for a chat, followed by my boy patient and often his father, and one or two Nepalese doctors. Then we go with the child to some part of the palace grounds and give her exercises and massage and teach her to walk. At 1 p.m. we go to treat the Maharaja's sister, a dear old lady who can speak no English. We then go home for tiffin. Later we go for a walk and peer into shrines and temples and look at the marvelous wood carving on window frames, doors and balconies; there are sacred bulls walking everywhere about the streets.

The evening's work is a riotous affair. It starts with Musical Chairs played with Nani and her ladies-in-waiting while General Krishna plays the pianola. Then I have to play the piano and my boy patient sings Harry Lauder songs with a broad Scots accent that he acquired goodness knows how. All this in the intervals of exercises and manipulations designed to strengthen Nani's weak muscles. Usually about four or five of the younger generals come in and join in the fun, and we have Nepalese songs on the gramophone alternating with the latest foxtrots. We get back to the bungalow about 7:30, bathe and change, have dinner, and read or write until bedtime.

Peggy and Nani in Nepal, 1926.

One afternoon shortly after my arrival there was a grand gymkhana affair on the Maidan. We put on our good clothes and arrived in state in our carriage and pair with the havildar or subadar [captain] sitting beside the coachman and two syces perched up behind. A bicycle bell is rung to make the people get out of the way. I was introduced to His Highness the Maharaja, who welcomed me to the country. Then the King arrived, in greater state than we had, and we all settled down to watch the events, consisting of running races, a bicycle race, gymnastics, pole jumping, etc.

I had quite a fright one evening. Driving to Singha Durbar in the moonlight we met the one and only steamroller of Nepal chuf-chuffing down the road. The horses took fright and plunged and turned sharply around until they were at right angles to the carriage in a narrow road. There was much shouting and excitement but finally the syces got to their heads and they were led past. Every night a gun is fired at 10:30, and anyone on the streets after that is put in prison.

It is a mixture of all seasons here. The flowers in my sitting room now are poppies, purple irises, sweet peas and marigolds, while the Brufords have daffodils and hyacinths. All fruit trees are in bloom and the palace garden where I spend the morning has orange trees in bloom and yellow roses. The oats and barley will be turning color soon and yet some of the trees are only just in bud, while the grass is yellow and burnt up. Sometimes in the middle of the day a tremendous wind gets up quite suddenly from a dead calm, doors and windows bang, and before you know it the house is full of dust. It only lasts about five minutes.

So far nothing has been said about my hospital work, but if I go on getting private patients, at this rate I shan't have time for it.

The English

The [British] Legation has a nice two-story house, not improved by a roof of red corrugated iron. The Envoy, Mr. Wilkinson, is the big noise and has the best house. He is 53 and looks 40 with a very pleasant humorous face, rather lined, slim and athletic, even desperately energetic. His wife, unfortunately, is not here as she isn't strong enough to come out. They have three sons at school. Mr. Bruford, the electrical engineer, is employed by the Nepalese. Once or twice a week Jessie and I dine with the Brufords and play bridge. The Brufords and I have been given a tennis court and General Krishna has provided me with a piano. He is most kind and always thinking of something new to do for us.

Feminine society for me is at a bit of a discount. Mrs. Bruford and I are the best of friends and she is the nicest little woman imaginable, but there it finishes. We have really nothing in common. Mrs. Hartland, the Training Officer's wife, is a delightful baby to whom very little on earth matters except dancing and clothes. She and I would have had a lot in common if I were eight years younger. Mrs. Hartland has decided that I am the last word in old fashioned-ness and is determined to smarten me up. She is going to chop me a fringe and do curled side pieces and says I must put them in curlers every night and every afternoon. It is too comic for words!

One Sunday we went for a picnic to a place in the hills where General Krishna has a bungalow. The entire British population (five in all) went. It was ten miles by car, passing through the famous town of Bhatgaon where I photographed the golden door, to the foot of the hills. Mr. Bruford and I rode, Mrs. Bruford was carried, and Mr. Wilkinson and Jessie walked. The Snow Mountains showed gloriously, all 200 miles of them. I saw Mt. Everest (thrill of thrills) but it looked very insignificant compared with some of the others being so far away to the east.

The whole valley of Kathmandu was spread out in front of us. There were hedges of white roses and trees of pink peach blossom and white blossom, and what with all that and the light on the hills, red soil and vivid green of the young rice, surely there could be nothing lovelier in the world. They say Tibet is grander, but oh! The sun setting on the snows turning them to glowing flame, then to deeper and deeper pink and finally to the red of fire. It just left us breathless with its magnificence. We walked down in the moonlight.

We have regular Sunday picnics and panting climbs up a hill. Mr. Wilkinson is tremendously keen on walking. I like him very much; he is such a cheery soul. In April, Mr. Wilkinson and I had a tremendous outing that left me dog-tired. We started on ponies at 8:45, left them at the bottom of the hill and walked until 5 p.m. when we got on the ponies again. We had two little lunches on the way and tea when we got back to the Legation.

Tibetans think Nepal very hot, and Indians think it is very cold and the English think it is just right. It is just over 90° in the shade at midday nowadays. It never goes over 100°.

On a Saturday in June on the King's birthday, Mr. Wilkinson gives an annual Garden Party at the Legation. All the Europeans go and the Maharaja, "with any members of his family and staff that he cares to bring." There are sports and horse leaping for the Legation Escort, and tennis or squash rackets for those who like it. I am to motor over for it.

We were unpleasantly thrilled yesterday by hearing from Mr. Webb that the Burmese pony he was riding on the journey backed over the khud with him. He managed to throw himself off, and the pony went down sheer 700 feet and was killed.

I had a very dull Sunday. Mrs. Bruford and I were to have gone for a picnic with Mr. Wilkinson, but it rained and when he asked us to spend the day at the Legation, Mrs. Bruford wouldn't go because she wouldn't leave "ma husband" who was unexpectedly at home. Such are the conventions here that it wouldn't have been proper for me to go alone. I played five sets of tennis with "ma husband" but I was rather bored.

Royal Life

When you see a great crowd in the distance you know it is His Highness going for a drive. Syces run in front to clear the way, then comes his closed carriage followed by a mounted guard with rifles loaded and cocked, then a lot of men running carrying fixed bayonets, and a miscellaneous crowd of people galloping along on little ponies.

There was a Durbar one day to welcome Mr. Wilkinson back after his shoot. It was in the great hall of the palace. The walls were lined with generals and colonels, magnificent in full dress uniform and head dresses with waving bird of paradise plumes. The King had a gorgeous one encrusted with precious stones, uncut diamonds, and emeralds the size of a blackbird's egg. Everyone wears jewels here; the diamonds in small Nani's ears are the size of peas.

When Mr. Wilkinson arrived, he and the Maharaja walked up the hall hand-in-hand, and the King then made him a little speech and poured some scent on his handkerchief. Then after a little chat the King removed his headdress with an audible and visible sigh of relief and the ceremony was ended.

There are continual processions past the house at all hours of the day and night and much singing and banging of drums because it is the month of marriages. I went to a wedding, a granddaughter of the Maharaja marrying a small Indian rajah. There was a grand reception at the Singha Durbar, all the generals in full dress uniform, bands playing, guards of honor, procession on elephants, and fifty bridesmaids. We each had scent poured on our handkerchiefs, and a little package of "pan" [a sweet] wrapped in gold paper to take away.

One day we went over to General Krishna's new palace, an enormous place with accommodation for hundreds of people. Here all the sons and their families live with their father until he dies, so most of the big places are empty and waiting for their occupants. Most of the big rooms are furnished with some lovely things, but they seemed to me so uncomfortable and dreary, and a lot of it is in such bad taste. Nice carved woodwork painted over in the crudest colors, plaster pillars painted to represent different sorts of marble and so on. The orthodox dining room had nothing in it at all. A marble floor and white tiles halfway up the walls, as their first meal of the day of rice has to be eaten ceremoniously after bathing and putting on clean clothes, and the floor has to be washed before and after.

Afterwards we went on to the Legation where Mr. Wilkinson was giving a children's party. These Nepalese children are simply adorable. The small girls each remind one of a flower, they are so perfect. They have wonderful manners, but one never hears their parents reprimand them for anything. Even the stern middle-aged General Sir Baber was playing games and enjoying it immensely.

In late August there was a lovely sunset. No sun or light in the west, but high up in the sky, the edge of a great mass of white cloud caught fire and grew brighter and brighter and then the sky all round it turned to a deep pink, then gradually faded. I was supposed to be watching a festival. My carriage and pair drew up at the front entrance of the Singha Durbar with a flourish. I was met by a man sent by General Krishna to look after me, conducted to a solitary chair, and the play began, which resembled what you might see in a booth of a small village fair. The heroine (a man) dressed in pink satin with pink cotton gloves sang a melancholy song about the absence of her lover. Then he (the lover) appeared in a pseudo shabby sort of court dress, and they began an interminable duet that was finally drowned by a brass band heralding the approach of the juggler who turned out to be a rather indifferent conjurer.

I had to go and see her Majesty again yesterday. The three little princes were all standing in a row, Mahendra, Himalaya and Basundhara, each wearing a large grey Homburg hat and an enormous diamond crescent pinned on to their coats. I should think the eldest was about eight [Mahendra, who ruled as King 1955–1972]. Their father the King is only twenty-three.

There is a runner who takes the mail down to Raxaul. He has a bell that he rings to warn off the wild beasts in the Terai and a spear to defend himself if he should be attacked. (I learned long afterwards that if he did not run fast enough, he would be terribly punished. One account said "Arms and legs tied up behind him and be left for a long period on rocks in the sun." I can't vouch for the truth of this.)

Domestic Life

Jessie departed and I was left in sole possession of bungalow, servants and dog. The servants are Shumlal the bearer, Bakermuni the wash up boy, Bereman the sweeper, Mohany the ayah, Jit Bahadur the cook, the havildar, two policemen, water carrier, Mali the gardener, syce and dhobi [washer man]. Twelve in all! The dog is a Japanese spaniel, a very good housedog though this virtue is quite unnecessary here where I am so well guarded. He is not beautiful to look at. He is fed entirely on curry and rice and can walk 20 miles without seeming tired. Occasionally he gets fits of neurosis when he rushes round the room and makes odd noises. I am quite fond of him.

What a marvelous ayah I have; really, she is a wonder. There were a whole lot of bullock carts in the road, and they wouldn't get out of the way of the car and the havildar was quite powerless to make them. But Mohany hopped out and took my big stick and flourished it at them, and in about two minutes the road was clear. My cook hasn't turned up here, and there are no stores but my ayah is cooking a dinner out of nothing as far as I know. Just been having a long discussion with the dirzee [tailor] interpreted by my ayah about my divided skirt which he has made far more divided than skirt.

I am afraid I am spoiling my servants though; I shall never make a good housekeeper. I hate finding fault with them and lots of things amuse me so that I can do nothing for laughing. At the present minute I am watching through the window the little cook, Jit Bahadur, clean the meat safe by throwing buckets of water over it. The floor is an absolute lake and the other servants are standing round fearfully interested and chortling with laughter as he *is* getting so wet.

I am getting tired of ordering my meals. Diet is mainly chicken and duck. If I want mutton I have to eat a whole sheep so I haven't embarked on one yet. I have been experimenting with Nepalese food lately, having rich people's lunches and poor as well. You have a plate of leaves stitched together on which is a pile of cooked rice, about ten little messes are laid out in front of you, all cooked in ghee and very hot with curry powder and pepper and greasy sweetmeats. I disliked most of it intensely. We eat Indian corn cobs here, very nice when they are young. I have also sampled their toddy which tastes like beer and wasn't nice. I had a jackfruit the other day, so big I could only just lift it. When you cut it open the smell! but the taste is rather like a mixture of anchovy, banana and cream. His Highness's sister, who is my patient, has sent me all sorts of wonderful fruits and vegetables. I can't say I really like any Indian fruits much, and mangoes not at all. The wild raspberries here are awfully good and there is a fern that we eat as a vegetable, besides getting all English kinds of vegetables. No mosquitos here but lots of other things that bite.

I finally killed my sheep, or rather had it killed, and am having mutton in every conceivable form for every meal. I have a hen that lays eggs now. Every day my boy brings in a tiny white egg in an eggcup that he shows me with great pride and then puts on the sideboard as an ornament. I hugely enjoy doing my housekeeping and writing the stores list for Calcutta.

I pictured myself having tons of time in the long and lonely evenings to read and write, but the reality is very different. I often don't get back to my bungalow until after 8 p.m., and by the time I have bathed, changed and had dinner there isn't much evening left. I have managed to catch a bad cold, and am not quite so fearfully cock-a-hoop as usual, but tomorrow the Envoy Mr. Wilkinson and I are going to climb one of the big hills on our own feet so I must pull myself together and not be outdone by a mere man. Just had my fortune told and am going to have great distress in connection with a fair man; hope it isn't Donald.

It will be funny when I come back to England to walk about without being escorted everywhere, and to carry my own belongings. Here I can't carry a newspaper from my house to Mrs. Bruford's. My mind is an utter whirl of a strange language, servants, housekeeping, patients, temples, queer gods, wonderful carvings, ponies, hill picnics, and the necessity of writing about a dozen or more letters before the mail goes. I am having lessons in the language and am beginning to pick it up.

The Tibetans say "It is a poor horse that cannot carry a man up a hill, and a poor man that makes his horse carry him down." I am not quite used to jumping brooks in motorcars and to going up steps on horseback. But if I stay here long I shall be used to *anything.* I never felt so fit in my life as I do here, and no amount of exercise tires me. It really is a perfect climate, warm during the day and cold enough for a fire in the evening.

Easter at Kakani

I had a splendid Easter weekend at Kakani. We started early on Saturday, drove to the Residency and then I got on my pony. Mr. Wilkinson and Colonel Russell rode and Mrs. Russell was carried. We went about five miles on the flat and then a climb of about 3,000 feet with a gradient of 1 in 1 in places that my pony made no bones about. I should think he is the best pony that ever came from Tibet, pure white, very long tail, stands about 14 hands, I think. I hang onto his mane to stop myself slipping over his tail. He has a mouth like iron though, and if you canter him in the direction of his supper, you have to pull like Old Nick to stop him.

There is a tennis court and a 9-hole golf course, but it pays to be a poor smiter because many of Colonel Russell's drives cost him the ball, as the ball that went over the edge was goodbye. We had an awfully cheery time, only spoilt by the fact that the fire smoked so badly we had to sit most of the evening with our eyes shut. One day we took our tea to a still higher place and with hardly any warning a terrific thunderstorm broke on us, and before we got back to the bungalow we were like bits of wet rag and my stockings turned a brilliant orange color.

The first night I started with my shutters thrown wide open as usual, and then I suddenly thought how awful it would be to wake a see a panther's eyes glaring at me. So I got up and shut them.

There were lovely white and purple orchids growing up there, and we had hill honey and tiny little fish from mountain streams. We got up at 5:30 next morning and at 6:00 every snow mountain was glowing in the sunrise and peaks 30 miles away looked near enough to throw a stone at. I was quite sorry to come down to earth again, although this bungalow feels like home to me now.

Nani

Before she left, Jessie and I made Nani a new plaster jacket and took a cast for future use; we did a complete electrical test, designed a saddle for her, and got her onto a pony, entirely Jessie's idea. I took Nani up to the Legation and four of the Nepalese generals went, too. For an hour and a half there was the astounding sight of ten grown-ups rushing madly about playing hide and seek solely to amuse one small girl. It was very hot and most exhausting, especially for me as I had to carry her.

One day we took Nani to a place of hills. We drove to the foot and then she was carried up on a servant's back. There was a large pool full of sacred fish (carp), Balagi it is called. Percy Brown in *Picturesque Nepal* [1912] describes the fine spring water, gushing out of the hillside, which is collected in a number of clear ornamental ponds. Below the terrace of fishponds, out of the castellated and buttressed retaining wall, more than 20 gargoyle-headed spouts throw out streams of water that fall into a tank beneath. They are carved in stone and are brightly painted in vermilion, blue and green. Reclining full length in a small tank at the side with all but the face submerged is a carved stone figure of Narain, framed with a hood of snakes' heads. Narain is the creator, Brahma. A man sang Nepalese songs on a guitar. It was a beautiful day and we had picnic lunch and tea.

Another day Nani and I went out for a picnic and there nearly was a tragedy because the key of her tiffin basket got broken and no how could it be opened. Men were flying in all directions. One ran a mile to a little shop and got another key made and then it didn't fit. Eventually we coaxed it open with a corkscrew. She wouldn't have been allowed to eat any of mine so she would have had to go hungry if we couldn't have broken it open. Then the rain came down in torrents. Luckily there was a bungalow to shelter in and we had a pack of cards.

On one occasion, returning with Nani and two of her ladies and the usual escort of subadar, servants, coolies, etc., General Krishna rode out to meet us with one of his brothers. All the way along, we met more generals and people until at last the carriage was escorted by 15 outriders all galloping behind and alongside. When we got back to the bungalow they dismounted and came in, and one or two of them sang songs. Then we went back to the palace and played hockey on roller skates in a big room at the top while General Krishna's wife and Nani and the ladies made the audience. We had the hugest fun and all enjoyed ourselves enormously.

I am worried about Nani. She is all swollen up under her eyes and I can find nothing to account for it. Hope to goodness it isn't nephritis. It is sickening just as she was getting on so well and riding her pony every morning.

There have been tremendous thunderstorms off and on all the week, which mean havoc for the crops. The lightning and rain are exactly as you see them on a cinema film, with almost continuous flashes lighting up the whole place with purple light. We were caught in such a violent thunderstorm yesterday driving back after a day out with Nani that we had to stop and shelter at one of the general's houses. We waited in what was a thoroughly English sitting room leading out of a magnificent billiard room, and I was introduced to his wife and three delightful children, named Tuli, Myli and Kanchi, meaning eldest, middle and youngest, Nani's cousins. General Shingha played the gramophone to us and Kanchi, an adorable chubby little thing of three years or so, danced for us, smiling all the time. She was dressed in a close little bonnet and a frock down to her ankles of white silk edged with gold lace. She was rather worried by her heavy gold anklets so her father took them off and she danced on.

When it stopped raining General Shingha showed us over the huge garden with fountains and goldfish pools and a summer and a winter pavilion, orange trees loaded with fruit and blossoms and so on. When we left and I thanked him for his kindness he said, "Please do not do so! She is my niece, and you are scarcely less than one of our own family."

One morning, we saw a huge monkey, whereupon Nani was wildly delighted, and we had to chase it ever so far, the young Maharani being pick-a-back with her diamond earrings shaking in the breeze. She has a special servitor who always carries her.

Nani is getting on well. She is wildly keen on puff billiards [game with rubber bulbs to blow a cork ball into a goal] at the moment, which I encourage because (a) it is very good for her hands, and (b) I like playing it myself.

The much talked-of celluloid jacket is at last almost completed. I wonder what it will be like when I dare take it off the cast. It was comic. Four doctors came to see me make it and I'd no more idea what it should look like than the man in the moon.

Alas, the celluloid jacket, which cost me so much time and labor, is pretty badly warped, but it may do until I can make another. Nani nobly said it was splendid when I tried it on, and much lighter than the plaster, but she is an angel child and would say anything so that I shouldn't be disappointed.

Godaveri

In June we travelled to Godaveri, nine miles from Kathmandu, where General Krishna has transplanted his family for a change. The Princess especially loves it here. I hope it will do Nani good because she is delicate beyond belief. Two nights ago she had a temperature of 103.6 for no reason as far as I could make out, except that she had had some raspberries to eat. I have a big bungalow quite near to theirs. This is different scenery from other places I have been to in the valley. The hills are very heavily wooded, and there are fascinating glades and little streams everywhere. I feel almost intoxicated with beauty. Sometimes after dinner at night I walk about round the bungalow in a forest of fireflies that is almost dazzling. Then one sees the moon coming up over the hills. I get sleepy very soon in this air and go to bed about 9:30.

I haven't spoken to an English person for a week but I don't miss them much, if at all; these people are such darlings. The rains may start at any time now. I am going to motor into Kathmandu to see two patients and have lunch and tea with the Brufords. Poor Mrs. Bruford is very lonely as her husband is in camp and she only sees him at weekends.

Learning About Hinduism

August is the month of devil dancers. They have hideous big silver masks and purple wigs and a double row of bells round their hips, and they dance to a band played by sepoys in the courtyards of the palaces.

We went to watch a big religious ceremony called the Dussehra Festival, or the Durga Puja. Percy Brown says it commemorates the victory of the goddess Durga over the demon Mahishasur who usually takes the form of a buffalo. The poor buffaloes are killed by the hundred, which I did not go to watch. The Gurkhas love this part of the festival for each beast has to be decapitated by one stroke of the kukri [machete].

For nine days, all the people are dressed in red, worn at their morning puja. It is to please one of the goddesses, Kali by name, whose favorite color it is—she is a very bloodthirsty goddess. I met two or three of the Generals in scarlet shirts and skirts and asked them if they wouldn't go for their morning ride like that to brighten up the Maidan.

I was talking to General Krishna about Hinduism the other day and he said, "The best of our religion is that there is a god to suit everyone's taste, both peaceful and bloody, but it is always the same god who takes many different forms."

The Hartlands have done an awful thing in going by mistake into one of the holiest places at Pashuptinath where Siva's huge golden bull stands beside the great lingam or phallus. With their shoes on, making it even worse. It means that they have polluted the temple and there is a lot of feeling about it. One has to be so careful to ask where one may or may not go in their holy places.

Tomorrow morning I start at 6:45 a.m. for a place in the hills to meet Mr. Wilkinson who has been for a week's camping tour. The Hartlands were coming but have decided not to as she has got no topee [pith helmet] and it is blazing sun all the way. Nothing would induce her to wear one, says they "are so unbecoming," which of course they are. They leave on 1st November and I shan't care a bit.

On Thursday, November 1, Mr. Wilkinson, Major Arnott and I climbed Phulchoki, the highest of the hills surrounding the valley. It was in the shade all the way so it wasn't very hot. We did the 4,000 feet in three hours. Not bad going was it? It was quite chill-some on top and the aneroid [barometer] made it 9,200 feet. We could see the plains of India helped by a little imagination. Then we had an enormous lunch of eggs and sandwiches and curry puffs. We came down in two hours. It was dreadfully slippery, I fell down six times and got very muddy, but there were no leeches, thank heavens.

Christmas 1926

I am going to try and rig up a Christmas tree for Nani. She would love it. My Christmas presents are all going so late. I am sending Donald something queer and, I am afraid, ugly. It is a brass devil-dancer's mask.

I leave here next Saturday for Bombay where I shall be for about two months. General Krishna is taking a house, and I am to live in a hotel. On the way back we are coming via Agra. It will be nice to be in an English community for Christmas and go to church on Christmas Day.

I am taking my havildar and ayah and dog with me so I shall be well looked after. Nani will love Bombay. I am going to rig her up in splints she can bathe in; seawater would be so good for her. General Krishna is paying all expenses like the angel he is. I never ask to do any of these things; they are all proposed by him, such as seeing Agra.

Raxaul

I left my little homestead and rode and walked the 20 or so miles of divine country to the Sisagarhi Rest House where I stayed the night. There was a glorious deep red glow all over the west that went on until it was quite dark, and perfect stillness only broken by a bugle from the valley 2,000 feet below. I heard some animal jump into my room in the night but hoped it was only a dog or cat and went to sleep again.

The next day after walking down the Pass, I motored to Raxaul, passing General

Krishna and his party on the way. They had a tremendous bandobast and no mistake, palkies, coolies, running men, five elephants, cavalry escort and dear knows what. I had a little chat with them and then went on. The last 14 miles were horrid; they are making a little railway along it and consequently had used the only road. We had to bump along in a foot of dust alongside and kept coming up against a load of sleepers or a big hole and then having to turn back, bump over the railway, and try and get along on the other side. I had sent on my heavy luggage by coolies. I caught the train to Lucknov.

This is warm and flat after Nepal, that land of milk and honey. It seems so odd to be outside the Maharaja's jurisdiction here. The awful threat, "I shall speak to General Sahib about it," would strike no terror. It is a case of "It will have to be reported to the Envoy." I must say the Envoy's little bungalow is quite charming with such a pretty garden and lots of flowers. I am going to stay a night at Lucknov, as I want to go and see the Residency and have a good look round. I shall then go straight to Bombay.

I went over a rice mill this morning. The nice little "Babu" overseer took me. All the buzzing machinery was a great contrast to the Nepalese squatting peacefully in the sun outside their houses, shaking and shaking the rice to get the husks off.

Christmas in Bombay

I am living with Colonel Hutchinson as a paying guest. It is a million times nicer than being alone in a hotel. I have joined a tennis club and have had three baths at Juhu. I have been twice to the theater, going to the pictures tonight, am learning to play billiards and am going to do lab work in Colitt's Hospital. Another thing I have done, which I always vowed I never would, is go out to dance with a man of color, even though it is General Krishna's brother-in-law, a very nice man. I couldn't have got out of it without hurting their feelings, which I wouldn't do for anything, but all the same, I imagine that English people would look at it askance.

It was rather comic. He was to call for me at 6 p.m. and there was a party of English people to tea, just off the boat, out for the first time. They were telling me how dreadful it seemed to them to see English girls dancing with Indians on board ship and didn't I think it was awful, etc., etc., and there was I sitting waiting for this rajah to turn up!

Nani is flourishing apace and gets more adorable every day. She simply loves being here. Her father showers toys on her. Her little Princess mother is enjoying herself too. She has had a paddle in the sea, been to theaters, cinemas and motor drives, so everyone is happy. But Bombay is too physically wearying for words. You wake up rather tired, do your morning's work, and lie down for two hours in the afternoon and then have a cold bath before tea. Energy begins to flow in about six or so. Unfortunately then it is beginning to get dark. I went for a little walk the other day and was so beat I had to get into a taxi. True, it was silly of me to go at 3:30 p.m. when the sun is still so hot. I have got some lovely new clothes—the frocks I took to Nepal are all worn out.

I went to a Reception at Government House. Fearful scrum. I stood in a queue for an hour to shake hands with their Excellencies, then had a drink and came home. Crowds of people, Indians and English pretty equally divided.

We took Nani to the zoo, not a very good zoo. There was a tree (not in the exhibits) that was black with bats, literally hundreds, all hanging by one leg.

I was getting tired of an idle and frivolous life in Bombay and had my fill of gaiety. Still I must say I enjoyed the Yacht Club Fancy Dress Ball and the Byculla Ball very much at the time. I attended the big Fancy Dress Ball at the Willingdon Club in Nepalese dress as a Newari woman, correct in every detail. The Willingdon is the only Club where Indians and Europeans can spend a social evening together. I never attracted so much attention in my life. No one could make out what I was, but all seemed to agree that I couldn't be English, although they couldn't place the part of India that I came from. General Krishna introduced me to an Indian, whom I had met several times before, as his sister. The man made me a very low bow and was too overwhelmed by the honor to speak to me. When I went off to dance he told General Krishna how beautifully the Rana Sahib spoke English. When he was finally told who it was he was completely incredulous and couldn't believe that I was British.

I drove to the dance with the Princess and another Nepalese lady, and it felt so comic asking where the Purdah Pavilion was and taking them into it. I thought I should expire from heatstroke halfway through the evening, wearing a large cummerbund, baggy trousers, long sleeves, high neck, two bodices, a petticoat to the ground and a sari of six yards of crepe de chine over the top of it all, besides a wide tight velvet belt. And all this in a temperature in the mid–80s.

The dresses of the Parsi women are too heavenly. Silks and satins and chiffons with gold- and silver-edged saris. Great ropes of pearls (real, I suppose) and little satin slippers to match their dresses. They are very emancipated and drive their own cars, play tennis, do everything in fact like us. Those I have met I like very much. They are Persian in origin. The Parsi men are very Jewish looking and mostly pretty narrow and commercial minded I think.

On a Saturday in January I went to the Races with General Krishna. He made 250 rupees and I lost 12. The Races are held in the prettiest place imaginable, with shady green lawns, flowering trees, gay flower beds, and lovely little shining Arab horses being led round the paddock.

It is sad that owing to the growing industrialization and the low rates of pay, the wrong type of Englishman is here in ever-increasing numbers, and the "sahibs" are getting fewer. I feel quite ashamed for General Krishna to go to dances at places like the Town Hall here and meet the vulgar crowd whose main concern is with chota pegs [a measure of whiskey] and often burra not chota. Things are all wrong. They are not the ones who ought to be in command, teaching the Indians how to rule their country. This is a dreadful climate I find.

A New Year Working in Kathmandu

Following our two-month Christmas sojourn in Bombay, we returned to Kathmandu. Colonel Hutchinson, with whom I stayed in Bombay, is here on a visit. He is company for me in the evenings, comes over and we play piquet. Today we went to see a certain temple on the top of a hill. Dandies were sent to convey us the last part of the way, but I infinitely prefer to go up on my own legs. Colonel Hutchinson was most worried because he was getting tired and wanted to go up in the dandy and said he couldn't if I walked, but I at last persuaded him. Poor dear, he has lived in Bombay for the last 20 years, which isn't conducive to physical fitness. It is so nice having him in the bungalow opposite, someone to talk to in the evenings. He is trying to inspire me to get my spare room fitted up as a biochemical lab and do bugs and things there. It certainly would be a great interest; I suppose I could learn to do most of it from the book.

We have had an orgy of dinner parties for Colonel Hutchinson's departure, and then it was put off so they had to be given all over again this week. I'm rather sorry he has gone. Last Sunday I had quite a lot of exercise. Up at 4 a.m. for a case, then a walk with Colonel Hutchinson before breakfast, then a picnic walk with Mr. Wilkinson at 11:00, getting back at 4 p. m. and after tea, three sets of singles and dinner and bridge at night.

I am getting to be more and more a slave to exercise and have to walk further and further. In the afternoons when I don't go to patients or have lessons in Gurkhali, I walk until 5 p.m. and then get back very hungry for tea with a nice wood fire waiting for me. When the 200 miles of snows have changed through golden and pale pink to dark rose color and finally to a cold silver white, then I leave them. I never get tired of gazing at them, and I try and impress them on my mind so that they will be there for life.

Practicing Medicine

I have been awfully busy. When I am not being lady nurse, I am a consulting physician and gynecologist. I drive to see my cases in the inevitable carriage and pair. The family doctor awaits me and asks exactly what I would like done. I only hope I shan't make some fearful mistake sometime. I charge Rs10 a visit, after consulting with General Krishna, which I think is quite enough. I badly want to get into the hospital as there is apparently so much that needs to be done, but nothing can be rushed here and I must bide my time. I pin my hopes largely to the new Legation Surgeon who hasn't arrived yet. If he will only collaborate and talk over cases, we ought to be able to do a splendid amount of work.

Thank you, Donald, so much for sending the *Pharmacopoeia* straight away. I am so glad to have it. The other day I had to prescribe Santonin in a hurry and although I knew the dose I didn't know what to give it with. The Indian doctor came to the rescue, however. There is one Nepalese doctor and several Bengalis. I have found them all very nice and polite and we are very good friends, but I must say I like the Nepalese one best. With the Bengalis, as with most Indians I suppose, you are never quite sure what they are thinking and there always seems to be a slight barrier. With the Nepalese, however, you know exactly where you stand. Their mentality seems to fit in with an English mind so well, and they are so simple and kind-hearted.

I do think an MOH would be a grand person to have here or a sanitation officer, or something. Every roadside ditch and everywhere in fact but the middle of the road seems to be a public latrine.

The other day the two Indian lady doctors had a disagreement over a diagnosis and I was called to the hospital to settle the question. I do feel it a most terrible responsibility but I can only do my best, I suppose. The Indian doctor who took me there said of the lady doctor in charge, "Of course she is very young," (she looked quite thirty) "and has only been practicing five years!"

There are times when things are very depressing. I make beautiful plasters that are uncomfortable, or my patients desire to see Colonel McConaghy. That makes me furious if they are getting on really well under me. These people must see every doctor in the place before they are satisfied, however, all except General Krishna who allows no meddling with Nani by other people.

I've had my first midder [midwifery] case here in Nepal and been called up in the night for it, as a consultant at that. It is awful being expected to be a mine of wisdom, and it was my first case since I was qualified. All was well, however. I was asked by the doctor attending what were my fees for midder cases and I was completely stumped, never having thought about it. I bitterly regretted not having paid more attention to midwifery when I was a student. One case was most humiliating. There seemed no reason why the baby should not be born, but hour after hour went by with no progress. At last I swallowed my pride and asked Colonel Hutchinson's advice. He was up on a short visit to Nepal. He grinned at me. "Didn't you ever think of puncturing the membranes?" he asked me, and did so, whereupon the baby appeared in the next few minutes. Once a patient had a retained placenta. I waited and waited day after day, too scared of sepsis to remove it manually. But the patient seemed perfectly all right, having normal pulse and temperature, inoffensive lochia. So I left well alone and in exactly a week the placenta appeared and everything was normal!

Today I was sent for to see the wife of His Excellency the C. in C. [commander-in-chief], a dear old lady whose chief complaints were rheumatism and indigestion. She said she preferred to keep her dyspepsia rather than alter her diet so that was easy. I have ordered radiant heat and am debating about ionization, but don't remember very well how to give it and certainly no one else can.

I have two new patients this week. One turned from a threatened to an incomplete abortion, which is a nuisance, but I am faithfully following Fairbairn in "adopting an expectant attitude and giving ergot." The relations are getting most painfully expectant, poor dears; they can't think why I won't do something drastic, however much I explain to them.

One gets used to seeing horrors here such as would be undreamt of in England. The other evening, having a quiet stroll by the river, I saw a dead baby wrapped in a cloth waiting to be burnt, a living skeleton waiting for death so that when the moment came he could die with his feet in the sacred water of the Baghmati River, and far out in the river a large vulture standing on something which my policeman escort with a cheerful smile told me was a corpse. The vulture was striking repeatedly at it with its beak. The other day I saw a dying cow lying in the blazing sun smothered with flies. Nobody would dream of killing it to put it out of its misery because cows are sacred, and it is a crime to kill them. There are some pretty awful smells in places as you can imagine. Still the sun shines, the flowers bloom and nearly everyone seems happy.

Donald

I suppose from your last letter that you have definitely got the job at the General [General Hospital, Birmingham]. You are very good about writing to me when you have so little time to do it. I get thoroughly worried thinking of you at the General, getting whiter and tireder and tireder looking. Where have your excursions into literature brought you to now? I have become converted to Maurice Baring and I think *C* [a novel, 1924] is a wonderful book, have you read it? I rejoiced to get a proper letter from you and a most delightful photograph. I will send you a nice little snapshot of me as soon as I get some printed; it is so flattering I think I shall publish it.

I am having breakfast on a shady balcony looking over to the hills. To be perpetually *in* wonderfully beautiful surroundings is such a joy. Oh Donald, I should like you to come and see the fireflies. When it is dark the air is alive with them, and to see them over water is just too lovely.

You wonder why I really came here. I think it was settled for me by some power arranging my life, just as it was that I should take up medicine. I wonder what it will decree that I shall do next. I often feel I am a failure with the child, but I can't force muscles to work with hardly any nerve supply. I love her, very dearly, and often feel that my professional instinct is swamped by a hitherto undiscovered maternal instinct.

Rest House on the Way Back to Kathmandu, 20 March 1927

Donald dear, got your letter today. So you're throwing me over again! I am getting quite used to it now and don't take any notice. Look here, let's leave the question of marriage in the dim distant future to Providence and just see how things manage themselves. You often told me that you hoped we'd always be friends, and I don't mean to lose your friendship if I can help it, so unless you definitely want to stop writing, I shall go on as usual.

I must try and make you see what I am seeing now. Dusk, with dull reddish gray in the west over the valley 2,000 feet below. Ranges of wooded hills to the right of me, with their trees standing out against the sky and a big protecting hill curving round on the left, and the clearest purest air that ever was. Oh I am glad to be back in the hills with the quietness and the space.

I had a wonderful time at Delhi and Agra and the beauty of the Taj passes description. I have seen so many wonderful things my mind is overflowing! Rose red cities, Fatehpur Sikri, a mixture of red sandstone and white marble. Glorious marble halls, the walls inlaid with precious stones. Akbar must have been wonderful. You know, I suppose that he took the best from all the great religions and so far as he could, acted in accordance with them. It was a curious idea to have a Hindu, a Christian and a Muslim wife, and they each had a palace built in the style of their religious architecture. They used to meet once a month and go up onto a minaret together to greet the full moon. I had some time at Cawnpore but it is a sad place, full of graves with inscriptions like "In this spot lie 150 women and children massacred during the Mutiny of 1857."

I had three nights and two days in the train, all quite comfortable except for yesterday morning. On the birthday of Krishna, Hindus throw red stuff at people, a sort of powder (the festival is called Holi), and every ten minutes or so along the line there was a wild yell and splosh, handfuls of mud and cow dung against carriage windows and some sharp stones came into mine as well. I shut up all the windows and was reading peacefully, when crash! Half a brick came in, missing my head by a few inches and filling the carriage with broken glass. Then I put up all the shutters and stood in darkness for over an hour because there was nowhere to sit. I got to Raxaul at 6:20 this morning and just had time to go to the bungalow and have a bath and breakfast. The Nepal Railway has just been opened, and I thought I should be able to say when I wanted the train, but dear me, no, it started at 8 a.m. punctually. Not very speedy, however; it took exactly three hours to go 20 miles.

I bethought me I had never ridden an elephant, so I told General Krishna and he said quite ordinarily, "I'll send one to your house at 5 o'clock today." I don't think I shall ever crave for one at home; they are very uncomfortable to ride.

This morning I had a cable advising me to apply for a house-surgeonship at the Shropshire Orthopaedic Hospital. I wired back to ask the date of vacancy, but it will, I expect, be before May. Annoying really, as I was certain of it, considering who told me to apply. My inward self is in turmoil, having tried so hard to decide on my line in life and being unable to decide anything. I want to go home and to stay out here; to marry and to have my freedom and independence; to go all out for surgery, the same for medicine; to drift along peacefully and take what offers. And all the time with a firm conviction that if I wait and don't fuss, Providence will arrange it all quite nicely.

What is the good of my coming home? I couldn't bear to work in a town again. I feel strong bands tugging me to stay out here, although the people I love are in England. I am disconnected from living for two months as one of the world's rich. One loses one's self-respect terribly. I do like to play hard and work hard.

Leaving Nepal

I am leaving here mid–May and going home via Lloyd-Triestino. I shall be at home for the summer, and Mother wants me to go to Scotland with her. Then in September or October, I am going to the London School of Tropical Medicine to sit for the Diploma and then try fearfully hard to get work in Kashmir. I think it will be rather fun going home, sad as I shall be to leave this wonderful country. I am very glad, though, that I shall leave the child much better than I found her, which is always satisfactory.

I have promised to stay here until the end of April. One of the General's wives is having a baby then. She is only fourteen and he particularly wants me to attend her. Pray that nothing goes wrong in my "really competent hands."

Chapter 3

Leaving Nepal and Returning, 1927–1930

by Peggy Lovett Wilson

I left Nepal in May 1927 after sad and touching farewells. I was overwhelmed with delightful presents in silver, enamel and ivory. I was given for my own the ruby and pearl necklace that the Princess put round my neck the night of the Fancy Dress Ball at the Willingdon.

I went by a Lloyd Triestino ship to Naples. It was a very hot voyage and Italy seemed very hot as well. Still, I had a lovely trip although I was very seasick for part of the way. Three young men, an American, a Welshman and a Frenchman and I made great friends. We played most energetic deck tennis and drank innumerable lemon squashes in the day. The American and I got off at Naples and the others stayed on the ship. We saw Pompeii and we climbed Vesuvius. We were indefatigable tourists without cameras and all through the heat of the day. Then to Rome where we stayed two days or so, but really it was too hot. Then we went by train to Paris and dined and wined superbly, and finally to London and home.

While I was attending the course at the School of Tropical Medicine, I lived at my pleasant club in Queen's Gate. Four pounds a week, I remember, which my generous father insisted on paying. For that I had a nice bedroom, but oh dear, on the fifth floor and no lift, so if one came down ready to go out and one's latchkey was left upstairs, well it was just too bad. The food was very nice and served by an efficient manservant. However, as I began to make friends among the doctors also doing the course, I got asked to theaters and dinners out and dances and suppers until I realized with shame that I was only working at home about one evening a week. I found the work very interesting, but I simply couldn't resist the gaieties. Evening after evening we dined or supped at the Savoy or the Dorchester or the Mayfair.

My main escort was a bachelor, aged 47, on leave from West Africa, also doing the Diploma of Tropical Medicine course. I remember an amusing letter he wrote to me when he was laid low with malaria. He ended by saying that all his little trophozoites and gametocytes joined in wishing me a fond good night. What a winter of delirious fun. He loved taking me out and found me very attractive. Much later he proposed to me by cable from Sierra Leone. I wouldn't have dreamt of marrying him though, but it was fun to tease him. He came on leave determined to find a girl, or rather a woman, to marry. "If only you were forty instead of thirty," he would say.

The winter passed very quickly and suddenly I realized there was only a month to go before the exam, and that my ignorance was abysmal. I knew a nice and very hard-working Eurasian girl also in the course. I persuaded her, without much difficulty, to coach me several evenings a week. She loved coming to dinner at my club and was fond of me so it worked splendidly. I passed without much trouble, much to my father's relief.

Well then, what to do next? I went to the India Office but they were very discouraging and said they were recruiting as many Indian lady doctors as possible instead of Europeans. I had an offer of employment from Malaya and another from West Africa for school medical work and for public health work respectively. Neither attracted me at all. In any case I didn't want to spend months in getting a Public Health Diploma right after the Tropical Medicine course.

Just then, I had a warm letter from General Krishna, asking if I would consider going back to them. I couldn't resist, so I replied that if I could have permission to work at the Women's Hospital on a voluntary basis whenever I had time to spare, I should be more than happy to return.

I felt an urgent need to know more about midwifery so I arranged to attend a short post-graduate course at Queen Charlotte's Hospital. I found this valuable although the time I had there was shorter than I would have liked.

While I was there, Donald, who had quarreled with me or I with him, asked me to meet him. He came across the park looking so smart and attractive in his dark blue overcoat and bowler hat. I was delighted to see him again. It seemed quite mutual. When I came up to London with my father before I sailed, we went out together nearly every evening, dining and dancing. "That's a very smart, good looking young man of yours," said my father. On our last evening Donald asked me to promise not to marry anyone until I had been to visit him in Africa.

I was booked on the *Rajputana*, sister ship to the *Rawalpindi* in which I went to India the first time. This time I had with me a little Italian microscope, price £14, various midwifery requirements, and some new medical books.

May 1928, Kathmandu

I feel completely exhausted, my first week here being the most strenuous on record, and coming on top of the very hot journey across India. Yet the place is as beautiful as ever and the people even nicer if possible.

General Krishna and Nani

I spent about two hours one day helping General Krishna choose a new carpet and cretonnes for one of his drawing rooms from patterns. An awful responsibility as the carpet is to be ordered from Maple's. His kindness to me simply passes belief. I feel I do so little in return. If only I could cure Nani for him. You should see him sitting beside that child helping her with her sewing and playing games with her, teaching her to read, and all sorts of things he does. She knows nearly all those poems in *When We Were Very Young* [A.A. Milne, 1924] by heart but can't get over the indignity of the king sobbing about the butter for the royal slice of bread. She and I play golf every morning. One man carries her tiny little bag of clubs, one holds an umbrella (as a sunshade) over her head, another puts down the balls for us and they all count the strokes. Tremendous excitement reigns when she wins a hole. She has to be held by another man, of course, and can use only her right hand, but she has a wonderfully straight eye.

We had a grand day out at Gaucher where the golf course is. Nani and I went in the morning in General Krishna's big Buick limousine. The way it rocked and swayed and bumped over the ditches and hillocks on that truly appalling road was quite frightening. And little boys *will* try and hang on behind, which is very dangerous. The driver thought to make an example of one who was most persistent. He knocked him down and then kicked him three times so I should think he won't do it again. For the first time I drove my ball over the big mullah and not into it, and from the men's tee. I began to like golf very much.

Nani's favorite song just now is "Hallelujah." I have to play it for her to sing every evening. She says if you feel sad it cheers you up so much, not that she ever seems to feel sad; she is the happiest little soul. I do wish I could get her to put on some weight. She is 4'1" and complete with leather jacket, calipers and clothes, weighs 2 stone 13 lbs. At the moment I am very sad over two recent failures. One that was to be a beautiful corrective plaster jacket for Nani turned out a complete dud after an hour and a half hard work for everybody. The other was a cataract operation I did yesterday and had loss of vitreous, which is worrying me dreadfully. Not as much as it would if I was conscious of having been careless or done it badly, but I did it, as I thought, quite well and as gently as possible. The lens came out beautifully, and then this beastly vitreous after it. I can only pray it won't go septic.

I took my tea to Swayambunath, the lovely old golden Buddhist shrine on top of a wooded hill. I found a mossy bank and a cool rock for a pillow with trees meeting overhead. Looking down on to the bright green rice fields and little red brown houses all hot in the sun reminded me I had a three-mile walk home and it would soon be dark. A peace that passeth understanding seems to belong to that shrine. I always feel quiet and rested when I go there. I lay there until raindrops began splashing down through the trees.

Women's Hospital

My ambition is attained, and I have got into the Women's Hospital. I started as tactfully as possible by asking the lady-doctor in charge to tea. She is a great improvement on her predecessors. She is an American Asian and very black, a good sort and keen on her job. She has done wonders to the place, got it cleaned up and the attendants into white dresses. I earned much kudos on my first visit by giving an intravenous NAB [novarsinobillon] with a very stiff old syringe quite successfully, thanks to my guardian angel. There are quite a lot of interesting cases. I am going to operate on a malignant growth of the eyeball and do some cataracts.

I saw a curious case the other day, a child with paralysis of both quadriceps following smallpox. I have taken my microscope to the hospital and have a free hand about examining bloods, etc. It really is fun and fills a great need in my life.

I am now thoroughly cross. The hospital has run out of NAB. The bacteriologist at the other hospital has gone to bed ill and I can't get any stains! The German who is up here manufacturing gunpowder for the Nepalese has a very loud and powerful gramophone. His bungalow is about 20 yards from mine, and our gramophones blare defiance at each other most evenings.

I walked up to the hospital this morning, and not having to go to the Singha Durbar, I stayed there from eight until ten. One little girl brought by her mother had an ear in almost two halves. They had dragged an earring through it I suppose. We had just got things ready for me to try my hand at a neat patch-up when she vanished. I am ashamed to say I can't make head or tail of quite a lot of cases. The lady doctor *will* open TB abscesses in spite of my earnest advice. The latest was an ankle.

Sunday morning I partially straightened a woman's knees under an anesthetic and put them in plaster. They were completely flexed from contraction of the hamstrings. Two more goes will get them straight. She hasn't walked for four years so what a thrill if I can achieve this. But will she stay the course, I wonder?

Struck by Lightning

I feel very lucky to be still alive, as a fortnight ago we were all staying up at the Envoy's hill station Kakani, which is on a very high exposed ridge, and it was struck by lightning during a violent storm. Three of the servants were struck but only shocked and temporarily paralyzed. There was surprisingly little damage done, but it was a horrible experience and we were all badly frightened. I have a mental picture of us all cowering down over the dinner table, faces white as chalk, and afterwards all trying to be frightfully cheery.

Disease and Worry

There is a terrible lot of smallpox in the valley. People won't bring their children to be vaccinated. There is some cholera, any amount of tubercle and always-odd cases of enteric. The lady doctor makes the most surprising diagnoses. She labels obvious phthisis as asthma. Practically every case of diarrhea gets emetin. She opened a psoas abscess before I got a chance to tell her not to, and now it is secondarily infected and there isn't a splint in the place. I've seen to it, however, that there's jolly well going to be. One solitary pair of crutches was available for a TB ankle and now there aren't any others. She calls a case sprue without having seen the stools or looked at the tongue or asked if it was sore. For all that, she is a very nice woman and takes my interference in good part. I have insisted on chart boards for the patients as it is sometimes helpful to keep a temperature record. I can't get any plaster muslin to make bandages or felt or anything of that sort, and I can't supply everything myself. Equally, I can't very well grumble to the authorities as I am working there quite unofficially. Little Colonel Husband, the Legation Surgeon, is a brick. His hospital is decently run, of course, and he is always ready to talk shop.

Hospital has been very depressing lately, a lot of deaths. Two of them I hadn't diagnosed at all—general edema and loss of knee jerks, absolutely no other signs or symptoms, no heart trouble or nephritis. We get such awful cases of myiasis [parasitic infestation by fly larvae] it makes one quite sick to see them. Had a prolapse of cord the other day, with a shoulder presentation. I managed to do version with great difficulty and delivered as a breech. I thought it would be less injurious to the mother than a destructive operation as things were, and it all turned out all right.

Also I have been awfully worried about one or two people who have been bitten by mad dogs. They *may* not develop rabies, but there is no possibility of treating them here, and I can't send them all off to Kasauli on spec. They wouldn't go anyhow. The only way is to get hardened to these things, I suppose.

The early morning autumn mists are just beginning, and there is a lovely fresh smell in the air. From now on the weather gets more and more perfect. My zinnias and asters and cannas are a wonderful show now.

I have found quite a lot of ankylostomiasis [hookworm] here and discovered clonorchis sinensis [Chinese liver fluke] the other day, rather to my surprise. Also I find malaria among the natives. I was awfully thrilled when I first found the parasite. What I should do without the movable stage Donald got for me, I can't think.

I have got a mood now of feeling that my work is positively futile, owing to having entirely failed to improve a beastly elbow, and having messed up a cataract and failing to diagnose a queer case with a large liver and no other sign or symptoms, and heaps of other things like that.

Christmas in Bombay

We are going to Bombay about 18 December, and Mr. Girdlestone came out from Home to do a tendon transplantation on Nani. Nani nearly died of acidosis after her operation. It would have been my fault through ignorance that I should have given her plenty of glucose beforehand. I didn't know and I should have had that burden of guilt forever if she had died. But she recovered and is now very well.

We had a wonderful camping tour in Nepal before I left. We walked and climbed and rode all day for a week through every imaginable form of scenery. Icy cold air and the most marvelous lights on the hills, and then one would drop down 4,500 feet or so and have tea in the shade of a mango grove beside a foaming blue river straight down from the snows. One day we saw a panther slinking through the jungle and stalked it with great care, but it disappeared much too soon. Then I had three wonderful days in Delhi. The 3rd Gurkhas were in camp there, and they did give me a good time.

I've been here in Bombay for a week and swallowed up by the usual delirious round of dining, dancing and feting generally, which I try to despise, but gets hold of me completely against my will. I did enjoy Pavlova [Anna Pavlova, Russian prima ballerina] yesterday and am going again tomorrow and in fact, every night of her stay in Bombay, thanks to General Krishna and the Princess. They both enjoy her wonderful dancing tremendously.

You would have been amused at my efforts to go to church this morning. I thought there would surely be a morning service somewhere so I got into a taxi and told it to take me to the Cathedral. After many miles they landed me at a Baptist Mission Church where I heard the last quarter of a sermon on gold, frankincense and myrrh. Sang a hymn and was heartily shaken by the hand, wished a Merry Christmas by a kind lady and the parson and found myself in the street again 10 minutes after I had left it. When I got back to the hotel, I found a wonderful casket of scents and soaps from Nani and an amethyst and aquamarine pendant from her mother.

Back in Kathmandu

On Monday I am having my first lesson in driving the new Chrysler. General Krishna really is a brick to let me. I shall be awfully proud when I can drive it well.

I went up in an aeroplane the other day and loved it. The wind at 100 mph is terrific; it quite numbs one's face.

Nani has a half-size billiard table and is desperately keen on the game. She scores about 10 in an hour but is quite undaunted and struggles round and round the table. Her very weak left hand and useless triceps are a great bar towards making an efficient "bridge," but I encourage it all as much as possible.

There are some very interesting cases in the hospital now but how I long for the wisdom of a serpent. I was awfully angry the other day. We had a youngish woman in with a dreadful heart, failing badly, just beginning to improve with rest and digitalis, when her husband insisted on taking her home as there was no one else in his house to do the work for the forthcoming festival of Dussehra. These women work on with swollen legs, panting for breath until they just have to drop. He'll probably bring her back moribund and then say we killed her at the hospital.

I have had to refuse to take what sounds a most interesting research job in Bombay on Anaemia of Pregnancy, £900 a year for two or three years. I don't want to do it; I want to marry when I leave here. Anyway they would want me to start this September and I'm not free until next spring and three years in Bombay would do my health in completely.

February 1929

I have had the hospital on my hands for the last fortnight, one doctor on leave and the other ill. I endeavored to cope with 50–70 outpatients daily besides the in-patients, and it included all the abscesses (such frightful abscesses as there are here), NABs, painting cervixes and whatnot, besides fractures and all the prescription writing. Besides

Peggy driving the Chrysler in Kathmandu, 1929.

that, perhaps you have an acute pneumonia upstairs, a dying dysentery, a big tear waiting to be stitched, and no one in the place besides yourself who can even take a pulse. What with trying to keep the place clear of dogs and cows who will keep walking in, and having to get your directions given in Gurkhali translated into Newari for half the patients, I found I was so blinking done up I couldn't sleep at night until all hours. I enjoyed it, however. The one doctor has come back from leave and things are quieter.

Letters to Donald

You will be getting ready for the Tropical Medicine School when you get this. I hope you will like it. I wonder if anyone else roasts chestnuts over the Bunsen burners. I found it a lovely way of eking out a dull hour or so and was quite popular on my bench in consequence.

My new blue dress has come and your earrings (chalcedony) worn with it revive all youth and vanity but there is nobody to see it. The books have arrived and thank you most awfully.

I'm just as pleased as Punch to hear that you've got your job. Really it is grand to think that your heart's desire is coming true so soon now. Of course I knew you would get it; they would never dream of turning down a man with your qualifications. I should say you'll pass the doctor all right, your heart used to beat pretty strongly if I remember rightly. I'm sure you'll like all the Protozoology people most awfully, especially Thomson. I'm sure you were hugely tickled at being taught how to clean slides and how to make a blood film. Are your fellow students a nice lot and what is the feminine element like? They were mostly rather earnest missionaries last year.

When you get this it will be near time for the DTM [Diploma of Tropical Medicine and Hygiene], but I haven't any anxiety about your passing it. Manson-Bahr passed me on knowing the life history of microfilaria.

Donald, 1929, on the ship to Tanganyika, wrote in his diary: "How glad I am to get a letter from Peggy. I know how glad I will be to get her back again. But if she were willing, ought I to stay alone for the parents' sake? That I have to decide."

Thoughts on Tanganyika

May 16, 1929. I just got your letter and have been trying to construct a picture of it all, Tanganyika. I can imagine Kilimanjaro. Has it always got snow on it? I suppose you are rather fed up being a Health Officer. What is the language called and is it hard to learn? As MOH it will doubtless be your almost impossible job to exterminate the flies. What happens when your new car sticks in the mud—are there generally some convenient and willing coolies to shove it out for you? I wonder if the baksheesh question is as trying as it is in India, and don't you sometimes feel like saying, "Here, take all I've got, only for God's sake, go." I am afraid I don't know the first thing about the politics even. I suppose they are fussing for self-government as in India and not in the least fit for it.

June 9, 1929. This is the day I have my wretched little V.D. clinic at the hospital that I started with such high hopes. Patients come about twice for their injections, and then when they find their symptoms disappearing they think they are cured and never come again. It is most disheartening.

I am thinking of going to stay with a cousin in Rangoon next winter and if I do come and see you, I would come after that, but don't count on it definitely. It rather tickled me your saying "There is no gay social existence in these parts," as if I should immediately demand a Palais de Danse or a cinema. This place isn't very gay socially at the moment, only the Kilburnes and me here. The rain is coming down in real earnest now. I suppose the next two months will be hateful as usual.

My father has had a wretched time since Christmas. The gardener got pneumonia and Daddy was trying to do his work and somehow fell down the well and hurt his shoulder badly. He is having massage and diathermy but nothing does it any good. Oh dear.

This is an amazingly peaceful place. You never see quarrelling and never any ill treatment (purposeful) of children or animals. I am as usual weighed down with depression about my patients. People here are beginning to know that I have a slight trend towards orthopaedics and I get various TB hips, spines, deformities, etc., brought to hospital. I've no proper splints, and there is no one to do any nursing, and in any case after a month or so, the parents insist on the removal of the splints and take the children home. Colonel Smith (Legation Surgeon) says, "Why bother? Don't tackle anything of the sort," but my inconvenient conscience puts me to all sorts of bother, generally quite unavailing.

I got your last most interesting letter when I was having a week's rest cure up at Kakani. I was rather ill for a fortnight. I don't really know what with, but the time at 6,000 feet up in the clouds has restored to me what Captain Tottenham calls my raw-beef complexion and a huge appetite.

I am so thrilled with the new car General Krishna has provided for my use. It is a new Ford two-door, four-seater sedan. So nice in the rains with big windows and no need for side curtains that are always such a nuisance. I suppose your Tanganyika roads are wonderful compared with these that have great fissures and holes in them and take a devil of a lot of navigating even at 15–20 mph.

Our monsoon is nearly over now, we only get occasional showers. But oh, the leeches all through the monsoons are too dreadful. One goes for just a little walk in the foothills and there they are, the nasty thin black things waving from every leaf and blade of grass eager for blood. They go up one's legs, through the eyelets of one's shoes, everywhere. And then they engorge themselves on one's blood. If you pull them off they irritate and bleed for ages. Salt makes them let go or a lighted cigarette pressed on to them.

I am sorry you had malaria and I hope you will religiously take your quinine for two months. Your patients sound very like these, really. I never can get any sort of reliable history out of the coolies' class, and worse than yours, when asked their age they generally say they have forgotten. We nearly always start by giving them Santonin whatever they complain of.

The hookworm cases here are very few and far between, I wonder why there aren't more because here such a thing as sanitation, including latrines, is utterly unheard of, and there is no MOH.

Yesterday we had a woman in who had her face rather badly mauled by a bear that sprang on her when she was cutting grass. They always go for the face and we've had some rather bad cases. The other out-of-the-ordinary case was a woman who had dislocated her jaw eating a cucumber!

You must have been cursing me for not letting you know at all when I proposed to descend on you. Since I wrote it has been decided that my successor is arriving here about the middle of January, so by the time I have visited Cousin Audrey in Rangoon and got from there to East Africa, I imagine it will be about the end of February. I don't quite know what I could do if I arrived and you weren't on leave. I imagine I could hardly take a tent and trail round after you, pitching it at a distance that would appease the proprieties. I will certainly arrange to stay about a month as you suggest, in Africa's sunny clime.

Donald's State of Mind

Really I don't know what to do about your lamentable introspection. When I first knew you at 23, I used to think you would grow out of it. Now I begin to be afraid you never will. You want the moon, Donald dear. And you are right in saying that you will never recover youth's idealism. Well, you've got the memory of the atmosphere of it, the fragrance. But the peach tastes as good without the bloom. I suppose I can understand the state of being that knows that life must be worthwhile but doesn't feel it is. I'm very sorry for you and all the other men who feel as you do, but I have no satisfying philosophy to offer. Personally I take my disillusionments as they come, know that they will quickly blow over and that there is an unlimited amount of joy in life still to come.

Final Months in Nepal

I've been having a very cheery time lately. I went to Nani, then to the hospital, and then lunched with the Tottenhams. This evening Captain Tottenham and I had a good gallop on the Maidan, both riding Legation horses. Then I went to Nani again and we played billiards and piquet for money (it is the yearly gambling festival). After dinner I am going to take the people staying here through the bazaar in my car to show them the gambling booths all lit up. It is a very cheery sight. Days are getting cold and bracing here, fires and tweeds again.

November 23, 1929. I am up to my eyes in writing letters and doing up little parcels to send home but I am feeling utterly miserable. His Highness the Maharaja has pneumonia and is very ill indeed, and if the worst should happen, I should think the appointing of a successor may bring difficulties, to say the least. In fact it would not be wise to write all that one fears and we can only pray that he will be spared.

Mr. Wilkinson has gone and now there is no British Envoy in the country. A new untried man may create difficulties instead of knowing how to deal with the ones he is sure to be faced with. It will be a terrible unimaginable loss to this country if His Highness should not recover, and feeling this, apart from one's personal affection for him, makes it all seem very melancholy. Mr. Wilkinson has accepted the post of guide, philosopher and friend to Indian cadets at Sandhurst. He will be dreadfully missed here, all the Nepalese are so fond of him, and Nani quite hero-worships him.

December 16, 1929. I am in a shocking temper and am going to let it off on you. It all arose out of the bad manners of an Indian doctor from Calcutta. Really the average Indian is insufferable I do think. I always make a point of being pleasant and friendly to all Indians, but when you treat them on equal terms they take advantage of it and one can't lower oneself to being rude in return. This particular little blighter, after seeing a case with me, remained on his chair when I got up to go and actually handed me my hat and gloves, still without getting up. And he a person supposed to know our customs. If it had been an English man in my place, he wouldn't have dreamt of doing it, which makes it worse. I suppose there must be some nice Indians that one could make friends with but I've never come across them. The Nepalese can't be talked of in the same breath. They are nearly all like the nicest possible English people; in fact in point of politeness, tact and understanding, they often put us to shame, and I'm proud to have them for friends.

I am beginning to feel it is time I left here, though I shall be very sad to part from

Nani, General Krishna, the snows, the fragrance in the hills, and all the wonderful colors of the countryside.

January 2, 1930. I have been having a terribly anxious time. A fortnight ago Nani got bronchitis. She had practically recovered from it in a week and I had no anxiety and went out for a day's climbing. That morning her father thought she was so well that he had her moved out of bed into the next room and put on the floor by an open window in the sun. When I got there in the evening I was seriously worried about her, and next morning I had Colonel Smith for a consultation. We found she had developed broncho-pneumonia and we have had such a fight for her life. She is out of danger today, thank God. We have used up nearly all the oxygen cylinders in Nepal!

My successor arrives here today. She is a spinster in her fifties, very kind and nice and a trained physiotherapist and orthopedist. I have a few little qualms of regret about handing over the bungalow and everything that has belonged to me for so long, but the longer I stay here, the worse would be the wrench of leaving. I have made so many friends among the Nepalese who I shall always think are the nicest people in the world, next to the English.

January 16, 1930. I have to tell you that my departure from here has been postponed for a month at the request of the Maharaja. He is rather pleased with my treatment of the Maharani and wants me to see it through and I didn't like to refuse, as everyone here has been so good to me. Thank heaven, Nani is better now.

My successor arrived nearly a week ago and I am trying hard to teach her some of the language and to drive the car. She had a few lessons in England but is so timid that it is going to take ages. She likes crawling along in second gear and I continually cry, "Accelerate, accelerate, change into top." If I can only get her to the stage of being able to go along the road at 15 mph in top I shall feel fairly happy. I shall be depressed at leaving Nepal, but I do feel that I have been here long enough and things are different now and we see so little of the Generals. This was deliberate policy on the part of the Maharaja because he feared we were all getting too friendly and he didn't want that.

I feel so muddled now about dates and addresses, and I don't know where to tell anyone to send anything.

Letter to My Father: Tiger Hunt, February 17, 1930

A Colonel Sprawson, DMS India, who is visiting, asked His Highness if he might have a shoot in the Terai and was given permission. I rather wistfully said how lucky he was, whereupon he immediately said, couldn't I come too?

The upshot was that General Krishna asked for me and the Maharaja said he will be very pleased for me to go! So on Saturday next Colonel Sprawson and I are going down to Amlekhganj [in southeast Nepal] to stay in the bungalow for three days and go into the jungle on elephants after tiger. We shall go to the place on pad elephants and shoot from a howdah [canopy-covered seat on the elephant]. I don't suppose I shall do any shooting at all—it will be immensely thrilling just to be there. I am frightfully lucky.

My great regret was leaving Nepal without having been to a tiger shoot. I was a little worried about whether the Nepalese would think it too unconventional for me to go alone with Colonel Sprawson, but apparently not, as General Krishna says they realize that our customs are quite different. Anyway one can't fuss over a trifle like conventions when it's a question of a tiger shoot, don't you agree? I am taking my trusty havildar who is immensely excited about it.

Yesterday I came down to Amlekhganj with Colonel Sprawson. We found we were to live in a nice little two-storey house. But dear me, in one of the two bedrooms, two beds had been put close together and moreover, in the bathroom there were two thunderboxes put matily side-by-side! Having got the furniture moved to our liking, we had a nice supper and slept well in our respective bedrooms. This morning we started off full of excitement, having had news of a tiger. They had tied up 20 buffaloes in various places. The Generals sent down a .275 Mauser rifle for me and a shotgun.

I have had a lot of new experiences today. First, getting on to my pad elephant, climbing up by his tail, and then a quite anxious time being rather afraid of falling off the pad. Finally I settled myself astride and went along with my loaded rifle laid across my knees. Until I got used to it, I was in a great fuss, nearly slipping off backwards going up steep mullah banks and trying to keep my rifle, which stuck out on each side of me, clear of trees and branches, as well as my face, although the mahout [elephant rider] was very good about it. The jungle was so immensely thick that the elephants had to knock down quite a lot of trees to get through. When we got to the place where the tiger was, we changed into a howdah and stayed still while our 18 elephants made a large ring, which gradually closed in. We were tense with excitement when we heard a very annoyed a-hoing from the tiger and expected him to break cover at any minute.

The last stage of the beat came when one of the trusted elephants went backwards and forwards across the small bit of cover left and nothing happened! The tiger had sneaked off without anyone having seen him go. Well, we hunted high and low but he had made off.

All we got today was a huge python, which my mahout saw a bit of sticking out of a hole. As it is really Colonel Sprawson's shoot, I thought he ought to have first blood, so I called him up and he shot it. It was 14 feet long and 18 inches thick. The men were all terrified of it and took a lot of convincing that it was really dead. We crossed several dry sandy riverbeds with tiger and panther pug marks in the sand, but saw none.

The jungle grass was as high as the elephants in places. There were lovely sweet smelling flowering trees and giant creepers hanging down like veils. It really is wonderful jungle if only there was a bit more wildlife in it. I do so hope we get a tiger.

Colonel Sprawson put up a little paper target on a tree early this morning for me to try out my rifle. I hit it twice from some distance and he seemed to think I was pretty good, so now that I am used to the elephants and know what is going to happen, I am to be in a howdah myself tomorrow and I do hope I shall get a shot at a tiger if we see one. After six hours on a pony yesterday and seven hours astride an elephant today I am tired!

Tiger Hunt, End of Second Day

No bag at all! I have *not* distinguished myself. We had news of another kill this morning, and set off at 9 a.m. After changing from our pad elephants to our respective howdahs, we went to the place where the tiger was and the elephants ringed him. Then in the distance I saw him, a great big chap slinking towards Colonel Sprawson's elephant. He fired and missed. We followed him up and I was on one side of the ring and Colonel Sprawson on the other. I was more excited than I have ever been in my life. Then we heard the tiger making very angry noises and suddenly he dashed into the ring and galloped past me going like an express train. I fired at him as he passed and missed. I reloaded as quickly as possible and sent another bullet after his tail. Once again he was found and this time I only caught a glimpse of him. He dashed past Colonel Sprawson who fired, but as he saw him so imperfectly, he missed him again. That was the last we saw of him and poor tiger, he had a very harassing time!

I feel dreadfully ashamed at not getting him and the Nepalese shikaris [hunting guides] are all very disappointed with me. Funnily enough, they said nothing about Colonel Sprawson missing him but everyone had something to say to *me* on the subject. Although I admitted it was bad, all the same, it's my first shoot, and as dear kind Colonel Sprawson says, "Just let them try and hit a tiger going at that speed and they'll find it is not so easy as they seem to think." We went miles round the jungle on the off chance of a shot at something, but it's my personal opinion that it is no use going after deer on elephant. By the time you've seen the deer, stopped the elephants and taken aim, the deer is miles away. We were eight hours on the elephants today without ever getting off. We had our tiffin in the howdah.

Peggy on tiger hunt in Nepal, 1930.

This morning brought news of yet another kill. They made the ring and we had beautiful positions and I was all primed to shoot to kill. The ring advanced, closed in, and no tiger. He had slunk off. I saw the place where he had been lying up, very snug in long grass. I also saw the kill, a buffalo calf with most of its hindquarters and part of its neck eaten. We went all round about and no sign of the tiger.

One of the askaris [local soldier] found a tiny deer, a kharka about a week old, which they gave to me. Then we got on our pad elephants and went separately "gooming" through the jungle to see what we could find. The shikaris were getting a bit fed up that we had got nothing. Suddenly my mahout pointed away to the right and I saw the antlers of a fine big sambhur stag about fifty yards away through the jungle, moving along not very fast.

I took careful aim and fired, and when we got to the place we found I had killed him stone dead with a shot in the neck. I must say I am proud of that shot. There was much shouting and all the other elephants came up. The shikaris asked if he was moving when I shot him and the mahout told them he was and everyone was very pleased. He is a huge chap and he was slung across an elephant and brought back. That's the only thing we got today.

I did wish poor Colonel Sprawson had been able to get a shot at something. The sambhur meat is being divided up among the men and I shall take the skin and I think I shall have the head mounted and send it home. (Alas, it was lost and I never saw it again).

No news of a kill today so we just went round the jungle to see if we could find anything. Colonel Sprawson had no luck again and had to go back at 12:30 to catch his train. I went on because they all seemed to want me to. I felt very grand moving off with 13 elephants all to myself, but I didn't get a thing. I saw one big stag but I could *not* get a decent aim and while I was trying, I lost him. The shikari again is disappointed with me! I felt a little frightened going through what I've learnt to think of as tiger grass, i.e., where they lie up. I kept picturing it all to myself—the tiger getting up—me firing and wounding him and then him springing onto the elephant. I must say I never reckoned on going tiger shooting all on my own and I am terrified of missing a good shot.

February 27, 1930. My shikar [hunt] is now finished and no tiger, alas. However, I shot two more sambhur stags but it wasn't such good work as the first one, and they both had to be finished off at close quarters. The first was fully 100 yards away. I had to fire several times at the poor brute. The second I thought I must have missed as I only saw him for a moment bounding out of the long grass, but apparently I had hit him in the neck. The shikaris came across him badly wounded. Those two were loaded onto elephants, and everyone's lust for slaughter was then satisfied and they asked me if I would like to go home, and feeling rather like a murderess, I said yes. There was plenty of meat for everybody. I am keeping the two skins, but the heads were not worth keeping.

How I wish I had my brother Dick's training and experience of shooting; I think I should have been a crack shot by now. As it is, I seem to be quite average with a rifle. As I am going to Tanganyika, which I suppose is the best place for big game in the world, I think I must have a rifle of my own. So please, will you get me one? I don't know what to ask you to get but that .275 Mauser seemed to suit me quite well. I am thinking of having a try for a lion if I persuade Donald to come. He seems to be turning into a useful shot by all accounts. I should like you or Dicky to test it before sending it to see that the sighting is accurate, and it must have a really smooth bolt. Some stick more than others, apparently, even when well oiled, and I want to be able to reload instantly. I know I can safely leave it to you.

Departure, March 2, 1930

I am feeling too overwhelmed for words. General Krishna has given me a check for £100 to buy a rifle! You ought to be able to get me the best in England for that amount.

I can't make up my mind whether to have one heavy enough for rhino, but if it is too heavy, I shan't be able to aim steadily. One of the Generals was very funny today, asking should he address his letters to Tanganyika c/o a lion!

Today was the unveiling ceremony of the late King's statue. His Highness honored me very much by sending for me to the special stand where he and the King and the Envoy were sitting and said he was so disappointed that I hadn't been able to get a tiger. General Padma said I was very lucky to have got the sambhurs as there are very few in that part of the jungle. I'm altogether too much in the limelight just now for my own liking and people are being really too kind. It will be a terrible wrench to go, but it seems the right time now that Nani has fully recovered from her chest troubles, and the Maharani is much better. Nani's left hand is now strong enough to strike notes on the piano, and her right one, being now normal, I hope she will soon learn to play. She is having grand times with her car (a small powered car specially built with only hand controls and brakes). General Krishna gave £400 for it. She is in a whirl of excitement over it. Her poor father anxiously shouts, "Don't go so fast, Nani."

Everyone has given me things. I was most touched at my bearer's old father whom I cured of dysentery sending me two cured fox skins. His Highness has given me a signed photo and Rs 1,000. Nani's mother has given me lots of lovely embroidered stuffs, and I have Nepali material enough to keep me in frocks for years. Nani loves the baby fawn, which I gave her. We decided to call it Daphne. I really am off on 5 March. My cousin Audrey writes that Rangoon heat is unbearable and they have taken a nice house at Kalaw in the Shan States. I am going up there with them from Rangoon.

So I left Nepal after heart-wringing goodbyes and went by train to Calcutta. I took ship for Rangoon and looked forward to a calm little voyage. I was pleased to hear that I had been placed at the Captain's table. At dinner on the first evening I was dismayed to realize that the Bay of Bengal was anything but calm and to avert calamity, I had to interrupt one of the Captain's best stories and excuse myself with all haste.

Rangoon

My cousin Audrey Bennett and her husband David met me when we docked at Rangoon. David was commanding the 26th Punjabis. They were in Army married quarters at Mingaladoon, a bare unattractive place, in a double-storeyed stone house among several. They had reasonably nice gardens but the whole place seemed to me like a prison.

One never felt energetic; however, David nobly played tennis with me on many evenings. It was too hot and dusty to walk anywhere. Audrey seemed very tired and unwell, mostly due to the climate I suppose. She had a very good Karen ayah to look after the three children, aged 6, 3, and a blue-eyed baby girl of 9 months. I wasn't too well at the time as I had very septic tonsils. It was arranged for me to go into Rangoon General Hospital, where an Army surgeon whose name I forget most efficiently removed my tonsils. This made a tremendous difference to my health.

Then the monsoon broke and the rain poured down, day after day. Insects, mosquitoes, and flying ants arrived in their myriads. In the evenings the windows had all to be shut to keep them out and one sat until bedtime, desperately hot and uncomfortable under the electric fan, which stirred up the stale air but did not give any coolness or comfort.

Mandalay

When the rains were nearly over I went for a lovely trip up country, first by train to Mandalay. On arrival I went to the Mission House. The girl missionaries were friends of a fellow student of mine. They made me welcome, and I asked if they would show me the town if I managed to hire a car. We gazed at the ornate and colorful palace of the king with its red lacquered teak pillars, much gold leaf and many little pieces of colored glass stuck on to the walls. The effect of all this glitter in the sunshine was quite dazzling.

Irrawaddy

I then boarded the paddle steamer up the Irrawaddy. For several days we went quietly and peacefully up the mighty Irrawaddy, tying up to the bank at dusk until morning. The Captain, Adamson by name, and I would walk through the village near which we had anchored, looking at the palm leaf houses built up on stilts to keep them from being waterlogged in the rains, and looking at the very attractive people, the women usually smoking huge cheroots. Even the small children smoked.

We arrived at Bhamo and next day began the return journey down river. I had a fascinating expedition to the ruby mine at Mogok. One approached the mines literally walking on precious stones as the path was covered with tiny chippings of rubies, sapphires, moonstones and the like. When we had gazed our fill at the wonderful gems on display, we went off to the bungalow belonging to a friend of Captain Adamson to be given a vastly different sort of fill, a Burma breakfast as it was called.

What a breakfast! It started with three gins apiece. I managed to get away with one small one as I never liked alcohol before breakfast; indeed, this was the first time I had ever had it so early in the day. Then there was fruit, porridge, eggs and bacon, fish, pilau, curry and rice, coffee, toast, rolls, jam, marmalade. No wonder people miss out lunch and perhaps just have a cup of tea and a biscuit to carry them on to late dinner in the evening.

Then we went down the hill to the river and boarded our steamer for Mandalay. I dined with Captain Adamson who tried hard to persuade me to promise to marry him and drew a delightful little word picture of the charming wife (me) awaiting him in our nice little bungalow on the river bank between his quite short voyages between Rangoon and Myitkina (pronounced Michenar). Somehow I felt that my life would be rather too restricted, and also because I was not in the least in love with him, made his case hopeless from the start.

David and Audrey met me with their car at Mandalay, and we set off to drive into the S. Shan States [Siamese Shan States, or northern Thailand] to Kalaw [then Burma, now Myanmar] where they had rented a bungalow. We went up and up through the teak forest round many hairpin bends and finally arrived at a nice bungalow in a garden full of English flowers and surrounded by green grassy slopes and larch and fir trees. It was a lovely place, cool and fresh, with charming walks over the hills. Audrey's health improved greatly in this pleasant climate and we enjoyed our walks in the hills.

Donald in Tanganyika

Donald despaired of my ever arriving in Africa. At the end of June 1930, he wrote: "Oh you pernicious, perfidious woman! I do so hate you, with stockings or without, I detest you—'Beginning in January, end of January, April, beginning of June, end of July latest.' And now no date at all except some figment of your feeble imagination. How about arranging for a nice walk during next long rains? We shan't meet in heaven you know, that's one of the reasons why I naturally gravitate to cool, windswept places. You, I'm glad to notice, are getting used to places like Rangoon. Seriously though, I shan't be in Moshi unless you come jolly soon and heaven knows where I shall be.

"Peggy dear, will you be wearing blue stockings when you come? Or will you have horn-rimmed glasses and your hair in a bun? And will you be an esthete and Aldous Huxley-ish? And will you have a portable typewriter and only eat toast for breakfast? And will only great thoughts and great silences be known in your presence?

"I shan't settle down till you've been and come and gone. And heaven knows how I want to see you and hold forth at enormous lengths on everything. You know at our last few meetings, I had no chance of telling you all about life and just how everything ought to be run. So there's a considerable accumulation of splendid imbecilities for you to hear. Remember, you don't have to argue—you just listen politely and then start telling about ... talking about walking sticks. And if that should by any mischance lead up to the question of force you say, 'How nice your cousin looked in a sword.' I will also give you my opinions on sport, on Eastern mentality, and mistakes in India when you arrive.

"Your rifle, which has come here, is religiously cleaned and oiled every week. I have been wandering around the mountain during the last week or two with a couple of agricultural officers. It's pretty cold work at 4,000 feet these days and a sweater is a very essential garment."

Poor Donald, indeed I was trying. About the stockings, I had told him that owing to the heat of Rangoon and Mandalay I had given up wearing them.

Kuala Lampur

I accepted an invitation to stay with my cousin Cis Baffles and his wife Peg at Kuala Lumpur as I wanted at least a brief glance at Malaya. So after a loving farewell to Audrey and David, I set sail once more. My ship went on down to Port Swettenham where I finally disembarked. I took a taxi to Kuala Lumpur as I had failed to tell the Baffles the day and time of my arrival, and so they were very surprised to see me.

Cis's wife, Peg, took me in hand on the subject of make-up and besought me never to show myself without lipstick, especially before anyone that I had ideas of marrying; she also took me to a wonderful dressmaker who created an evening gown for me with yards of black lace over silk and a rose and gold chiffon brocade bodice, the material being among the many gifts from the princess, Nani's mother. Then I had made, in case it should come in useful, a long white georgette dress cut up a little in the front and a big white hat with chiffon frilling round it. Peg said, "But suppose, after all, you didn't want to marry him or he doesn't want to marry you?"

I said I should take it home and it would do fine for garden parties in the summer.

Now my travel plans for Africa were finalized. I went down to Singapore by train. It took most of the night and I had breakfast in Singapore.

The light over the harbor in the early morning was rose tinted and pearly and magical. Cis had arranged for a Malay Forest Ranger to help me find my ship. Such a nice and good looking young man dressed in the attractive uniform of jungle green with a green silk puggaree. He was helpfulness itself.

Introduction to Tanganyika, 1930

The east African nation of Tanzania features a varied ecology. From the island of Zanzibar and the eastern coastal region, woodlands and savannah plateaus stretch west to the high mountains of the northeast—Kilimanjaro, Meru and Usambara—on to Lake Victoria in the northeast, and along the Great Rift Valley to Lake Tanganyika in the west. By the nineteenth century, hunters, herders, pastoralists and farmers representing the four major language families in Africa were adapted to these diverse ecologies. Political organizations included stateless societies, chiefdoms and kingdoms.

The coastal region had centuries of commercial relations with Arabs and with Islam. Traders based in Zanzibar negotiated long distance trade in ivory, slaves and products from the interior. With Europe's growing power in the Indian Ocean, the trade system increased dramatically in the nineteenth century. Arab planters on Zanzibar developed clove plantations using slave labor while Pangani emerged as a slave port. Ivory hunters moved further inland as elephants were hunted out. Porters carried imported cloth and firearms to trade for goods and food from the interior. The word Swahili describes both coastal peoples and their language, and like Islam, it spread into the interior. Slavery increased and continued throughout the German occupation (Iliffe 1979).

By 1885 five European missionary societies were in the country: French Holy Ghost fathers, Anglicans of the Universities Mission to Central Africa (UMCA), the Anglican Church Missionary Society, the London Missionary Society, and the French White Fathers. Christianity fed on generational conflicts as Europeans engendered intense internal rivalries and competition over land, water, and power (Iliffe 1979).

In the 1880s and 1890s, German occupation proceeded inland from the coast, as Germany claimed *Deutsch-Ostafrika*, or German East Africa. Health conditions in the country prior to colonization and capitalism were comparable to those in Europe at the time, though with different diseases prevalent (Turshen 1984). While the Germans re-ordered economies into colonial patterns, European invasion accelerated the diseases in East Africa, exacerbated by turn-of-the-century ecological disasters. German East Africa was beset by rinderpest, a disease that infected cattle and other ruminants in 1891, resulting in human starvation (Iliffe 1979). Invasions of bush pigs and baboons ruined crops, lions forced cultivators to retreat into forest fringes, and tsetse flies thrived in abandoned fields. Tsetse flies brought trypanosomiasis—sleeping sickness that kills cattle and people, becoming a major source of death

(Feierman 1985). Smallpox, sand fleas, locust plagues, drought, and famine also affected human populations. African societies had developed ecological controls that confined the most dangerous trypanosomiases in *Grenzwildnesse*, wilderness areas, "arranged so that people and cattle did not come into frequent contact with tsetse flies. The European conquerers destroyed a whole range of controls and unleashed a plague on Africa" (Feierman 1985, 87; Ford 1971).

In 1905 villagers arose in the Maji Maji rebellion against German rule and policies of forced labor for growing cotton. The uprising's brutal defeat in 1907 led to conversions to Christianity and Islam with native religious practices incorporated, particularly in music and dance, that were then adopted and adapted along travel routes. Dance forms (*ngoma*) like those that Peggy and Donald witnessed, expressed spiritual ideas, daily work and dramatic events, like the hunt, rebellion, and even the terrors of war (G. Hartwig 1969, C. Hartwig 1972, Iliffe 1979).

German farmers moved inland, joined by Greeks and Italians. Germans, Italians, and Greeks began growing sisal in Kilosa or coffee in Moshi. Railroads were built from Mombo to Moshi in 1912 and along the caravan route from Dar es Salaam to Kigoma on Lake Tanganyika in 1914 (Iliffe 1979, Tucker 2010).

World War I had horrendous impacts in German East Africa. After Germany's defeat, Britain took over the administration of the country under a League of Nations mandate, renaming the country the Tanganyika Territory (Iliffe 1979, 247). British colonial polices saw many German settlers and missionaries deported, revived the state education system, discouraged new settlers in the absence of sufficient labor, staffed the administrative system with recruits from British territories, reorganized the police force, abolished "slavery and racial distinctions in the legal system," and worked to improve the economy (Iliffe 1979, 263). Tanganyika was a large territory with isolated stations, so the European community was more scattered than in British East Africa (including Kenya and Uganda) (Crozier 2007, 9). As merchants recovered from the war, Asian presence increased, and English-speaking clerks and artisans emigrated from India. European companies and British settlers acquired former German plantations, while smaller sisal and coffee estates were sold to Asians and Greeks (Iliffe 1979, Tucker 2010).

In 1954 and 1955 the nationalist movement TANU (Tanganyika African National Union) emerged under the leadership of Julius Kambarage Nyerere to work for Tanganyika's independence and self-government. Winning elections in 1958, 1959, and 1960, Nyerere became prime minister as independence was celebrated on December 9, 1961. The following year, a new constitution was implemented and Nyerere became president.

After a revolt in Zanzibar against the ruling sultan, Tanganyika united with Zanzibar and was renamed the United Republic of Tanzania on October 29, 1964. The Arusha Declaration of 1967 defined the values and goals of the new nation, including universal human rights, freedom, equality, dignity, and universal education. A democratic socialist government, it defined the role of the state in control over the means of production, collective ownership of the country's resources, and the formation of cooperatives and Ujamaa (familyhood, brotherhood) villages. To implement this declaration, the Nyerere government announced a number of legislative acts in 1967, including the nationalization of banks and large industrial enterprises, and the Land Acquisition Act. The Acquisition of Buildings Act in 1971 nationalized houses, targeting especially Asians. In 1973 the Rural Lands (Planning and Utilization) Act was passed to create villagization, that is, Ujamaa villages and cooperative farms as the basis of the rural economy, and the Village and Ujamaa Villages Act in 1975 provided for the administration of villages (Dias 1970, Ibhawoh and Dibua 2003, Iliffe 1979, Nyerere 1967, Pedersen 2016, Scott 1998).

Donald Wilson went to Tanganyika as a Colonial Medical Officer (MO). Under British control, the country inherited the German infrastructure of roads, government buildings, and a telegraph system, as well as medical facilities, including three hospitals. One of these was at Tabora, where Donald and Peggy worked. As British policies went into effect, the health of indigenous Africans gained increasing importance; colonial medical services extended to rural areas, and Africans were trained as medical support staff to coordinate with native authorities (Crozier 2007). Donald's and Peggy's safaris, working initially with sleeping sickness, then malaria research, reflected this new agenda of work with more remote villagers.

Sleeping Sickness

Donald's initial work in Tanganyika focused on sleeping sickness, or trypanosomiasis, caused by the parasite trypanosome, carried by the tsetse fly. Sleeping sickness reached epidemic proportions in the late nineteenth and first half of the twentieth centuries, as cattle loss to rinderpest, war, and population relocations allowed the spread of tsetse flies. Tsetse flies kill wild game and cattle, but infect humans as well. The parasite trypanosome burrows into the brain; the name "sleeping sickness" results "from the behavior of victims, who lapse into sleep during the daytime but become restless at night" (Turshen 1984, 135, Iliffe 1979).

Malaria

Both Donald and Peggy worked on malaria research and treatment for most of their careers and both suffered from malaria. In 1930 there were 3.5 million deaths from malaria in sub–Saharan Africa. Malaria parasites infect mosquitoes and thus the vertebrates on which they feed. European colonization and agricultural plantations with more workers, poor housing and sanitation, and other environmental and economic factors increased the mosquito populations and the opportunities for malarial transmission to humans in East Africa (Packard 2007).

Four types of malaria parasites emerged in sub–Saharan Africa to infect humans through anopheline mosquitoes. These are P. malariae, P. ovale, P. vivax, and P. falciparum. The first three do not cause severe anemia, while P. falciparum causes severe illness and often leads to death. P. falciparum accounts for most of the human deaths from malaria worldwide (Packard 2007).

While on leave in England in 1932, Peggy and Donald attended a training course in Epsom to prepare for assigned anti-malarial work upon their return to Tanganyika. At the Horton Hospital, they learned how to identify the four known species of anopheline mosquitoes they encountered in Africa. They learned to dissect mosquito salivary glands, recognize the presence of malaria parasites (sporozoites), and recognize the presence of cysts in mosquito stomach walls.

Donald wrote in 1931, two years into his 31-year career in East Africa, "the vast bulk of sickness is due to disease that is either wholly or largely preventable, by specific preventive measures, more by education in the causation of disease, and most important of all, by a general raising of the standard of living." For a century there has been a lively debate in the malaria research world about the role of malaria prevention and control in areas where populations have developed some immunity. Donald and Peggy Wilson and their work were central to that debate.—*Editor.*

Chapter 4

Africa, 1930–1932

by Peggy Lovett Wilson

My ship, the *Canada Maru*, looked very small, and in fact she was only some 4,000 tons. I had quite a nice cabin, however. The captain and crew were Japanese as she was a Japanese ship. It turned out that I was the only woman on board. There were two Japanese men passengers but we had no means of communication. The captain and the senior members of the crew such as the purser seemed fairly friendly.

I was glad when we arrived at Colombo [Ceylon, now Sri Lanka] as I became dreadfully bored with no one to talk to. The captain and first mate kindly asked me to go ashore with them and visit a friend of theirs who had a large jewelry shop. He also had a fine car in which we went for a drive about the island, finishing with tea at the Galle Face Hotel, the most celebrated in Colombo.

Then we continued the voyage across the Indian Ocean. I busied myself with trying to learn Swahili and in the evenings after the early supper, I sat in the bow of the ship in the moonlight, going towards Africa. A day or two out from Mombasa I received a wireless message from Donald. It said, "Trumpets and Banners. Seek emissary Mombasa." It was the first radio message I had ever received and I was thrilled.

Mombasa

When we steamed quietly into Mombasa harbor a day or two later, I looked with great interest at this, my first sight of Africa, except for brief visits on the outward voyage to Port Said and Fort Sudan. This sight of Africa looked dull and disappointing. Low, grass-covered slopes coming gently down to the shore, low cliffs, nothing to lift one's heart with excitement and beauty. No one to meet me, I wondered how to find the "emissary" Donald had spoken of. I went ashore through Customs and left all my twenty-one pieces of luggage to be collected later.

I made my way to the bank as I had no local money or indeed any sort of money at all. I had ordered a transfer of a reasonable sum from the Calcutta to the Mombasa branch of my bank but was dismayed to learn that nothing had been heard of it. I asked advice of the manager. He could only think of one solution and naturally rather an unwelcome and awkward one for him, which was to lend me money out of his own pocket to buy my railway ticket to Moshi. I then went to the station, bought the ticket and booked a compartment in the evening train as far as Voi where I hoped to be met.

By then I began to think about lunch so I went into the Manor Hotel. I tentatively tried out my few words of Swahili and said "*Leta maji*" [bring water] which was understood and produced what was wanted, but with no subjunctive tense, which is polite, and no please or thank you.

Sometime after I had finished my lunch the emissary named George arrived and made himself known. He was a cheerful smiling African who brought me a note from Donald, very welcome, a bag of money even more welcome, and assurances that I should be the *bienvenue*. Then my first and pleasant task was to return to the bank and repay the kind manager what he had lent me.

In the train we almost immediately began to climb, leaving the coast vegetation of coconut palms and mango trees towards the cooler uplands. I went along to the restaurant car for dinner. I supposed, rightly, that George was on the train.

Meeting Donald

At about 10 p.m. we arrived at the little station of Voi. It had then been dark for about three hours. I saw Donald on the platform wearing a white sweater and white shorts. We had not met for two and a half years. I had a very favorable first impression of him, so fair haired and sunburned. I have no idea what he thought of me after so long. He asked whether I would like to sleep in the Rest House at Voi or drive through the night to Moshi. I said it was up to him, but if he was not too tired I should like to drive on.

It seemed terribly cold to me, wearing my thin frock of Nepalese muslin. My thick clothes were in my luggage and his two-seater car with dickey behind was open. However, he gave me what he could of his clothes and we set off. I noticed from the speedometer that we were travelling at 50 mph, and I asked him how often he had driven on that rather rough unsurfaced road. Only once, it appeared, when he had come from Moshi to meet me earlier in the day. As he was holding my hand and therefore driving with one, I just hoped it was all right.

At about 2 a.m. he stopped and said, "Now we will have some supper." I couldn't think how this was to be achieved in darkest Africa as there was no sign of any human being or habitation. "You stay in the car," he said, "while I go and get some firewood." He soon came back with some wood and in no time had a fine bonfire going. Then from the boot of his car he produced a kettle, frying pan, plates, cups, eggs, bacon, coffee, milk, bread and butter. It was magical and when the fire died down a bit he cooked us a splendid supper. I suppose George had some of it but I can't swear to that—maybe he had some food with him. By the time we went on again we had decided to get married.

Moshi

Daylight came and my first view of Kilimanjaro. How cool, fresh, open the countryside seemed. No people, no houses. Donald got out his shotgun, handed it to me and said, "You shoot a partridge for our supper tonight." I had never fired a shotgun and so of course I missed, but he got one afterwards. We arrived in Moshi at the ordinary breakfast time. Donald gave me his bungalow and he stayed with the MO and his wife. During my first night a lion padded round and round the bungalow but quite silently, not even a grunt, so I didn't know about it until morning.

Marriage and Work in Tabora

There was a great deal of arranging to do. Donald was being transferred from Moshi, where he had been acting as Health Officer, to the western province in the Tabora District to work in sleeping sickness, i.e., trypanosomiasis. He had to see about getting a marriage license, write innumerable letters both official and unofficial, make all kinds of "bundobust." Donald wrote to his parents, "All this business of getting married seems very odd. As a matter of fact I don't at all want to get married; but there it is, I've never been able to escape from Peggy, and she is just the same, and very determined about it now. I find her entirely satisfying and about as ideal a person for this sort of life as you could wish to find. But I can't help feeling very sorry for her.

"If a Governor's license does not appear next week, we shall probably go off without being married. If it does, the idea is to get married at Arusha, have a breakfast at Provincial Commissioner Longland's house, and then go off on this shooting safari. I have got a most charming ex–KAR [King's African Rifles] named Ionides to come with us as a white hunter, which will probably ensure a fairly interesting shoot, a good deal of information and a margin of safety. The game ranger at Arusha has been wonderfully helpful in getting everything arranged. All the same, I am getting a little tired of making all sorts of arrangements, what with licenses and rings and money and clothes and lorries and one thing and another."

I wrote to Donald's parents: "My dearest Mrs. Wilson, I do hope you won't mind, but Donald and I are about to get married and quite soon. I'm nearly crazy with happiness and excitement. I love Africa and I shall be wonderfully happy here. I do hope you and Dr. Wilson will be pleased about it. I suppose we should have asked your approval first, but there simply wasn't time.

"Donald says that I will be able to help him in his work. I wonder if you can bear the idea of having me for a daughter. I will do my best to be a good wife to Donald. He is such a darling.

"He is looking splendidly well. He has lots of color and is hard as nails. He seems to have made a splendid thing of his work as a health officer in Moshi. The Roman Catholic priest at the leper colony is almost in tears at the thought of losing him. Nothing had been done for the lepers before he came and they are improving from his regular treatment. It is the same everywhere and everyone likes him.

"The roads are dreadful here, but Donald's car seems to be able to go through anything. He didn't want to tell people here about getting married because of all of the fuss that would be made. So I go around telling no one and nobody knows. I cannot tell you how happy I am: it is all like a glorious dream."

Telegram to Donald: "Received following cable, 'Request approval marry Peggy. Replied yes with love and good wishes, Lovett.' Peggy's father put it in the paper (fancy my engagement being in the *Morning Post*)."

Letter from Mrs. Longland to Donald's parents: "Dear Dr. and Mrs. Wilson, Your son Donald and his wife Peggy left this afternoon to spend their honeymoon on a shooting trip, and there they will write and probably tell you all about the wedding. You might like to hear from me also. I hope also to send a piece of wedding cake, though it's doubtful if it will be eatable when it reaches you. (In fact it came the same day and was very nice.)

"As it was not possible to get a padre, he's miles away and not coming back yet, the marriage ceremony was performed by the resident district officer at the Boma, the government offices. Peggy didn't much like the idea of being married in a room which had a desk and a cupboard and a lot of maps around the wall, and was very disappointed that it shouldn't be a church marriage. Still it was quietly and very definitely done, though so quickly over.

"Dr. Speirs, the government doctor in Arusha, came along to our house with his car to see how the bridegroom was taking things and to give him a hand if necessary. I went to help Peggy dress. She had been helping me with flowers for the lunch table and she looked very sweet in her long white Georgette frock and soft crinoline hat.

"We picked the best of the carnations for the bouquet, and Dr. Speirs drove the bridegroom to Boma and my husband followed with Peggy and me a few minutes later. After the ceremony we all came back to the house for lunch, not a big party, since Peggy hardly knows anyone here. We were 14, so filled one long table and had a cheery lunch after taking photographs in the garden.

Peggy's and Donald's wedding photograph, Arusha 1930.

"After drinking to their healths and eating cake we helped the two to change into safari kit and they started off in their car about 2:30 for the first night's camp. Their camp's outfit with all necessities went yesterday in the care of the white hunter who is directing the shooting expedition. Both bride and bridegroom looked very happy when they went off in the car, smothered with rice and confetti and with a good old shoe dangling behind, and a personal boy perched on the top of the luggage. They certainly took with them the best of good wishes. We were glad to have them here and give them a happy send off."

Instead of going-away clothes after the wedding breakfast, we put on shirts and khaki shorts and skirt respectively, then we shall motor 60 miles to the camp named Mto wa Mbu, which means river of mosquitos. Did ever anybody have such a glorious honeymoon in prospect, I wonder?

Donald later wrote to me: "This evening I was giggling over your arrival in Tanganyika, complete with your wedding dress. I think you should have brought a ring as well. I still wonder what caused you to change your mind so completely without my being there myself. But thank God you did, dear woman."

Wedding Safari October 1930: Lion and Oryx

Donald wrote to his parents: "We departed from Moshi 10 days ago, spent three days at Arusha, and now have been at camp here for a week. For better or worse, the deed is done and I confess to rather liking being married, though I shall no doubt regret it later on."

"Yesterday Peggy got an oryx—which is like a unicorn, and today an enormous lion. [Sylvie recalls: *The lion was sent to England and mounted in the drawing room at Spa House. Angela and I used to say, "How could you have shot that beautiful lion, Mummy?"*]. Peggy writes, My father got a wonderful rifle for me with General Krishna's £100, a .375 double-barreled Rigby. Besides my fine lion and a few small buck, I shot a fine oryx. It was a good clean shot at about 150 yards.

"The idea is to shoot one or two zebra, cover them with thorns to keep away vultures, uncover them at night, and stalk up to the kill in the first light of the morning. We've also spent a night watching a kill for a pair of leopards; although they grunted about a few yards away, they wouldn't come right up.

"We are at a marvelous spot: wildebeest, hartebeest, zebra in hundreds. Eland, impala, oryx, Thomson's gazelles and Grant's gazelles. Dikdik in fair numbers and lots of francolin and guinea fowl. Apart from everything else, it's good to be away from all work and people for a bit. Peggy has changed but little, and by some curious turn of mind, has become very fond of me. She fits into this atmosphere perfectly. It's cold and cloudy again, although I don't hear the crescendo of complaints of the coldness of Africa that I had expected."

I wrote to my mother, "We are staying with the Greenings, the DC and his wife at Mbulu. This house is an old German fort, surrounded by open rolling hills. It is 7,000 feet high and very cold. They have big fires at night.

"The Greenings had an awful experience in March. Plague broke out here and 12 of the hospital staff died. An MO who should have come up here refused, saying he couldn't get here in his car as it was in the rains. Donald was told to come and he walked for three days through deep mud and water. They were terribly glad to see him when he arrived. He burnt down the hospital and cleared the place of rats and got up a supply of vaccine by plane.

Peggy and the lion near Kwachinja, Tanganyika, 1930.

Donald described the experience in a letter in March: "...we got about 60 miles on a lorry without much difficulty and it was rather pleasant. Imagine it—mile after mile of smooth green grass, nine inches or a foot high. Here and there a herd of zebra, or a few gazelle, or giraffe where there are some trees, and sometimes other animals. No people, no houses, no villages. Above the blue sky and white clouds blown along by cool wind with sometimes a hawk flashing along or a flock of vultures. That's Maasailand.

"The first day we walked about 12 miles, the second 18, and the third 20, which doesn't sound very much but when all of it is done in soaking boots and a good deal of it in mud up to your ankles, it's rather tiring. At Mbogwe [near Mtu wa Mbu, the river of mosquitos], which is at the foot of the escarpment, it was stiff with mosquitos. I set off with two others at 2:00 a.m. in rain, and had the pleasure of wading through a small river at the start. You then do a two-hour walk to the foot of the escarpment and then go straight up 2,000 feet or so to a height of about 7,000 feet. And after that there's another walk of about five hours to Mbulu. I was intensely comforted to see Greening in a car six miles from Mbulu. The climb up here was described by Indian Clark as 'ascendance and descendance with not one descendent.'

"The plague seems to be over. I am spending my time in boiling things, burning huts, and shifting people about, then doing some sanitation. The first case was a child with bubonic plague and its mother who got pneumonic. She was shifted about in the hospital and nursed without any precautions, except injection from some six-year-old vaccine. The result was that all the hospital staff, with the exception of one dresser who ran away, and one sweeper who seems to be immune, died. The Indian Sub-Assistant Surgeon completely lost his head and things went from bad to worse until the District Officer took charge of the situation."

In another wedding safari letter Donald writes: "Our safari is nearly over. We spent about a week at Kwachinja [near Tarangire National Park], which was full of game. We then went on to Babati where a new hotel was just opening called the Fig Tree and we got a free dinner. From there we went to the Tsetse Research Station at Kikori [in the

Kondoa Region, south of Moshi]. We had an interesting time seeing their work, which is chiefly an intensive study of fly habits and movements and seems to be leading up to some useful results.

"We went from there around Hanang, a beautiful mountain in very lonely country, to Mbulu which is where we are now, spending a night at Dongobesh. It is blowing like anything and almost cold. To get here from Babati, you have to go about 120 miles, although it is only about 40 away.

"They are at present cutting a road to Oldeani with a view to getting down the much lower escarpment at Mto wa Mbu and from there direct to Arusha. We leave Tabora in three or four days for Uyogo, which is more or less between Tabora and Kahama. I shall be doing routine Sleeping Sickness work with four or five substations and a good deal of safari [trips, work trips].

Peggy writes: "I rather like Tabora, although you haven't the wonderful view there was at Moshi. The day before we arrived a lion killed a native here and was hunted up and shot on the golf links in the middle of the town. After Mbulu we next slept at the Rest House in Singida [central Tanzania]. The bluest lake, the greenest grass, and big grey stones—boulders really, sticking up out of the lake."

Dicky and the KAR

We got on the train at Manyoni [Singida Region] and to our great surprise, found my brother Dick asleep in the next compartment to ours. His surprise was really comical. It was so unexpected—I didn't even know he was in Africa. At Tabora we saw a lot of Dick and his brother officers in the KAR, charming lads for the most part but with hardly anything to do in the way of regimental duties. They started drinking about 6 p.m. and went steadily on through the evening.

They gave a dance, enjoyable for me but not for Donald. I wore my splendid lace and brocade dress and I was besieged by would-be partners. But Dick wanted me to dance with him the whole evening, which caused a lot of amusement. He was really glad to see me, but I was most inconsiderate of Donald. He knew nobody to dance with, he drank very little and so after a time he just left. I felt dreadful about it when I got home and found him in bed, and he wouldn't speak to me.

Tabora is an attractive place, red sandy roads shaded by avenues of mango trees, which give the best shade of any trees, and everything wonderfully green in spite of the lack of rain. It is a half-and-half sort of place though, with one good English store, golf links, cement floor at the club to dance on, and most people living in what seems to me a rather forced hectic gaiety—staying up late, one drink after another, that sort of thing. The KAR bands play here almost all day, and much as I love bands, it is almost too much. Dicky comes in nearly every day; he is dreading the time we leave here as he says he will be so lonely.

Donald went to a Guest Night at the Mess. Apparently he and Dick had a drinking contest. Donald came home in high glee saying, "I've won, I've won. Little Dicky couldn't hold a glass straight when I left!"

Uyogo via Kahama [in the Shinyanga Region]

We have arrived and are in our own house! We left Tabora yesterday, driving through miles and miles of thick forest. About 60 miles from Tabora we arrived at one of our houses. Whether to call it our town or country house I don't know. A quaint old two-storey thatched house with fireplaces that one couldn't possibly need, and the minimum of furniture, just I suppose what was left by the last possibly missionary inhabitants, almost certainly UMCA.

In the upstairs room there was a baby's cot and nothing else. We had lunch on the way, tinned tongue, brown bread and butter, and papaya sprinkled with lemon juice and sugar, sitting on one of the car cushions in the forest with the hot sunshine filtering through the trees. The delight of it was rather spoilt by the swarms of tsetse flies that buzzed round us on every side. We had a cup of tea at the house, and Donald had a talk with the dispenser and then started off again. There were heaps of elephant dung on the road. The locals say there are innumerable elephants about in the rains.

It was dark when we arrived at our next house. Dr. Coghlan, from whom Donald was to take over, had gone, leaving no note, nothing, not even the key of the cash box. The house looked dirty and dismal with its unswept mud floors, one table and two hard chairs. We were dreadfully tired, especially Donald, and finally we sat in the car until something was ready to eat. We opened a bottle of Chianti and drank most of it.

This is a thatched mud house with a low walled verandah, also of mud, and square pillars, really quite attractive. The rooms are all in a row: Donald's office, the sitting cum dining room, sleeping room, and then a combined bath, store and gun room. All have square windows with wooden shutters opening on to the verandah. No glass of course.

It all sounds quite grand but actually it is rather comic. When you drive nails into the walls the mud coating falls off in bits. The natives say that there are roan and sable antelope round here and hartebeest, that is, *kongoni* in Swahili. So when we get too tired of eating chickens, we shall go on an expedition in search of big meat. This house is on the slope of a lowish hill, and in front there is a clearing stretching for about 500 yards, with a few round native huts on it (the hospital in fact), and beyond, nothing but the tops of trees in gentle undulations right away to the horizon. It is wonderful to see the sunset from our verandah and then the moon and stars coming out. A sort of velvety warmth surrounds it and all is quiet.

Donald wrote to his parents: "We feel that we are really in Africa now. I think perhaps Peggy won't be such a failure after all. She is really quite good at unpacking and very loving even if not particularly useful. We are much engaged in putting in hooks, making shelves, cupboards and whatnot, all out of petrol boxes [wooden boxes holding 20 litre tins of petrol]. Now I am beginning to attempt to reduce everything here to some sort of understandable condition, and then we will try to find out what Sleeping Sickness is or at least what returns have to be made on the subject."

Peggy wrote: It is a brilliant sunshiny morning. The green trees and red earth look fresh and lovely after the rain. Donald is sitting in a rocking chair on one side of the window shutter table writing official correspondence. We have Donald's former houseboy Juma as cook, though at the moment he is ill. Then there is a perfect treasure of a houseboy who understands equally little of English or Swahili, but who I like so much that I am always trying to save him from Donald's wrath. Not that I need, because he obviously thinks the Bwana is wonderful and everything he does is right. There is a small boy who cleans the car and helps me to wash up, a boy who fetches water from the dirty little pool ¼ mile away for our drinks and baths, and a shamba [garden] boy who hoes and digs. You will be surprised to hear that I like cooking immensely, but I don't know what I should do without the invaluable cookbook from Donald's parents. Though I came rather a cropper over egg kromeskies [poached eggs, battered then fried] last night. Still Donald nobly ate them and said it was nice to have a change. Donald made a marvelous pie for dinner the other evening, cutting up with great malice the old rooster who woke us up every morning.

The local chief has just sent 15 men, at Donald's request, to help start the car. Being entirely on the flat as we are, only strong pushing could do it. After much shouting and pulling on the end of a rope it started. The battery was dead owing to the garage in Tabora having put it in the wrong way round.

My Hospital Work

The microscope work at the hospital takes a long time because practically every patient has to have his blood examined. It is not uncommon to find trypanosomes and malaria and relapsing fever all present simultaneously in the same individual. I do most of the diagnostic lumbar punctures, work I dislike. One makes the patient sit in a chair and bend forward and then push in the thick hollow needle in the 3rd and 4th lumbar interspace. Then there is the little scrunch as the needle goes through the dura mater and then the cerebrospinal fluid begins to drip, and when one finds trypanosomes in the fluid, the prognosis is poor, especially if there are many.

Christmas 1930

Donald's parents' Christmas cards are our only decoration because we could find nothing in the least like holly. I did manage to find some pretty red and yellow flowers growing wild. Donald bought a bullock and divided it up among our servants and the hospital staff and patients and then sent the servants off duty for the day. Donald announced that we must have flakey pastry for the mince pies. We had neither of us ever made it and the butter melted and ran away in the great heat so they were a sad disappointment. The egg soup and roast guinea fowl were very good, however. We spoilt the brussels sprouts by cooking them in their tin. Still one does learn a lot from doing things oneself.

We have been to Urambo [district of the Tabora Region], a charming place all green and shady with ripe pomegranates and mangoes everywhere. It is another of our houses. But I thought we should never arrive there. We were stuck in mud for six hours, and it always seems to happen in an open swampy place in blazing sun and myriad tsetses. We should have got out much sooner if it hadn't been for me. The four men we had

Stuck in the mud in Tanganyika.

taken and I were pushing for all we were worth and the wheels were just getting a grip when I slipped and fell down. Donald, thinking I might be under the wheel, had to stop, and there we were up to the hubs again in that smelly black stuff and all the excavating over again.

Lots more lovely presents from Donald's parents and a splendid hamper reached us at Urambo. I was specially thrilled to see curried prawns and pate de foie gras! Dick is going with us to Ussoke [near Tabora] tomorrow for six days leave. We come back here to Tabora for the KAR dance on the 17th. They are so immensely pressing about it, and I expect it will be great fun. I was so proud today, because one of Dunstone's famous ginger cakes arrived, and Donald said, "Yes it's very good but not as good as the ones you make."

Ukune

Tomorrow really ends our long safari. We have been travelling off and on ever since the end of December. (I wasn't feeling too well some of the time, as I knew by then we were going to have a baby). We were at Ukune [near Shinyanga] for two days. We arrived in the dark after a difficult journey because it was an unknown road through high thick grass. The inhabitants gave us such a welcome! For some distance out they lined the road, hundreds of them, and when they saw the car, we were nearly deafened with cheers and hand clappings. The Mtemi [Chief] has been most helpful and collected all the people Donald wanted to see. Yesterday I examined 100 or more while Donald wrote down my findings. A sad number were blind through having been given overdoses of Tryparsamide in 1929 or thereabouts when it was still under trial and the correct dosage not known. It is a dreadfully tragic sight when those fine big men totter in. Far too big a price to pay for their recovery from Sleeping Sickness. The Mtemi presented us with a very welcome present of a sheep. Yesterday a huge swarm of locusts came over looking like an immense cloud of red dust. Everyone rushed about catching them, and even we had some for tea, fried on toast. They reminded one of whitebait without the fishy taste.

Each evening a big ngoma [dance] has been arranged for our benefit. This evening there must have been 300 taking part, to the accompaniment of drums, singing, hand-clapping and whistles. The chief performers were very quaintly dressed, one with a long floating train of snakeskins, others in tunics and masks sewn all over with cowries; the so-to-speak chorus dressed in long white kanzus (nightshirts), holding white fly whisks, which they waved in time to the music. At the end of this evening's performance Donald made a speech to them all in masterly Swahili thanking them for the show and telling them how pleased he was with the way people had come to be examined. It was most successful and drew forth loud claps. The Mtemi translated it all into Kinyumwezi and then made a speech of his own and it was all quite a ceremony.

Uyogo, February 1931

Now we can settle down quietly at Uyogo and wait for the rains to break. Soon after our return, Donald fell ill with a high temperature. I examined his blood and found that he had relapsing fever (caused by Sp. recurrentis). I gave him an intramuscular injection of Bayoer 205. After a week or so his temperature shot up again and he had a dreadful headache. I sent a runner to Kahamato to ask for advice. When the reply came it said to give him a large dose (amount not specified) of NAB. So I gave him the top dose of 0.9 gm. intravenously. The result was most alarming. He collapsed and I thought I had killed him. However, he gradually came about, got over it, and did not relapse again.

It is such a joy being able to share our letters and parcels. We exclaimed over his birthday parcel this week with much joy. "Oh, another of these fascinating books," and "Oh, chocolate *creams*!" not having seen any for about a year. Hence squeals of delight.

We have gardened a great deal lately, and Donald will have a nice lot of vegetables through the summer. This morning we arose at 5:30 a.m. and went to look for something eatable to shoot. We walked for ages through wringing wet grass high above our heads and saw nothing until we were making for home, when coming on a little pool, two fine wild geese got up, one of which Donald shot and so we came home in triumph. This evening we planted out little tomato plants down at our shamba and dug up our first potatoes, quite nice ones. Donald wrote, "Peggy is getting more and more wonderful at cooking and has made some very edible mince pies. I shall be sorry to lose her." By then it was decided that I should come back to England for the birth of the baby.

Travelling to England, April 1931

It was settled that I should sail for England in May but when the time approached to leave Uyogo, it was pouring with rain and the roads would be impassable. There was nothing for it but to walk the 60 miles to Bukene to get the train for Dar es Salaam via Tabora. It was a horrid trip. Four days walking, often in ankle-deep water and bitten by tsetses. Then we had one spare day at Bukene to rest and settle last details of what I was to send up from Dar es Salaam to Donald. Next morning I caught the train to Tabora. I visited Dick who was in hospital with malaria.

Dar es Salaam is so pretty. Shady avenues of acacias, palms, white houses and a coral beach. Staying at the New Africa Hotel was very nice. I put on my black lace evening frock only to find that I was the only one in evening clothes. I do think it rather messy to be in day clothes for dinner, but I will do the same from now on. There is no point in being conspicuous.

We stopped at Zanzibar and at Tanga. After we sail today I shall feel that I have really left Donald behind. After a few days on board I began to run a temperature. I told the ship's doctor of the fever and that I had run out of quinine. I don't remember his giving me any and he had no microscope on board. A fellow passenger was a very friendly middle-aged major who was a Christian Scientist. Often when he went to his cabin he would say that he was going to do some "work on my behalf," but I don't know that his prayers made any difference. My new friend was very kindly and cheery and I found him a comfort. He asked me to have lunch with him at Marseilles, an interesting meal at which I first ate snails. But I fainted dead off at the end of lunch in my chair. Nothing to do with the snails I am sure.

I went from Marseilles to London by train. When we got to Paris I was intensely thirsty, and I drank two pots of tea and two carafes of water. I arrived at my club in Queen's Gate and was cheered by the exclamations of how well I looked (no wonder, I must have had a really high temperature). Next morning I sallied forth to buy a car; I chose a big Singer Super Six, second hand. Then I went to the Tropical Diseases Hospital and asked them to examine my blood. "I have either got trypanosomiasis or malaria," I told them. It was a Saturday and the technician didn't want to do anything about it then, but I persuaded him and said I would ring up in the afternoon. This I did, and was told that I had *P.falciparum* malaria. Someone kindly shopped for quinine for me and I took 20 grains. I did not know or realize what a risk I ran of developing blackwater fever by doing so.

Next morning I didn't feel up to much and before I was dressed, the Lady Manageress of my club came to tell me that the Tropical Diseases Hospital had telephoned that they were sending an ambulance for me immediately. I made no objections. I was glad to be taken care of. Almost as soon as they put me to bed a technician came and asked if I minded him taking blood films for demonstration purposes. He took about 200 and fool that I was, I never took one for myself. Then Sir Philip Manson-Bahr, whose patient I was to be, visited me. He listened to my baby's heart and said, "This little fellow doesn't mind falciparum malaria!" I must have been very anemic, as in a letter I wrote a week or two later, I said I was getting on splendidly and my Hb was up to 50 percent! "Don't be in the least worried about me and don't dream of coming to London."

My Family

My father appeared at the hospital. I was very cross with him for coming as he was not at all fit to travel. His nurse had come with him, however. It nearly broke my heart when he tottered into the room looking so old and ill and different. They are keeping me here about another ten days to be on the safe side. Everyone here is immensely kind. I have started solid food today and my temperature is quite down. This doesn't seem to have hurt the precious baby at all, most fortunately.

I had a delightful journey to my parents' home in Shropshire and drove 70 miles of it myself. I believe Donald will be pleased with the Singer and will love its smoothness and power. How I love seeing the buttercups and wild roses and tidy little fields again, in spite of it raining every day.

I was glad to get back at last, but it is a frail little household. Mother can only *just* walk and totters about the house on Daddy's arm. He, in his turn, totters about the garden on my arm. Nanny, although the oldest, seems the most active member of the household and suffers from nothing worse than *anno domini.*

My mother's existence is simply a burden to her and horrible. She only lives for Rosie's visits with her children. Try as I can, I cannot show her love and tenderness. I wait on her and bring things for her and she thanks me formally as if I were simply an acquaintance. It is, "Thank you for your help, Peggy, and good night." I pity her intensely, but that is all I can do.

Donald's Letter to Peggy from Tabora, August 2, 1931

"After I posted a letter to you only this morning, I think I must begin this now as I have only three more days in which to write it. That isn't the only reason; the other is that I feel like writing to you. Sometimes I write because it's time to, and sometimes because I have something to say, but now just because I love you and will get as near to you as may be. Why do I love you, I wonder? Is it chance just, or is it because you have charm? Or because I am a male and want someone to sleep with, or because I thought you were a rather superior sort of being? What is it makes me think you're the most wonderful creature in the world? You, myself, or a power over and beyond us? Like a master solver jigsaw puzzle, that's a simple problem compared with your loving me. The other wonderful thing is the more you show signs of loving me the more comes back from me to you. There's no sign or trace of anxiety in the foreseeable future. I think of you in so many different ways, too often with just a rage that I am not with you, others with wonder or tremendous thankfulness or pride. Again I rest on your love as a bulwark against the tides of life that, whatever disaster may happen, will still break away with me for something to cling to.

"All around Tabora the mangoes are splendid, covered with blossoms, cream or pink. They look like horse chestnuts in flower. But now I am at peace on a still, rather hot evening, a pipe, bottle of beer, bathed and clean, chewing the occasional olive. I begin to feel again that life is good and the God who planned it all, kind."

As Donald is packing up to leave Tabora, he writes, "I shall be sorry to leave this house, our first little home. I suppose there will never be anything quite like it, just us two to ourselves. I'm afraid I never stopped to think whether you were bored, so glad was I to have at last what I had so long desired. But luckily my imagination had not realized what the sweetness of the fruit would be. True, dear heart, I'm not just talking about what a lot of other little homes we should be able to make express ourselves, and turn empty houses into living things, even reflections of rather ordinary people. Tonight I seem to have recovered from my depression and feel quite excited at the thought of seeing you again and the recollection of the splendidness of life with you."

Childbirth, August 1931

Our baby, so desperately looked forward to, was born in August. Donald had insisted on my being under the care of a senior obstetrician in Birmingham. I wrote, "I don't think there'll be any complications. I am very well and apparently all is completely normal in every way." This senior obstetrician, Donald's own choice, killed our son. He did not discover that I had a deformed pelvis. Perhaps he should not be blamed for that, but he dragged him into the world as an unreduced occipitoposterior and he died of brain damage in three days. The only reproach I made to the doctor afterwards was, "Perhaps I shall never have another son." And I never did.

I initially wrote to Donald to describe the birth of our son. Then my letter turns to anguish, as I must bury this beloved child.

Peggy's Letter to Donald, August 16, 1931

"Dearest, It seems cruel to send you this letter. Yet as it is written, I think it should go. Precious, I'll just start my letter to you today because I love you so much and it makes me feel a little in touch with you, just the act of writing. To think that we have a son after all, our very own. Isn't it splendid? Little Ethelbet who isn't unready anymore. I wish I knew if you would like to hear the details of his arrival. Anyhow I will tell you and you needn't read it if you would rather not.

"I was driving in Birmingham on Thursday afternoon. At suppertime I began to get little sort of pains so we got things ready and I had a nice big hot bath and then Sister rang up D.G. [doctor]. He arrived at 11 p.m. and examined me and found it was an occipital posterior (but didn't tell me), just said I might have to go on for 40 hours or so, or it might be quicker. Gave me a sedative and said to go to sleep. That was all very fine, especially as I had pains every 2 to 10 minutes from then on until 6:30 a.m. when the membranes went and the second stage began. I should like to inform you and all practitioners that first stage pains are most abominable, they just grip you without you being able to do anything with them. They were so frequent that I couldn't walk about at all. I just lay as still as I could.

"D.G. came back at 8:30 a.m. I was too occupied to converse with him much. He went and fetched Dennis Fox who gave me medication with each spasm. It was quite useless, I thought, and didn't touch things a bit. They all sat there and waited and I began to feel quite guilty and apologize for wasting their time, and by then I had a grain of suspicion that my utmost efforts were making no headway. At 10:30 a.m. D.G. said, 'Well, she's had four hours of it so now put her right under, Dr. Fox,' and proceeded to get out his forceps. Ethelbet and I emerged from the struggle of being torn asunder decidedly bruised and battered. He, poor little soul with a swollen cheek and black eye and me with a central tear of the perineum, which D.G. just made continuous with the vagina so delivery more easily."

Three days later my joy turned to sorrow with the death of our new baby. I wrote: "I had him christened 'Derek Bagster Wilson.' On Thursday morning your father is taking our son to be buried at Dorrington. I simply couldn't bear the thought of his being buried in Birmingham and your father is to take the service. He was to have christened him. Sister went to see him this afternoon and took one of his gowns to dress him in, but she found that they had already put him in a little white robe and clasped his hands and put him some white sweet peas to hold. She managed to cut me off a tiny bit of his hair (he didn't have very much) because I wanted something of him to keep. Miss R. has given me a very quaint little old square brooch to put it in.

"I am being very self indulgent and I'm afraid selfish darling in worrying you with all this. I know perfectly well I ought to wait and write you a normal cheery letter, a 'Bad week but can't be helped,' sort of letter to escape the charge of being what? Soundly sentimental. But I know you'd give me your understanding if you were here. I think you would have shed a little tear too. The trouble is that everything just now seems connected with him and when I'm by myself I can't turn my thoughts away. If you were only here and could sleep with me tonight how lovely it would be. Your darling Little Mother has prayed with me a great deal and I know your father will too, but somehow for me it doesn't touch the place.

"We know that God doesn't—can't—deliberately send suffering and death or he would be a monster of cruelty like the Hindu Kali instead of being perfect goodness and love. We beseech him in vain repetition with an anguish of sincerity to exact a fraction of his almighty power and heal our baby, in the name of Christ. We believe that he hears it, and then we are forced to believe that he ignores it or waves it aside with a 'No, no. Things must work out according to my plan.' It doesn't hang together in my opinion, and I am firmly convinced that we have none of us found the right way of approach to him."

August 19. "Letters of congratulation and condolence keep coming. The one from Mother made me laugh. I must send it to you. Your father has been splendid, so cheery and telling me funny stories and smoking a guilty cigarette with me. I like talking to people because I want to get back to a normal frame of mind as soon as possible. After all, I've had a glimpse of motherhood and it seemed to provide untold joys, more than I ever dreamed of, but I do feel it is wrong not to make every effort to put away a grief."

August 20. "Derek was buried today. I enclosed a copy of your father's special prayer. A copy of the service he has given you I will send by next ordinary mail. I can't write more now. I am wearying for you to come back to me my own Donald."

This was a terrible time for me and for Donald. He was on safari round Lake Victoria on sleeping sickness work and first received a cable giving him the glorious news of the birth. Then, so soon afterwards, another cable shattered all his hopes.

Donald wrote: "My dear, I weary for you no less. Believe me my sleeping and my waking thought is of you. To be able again to share all my life and experience with you and not just these poor fragments of a letter. This seems but half life to me now, for you hold to my heart all the fabled stories of grand ladies, whether of beauty or strength, of tenderness, of faithfulness, or passion. Without you my tunes drop to a poor half cadence that is mocked by a half-heard lovely descant far away...."

I initially stayed with my parents in Dunstone in Shropshire, and also visited with my dear sister Rosie, her husband Thomas, her daughter Rachel and baby Hazel. My letter of September 8, 1931, describes my homecoming and the little grave for our son Derek.

"I have been back here for four days. *Petite mere* [Little Mother, Donald's mother] will tell you about coming home with me. A wretched day it was and everyone, especially Daddy, with such miserable faces. They didn't understand that that wasn't the best way to cheer me up. I saw Little Mother off at 6 p.m. and then couldn't bear it another minute and retired to bed. Mother had ordered a huge wreath of white roses, so next morning I put it on the grave—which is quite covered. It is in such a nice part of the churchyard, a new part, like a garden, just as if the graves were dug in a smooth green lawn, and rose trees near. It is only sentiment to care anything about the whereabouts of a grave, but I do care, and also that Derek's is at the foot of Jimmy Sayce's, who was an awfully nice little chap, died when he was 12, of pneumonia. I should like to put a tiny cross or headstone to mark our baby's grave, wouldn't you, Donald?

"Will you tell me what you would like and I will have it done before you come home, and should I put on it his name and the date and what else? I should rather like, 'All the firstborn are mine.... I am the Lord.' That is from the third chapter of Numbers, as you probably know, and it was the name of one of the poems in that book that Mrs. Kember sent me. I read them very often and grew to like them intensely.

"Two letters from you were waiting for me here. I really do think you must have had a premonition of what was to happen or why should you have thought of saying, "If anything dreadful should happen to him don't sorrow unduly," and you wrote that only just before it did happen. Your second letter.... Oh darling, you did have the joy as I had, for those three days. You will see that Manson-Bahr says the malaria had nothing to do with it. I have firmly decided that I should go back with you when you go, whatever happens."

As the terrible month of August gave way to September, I continued to describe my grief. September 15, 1931 "...This letter is not flowing easily. I do want my baby so much. When it's sunny I think how nice it would've been for him to be out in his pram on the veranda, and now it would have been his evening bath and feed time and he would have been all soft and warm on my lap before the fire and instead I've got what? Cigarettes...."

In another letter I describe the beauty of the coming fall, and my efforts to recover my strength: "The year has turned the corner now and is definitely on the downgrade. The September mornings are marvelous. There's a white frost and such a clear cold purity of air with the fragrance of late roses and sweet peas and hints of blackberries and mushrooms. One wakes to soft misty sunshine lighting up the orchard. In the front of the house the beds are full of rose and mauve asters—great big chaps—and others of scarlet and yellow dahlias. There is abundance of tomatoes and plums. I am glad to be back, the country is so satisfying. How I wish you could see it this morning. The lawn is glittering and the sky is clear soft blue, a really happy sort of day, quite a hot sun too...

"Mother actually walked downstairs yesterday with her nurse's arm, her perseverance is astonishing. Daddy can really do a fair amount of walking. I am going to use every bit of influence I have over him to make him go abroad this winter with one of his sisters...

"I'm beginning to feel much stronger but can only walk a very little way yet. It seems to take longer to get over this sort of thing than I used to think, but as soon as the local damage gets right I should be quite fit...

"I won't buy or order anything with a view to taking it out with us until you come, as you say we won't take anything extra. Our possessions take up so much room I sometimes wish I hadn't anything but a staff and a begging bowl. How it would simplify life.

"I picked a big bunch of sweet peas. They do smell so good, and I picked blackberries on the bank by the brook, and now I feel I have done a good morning's work. So now goodbye my Best Beloved."

I faced moving to Donald's parents home in Muker with mixed feelings. Donald's father, Horace Bagster Wilson, served for 34 years as Medical Director of the Birmingham Medical Mission in Birmingham, England. Donald's mother, Emily Marie Sylvie Buffat, had come from Switzerland to England as a teacher and met and married Donald's father. She too worked at the Birmingham Medical Mission. Horace Wilson was a deeply spiritual man and after he retired, was ordained as an Anglican priest and they moved to Muker-in-Swaledale, Yorkshire where he served as vicar.

Although I was very fond of my parents-in-law, I was dreading being fussed over and dreading personal family prayers. My worries were quickly dispelled, although I was still a bit overwhelmed by the attention to my spiritual well being.

October 1, 1931: Muker. "I feel positively ecstatic about this place. I'm now in my twin bed in our room and the moonlight is on the hills, which we can see from our beds, and the 'Cozey' stove is smoldering gently. I'm snuggled under a black and bois-de-rose satin quilt after a nice hot bath. Donald, you will love this place. It reminds me very much of Moshi but far nicer with its stone walls in houses, even the cow houses, and rippling stream. I am very happy. The whole place and this room especially seem to be just waiting for wonderful times to come when I shall have my Donald again.

"My spiritual welfare is being well looked after, you will be glad to hear. Devotional reading by my bed, family prayers after breakfast, a morning service on the wireless. Today a harvest festival at Grinton. I am afraid I shall have a dreadful reaction when I leave because I am so unused to living in such a pure atmosphere.

"But they are darling, your parents, and I do try very hard not to shock or hurt them. They're really very well on the whole. Your father is a robust help I should say. You will hardly know him, he looks so fit and is filled with energy. L.M. is pretty well, too and always busy, as you can imagine. I wish she had a better maid. I hoped I should be able to do a lot for her but I can't stand for more than a very short time and there

Left: Horace Bagster Wilson in uniform. Right: Sylvie Buffat Wilson.

aren't many jobs we can do sitting down. It is rather absurd after seven weeks and makes me feel quite ashamed of myself. I suppose it is due to the bit of local sepsis, which I still have to ask D.G. about when I go home. It is nothing to do with the tear because that was healed at last, thank goodness."

The Parish of Muker was enormous, consisting of 30,000 acres of fells, moors and valleys. My poor father-in-law, after much thought and discussion, decided to buy a car and learn to drive it. He was advised, ill advised I thought, by a friend of Donald's to buy a Jowett. Of all the rough and awkward cars he might have had, it was the worst. However, Donald's father persevered and finally became a very fairly competent driver, which at the age of 70 was no mean achievement. Even the easiest approach road, from Richmond, was narrow with many blind corners and humpback bridges. The other approaches are by narrow wild mountain roads, one from Kirkby Stephen, and that is joined by a desolate track from Brough and Tan Hill. Few mountain roads equal these two for wild solitude. And this was where Donald's parents, elderly and both suffering from high blood pressure, lived and worked. And how they worked!

October 1, 1931, "We have had some most amusing times with the car and fairly perilous too. It is rather an awkward little chap to drive, as the clutch is so fierce. Yesterday your papa drove us to have tea with someone about four miles off. I don't let him go more than 15 mph. He is so very uncertain of his steering, that with these sharp corners and narrow bridges it simply isn't safe. Going up a steep hill he missed his chance to change into bottom and we shot backwards; then he rammed it into gear and we shot forward even more suddenly, with an agonized squeak of 'Oh Horace' from your mama at the back and convulsive giggles from me. I refuse to take the wheel for him anywhere, except that I did just turn the car at the foot of the Butter Tubs [a hill near Muker]. I don't know when he'll be safe to go anywhere quite alone. These roads are certainly dreadful for a beginner, but he simply must drive as often and as much as he can to get used to it. When he goes out with Whit I imagine he too often says, 'You'd better drive or we shall be late.' Although he tentatively suggested it to me once or twice, I was quite firm on this subject. It is so expensive for him having to pay Whit every time he goes out with him."

At Donald's parents' home, I described a particularly "spiritual day": "Early service at which P.M., Mary and I were the only communicants, wireless service after breakfast, evening church, another service on the wireless and evening prayers to finish up with. I had to ask to be excused when the evening wireless sermon started. I felt I just couldn't bear it and I came up and smoked a cigarette on my bed. They thought I had had a sudden pain somewhere and I didn't disillusion them, but after all we only just finished a 20 minutes sermon by your father and as you know I am so unaccustomed to this intensive devotion that after a certain point I feel emotionally spent and want to take my leave. I wonder how well you'll take to it. Perhaps you'll rescue me sometimes? It is difficult to avoid being a hypocrite sometimes, but I told your mother that I am not really what she calls 'converted,' that I didn't miss church services in distant lands, that I didn't have any particular worry or misery if I neglected to say my prayers, and that often I couldn't feel there was anyone to hear them if I did. She talked to me for a long time about it—she and your father but especially your mother. She is the best example of a Christian that I have ever met.

"Your father preached very well I thought and not over the heads of the village people, which I should rather have expected. I wish he didn't shake hands with everyone going out of church and join in with talk and laughter and introduce one to all the congregation separately while still in the church with much handshaking. You would wonder why I don't like it but it goes against the grain dreadfully, makes me all uncomfortable and rumpled up inside."

Worrying about Donald's safety, I sent a cable and wrote, October 8, 1931: "I got into an absurd state of nerves about you; felt I simply must have an assurance that you are all right.... If anything were to happen to you it would simply break me up. My love for you has grown so deep and strong that it almost frightens me with its power of joy and hurting.

"We will have some splendid walks and climbs here and explore the place all round. But then I must be able to walk my 16 miles in the day. My poor 'best' thick shoes that I went to Bukene in are coming adrift at the soles and they are in Darlington being mended. Yesterday I went out in a pair of your red socks (which I am thinking of annexing) and a pair of your papa's shoes, which leak...

"Little Mother is scribbling away hard on the opposite side of the dining room fireplace with her feet up on a green velvet rocker, horn rimmed spectacles on nose, writing on a book on the chair arm. Your papa is clicking away to you on the typewriter in his study...

"There are very nice apples here for you and fine thick cream for your porridge. I know they'll try as hard as possible to fatten you up, and if you really wear that belt at the fourth hole you certainly need some fattening. All my love, Peggy"

Reunion with Donald in England

Donald arrived in England in November 1931 and Dick, too. Dick's wife Clare and I met them at Victoria. Dick and Clare went off to stay at the Regent Palace Hotel, and Donald asked me which hotel I had booked us into. "The Berkeley," I said very grandly, whereupon Donald collapsed onto a seat in mock horror. Comfortable and lovely and luxurious it was, and we loved it ever after.

I had made great preparations for his arrival in the way of new clothes and was rather dismayed at his disappointment not to have been able to choose them for me himself. Also I had had a permanent wave for the huge sum of £6 in London and had tight little curls all over my head. It was not thought very well of either. Still we were tremendously happy to be together again.

From November until February 1932, we divided our time between [my family's home in] Shropshire and [Donald's parents in] Yorkshire. How lovely the dales looked covered in snow round Muker-in-Swaledale, and what splendid walks we had over the hills surrounding Muker. One day in the rather early spring we walked up Shunner Fell and there we found on the summit that the ground was literally covered with seagulls' nests, many with eggs and some with young birds. We took a few eggs and tried eating them for breakfast but they tasted too fishy.

Malaria Training in Epsom

We are to be engaged in anti-malarial work when we go back to East Africa. So in February 1932 we spent two months at Horton Hospital under Colonel S.P. James' instructions. Horton is one of four L.C.C. Hospitals here containing some 14,000 lunatics of various sorts, some of them suffering from G.P.I. (General Paralysis of the Insane) are treated by means of infecting them with malaria (Benign Tertian; Malignant Tertian gives infection with *P. falciparum* and is too dangerous). With B.T. *Plasmodium vivax* one can let patients have 10 or 12 peaks of fever before curing the malaria with quinine. [Infecting mental patients with malaria to allow fevers was a common treatment.]

Our day's instruction was given by Mr. P.G. Shute. We learned how to make thick and thin blood films and to stain them with the appropriate dyes. Giemsa and Leishman were the two stains we mostly used. We learned to know the different stages of the malaria parasite in the four known species. Then we learned the taxonomy of anopheline mosquitoes and how to identify them from a key. We learned to dissect out their salivary glands under a special microscope and to recognize malaria parasites called sporozoites in the glands when present, and to dissect mosquito stomachs and recognize the presence of cocysts on the stomach wall.

We found comfortable rooms in Epsom. In the evening we had supper at the Nell Gwyn House, either steak or mutton chop, and did the crossword in the *Evening Standard.* Epsom is divided into two separate worlds, lunacy and racing. On the one hand you see giant asylums and the streets full of keepers and nurses and patients out for walks, and on the other, racing stables, grooms, jockeys and horses.

Return to Africa 1932

On board the Llangibby Castle of the Union Castle Line, so far we have enjoyed our voyage. It was such fun having a day and a half at Genoa and we went for a beautiful expedition to Levanto and bathed and sunbathed. Italy is such a smiling flowery country. The cherry trees loaded with fruit looked so pretty in the bright sunshine.

Our last night at Mombasa we were given a good dinner at the club and afterwards we went to the pictures. The Mombasa Picture House is quite a fine place and very well ventilated. We got back to the ship at 11:45, terribly thirsty, but as it was so late we had to be content with tepid water in our cabin and we shared an apple.

Donald's solo exhibition dance at the finish of the Fancy Dress Ball was quite the success of the evening. With a red fez on his head, he danced all alone to the band with all the other dancers standing round watching and clapping time. I can't say I was exactly *refreshed* by the voyage, first a baking and then a toasting.

Dar es Salaam

Since we arrived we have been staying with Lilian and Robin Nixon, the MOH. They were so kind and hospitable. Lilian has fair curls and blue eyes, is very pretty and great fun, and not above telling the odd "blue" story. This evening we are moving into a bungalow in Oyster Bay. It is four miles from Dar itself, and the drive there is very pretty, mostly near the sea which is a glorious deep blue, and the beach is white coral sand fringed with palm trees. We are to be here for three months. The lab where we work looks out onto the harbor, which is always so blue and lovely. The house has a good verandah and adequate furniture. With our own bits and pieces, including Bedouin, Chinese and Tibetan rugs, it is well set up. The storeroom and pantry are very nice with icebox, meat safe, and porcelain sink. The kitchen is luxury after Uyogo where the smoke from the fire could only get out through the door, there being no chimney.

I am working six hours a day in the lab, besides doing a good bit at home. My fingers are itching to grip my tennis racquet again but there never seems time for any exercise. The sitting room is long and narrow, with five windows. The settee is covered in brown silk with the topi skin thrown over the back and flame colored cushions. Above it hangs a Surrey sunset in oils. To one side stands an Indian inlaid table with a Burmese red lacquer cigarette box. A brilliant red and black Kachin bag hangs on the other side. The rest of the room is a deep green with cushions of different shades of gold. The curtains are made from a Nepalese bedspread, white with black and red birds flying.

Tomorrow we are having two men to dinner and this is the prospective menu: grapefruit, Benjamin's special egg soup, fish soufflé, roast chicken and potatoes, cauliflower and bacon, Cape gooseberries combined with a sort of fluffy yellow jelly and dessert. Not too bad for Africa? Dar es Salaam meat is the despair of any housewife. The more it is beaten the harder it gets. The weather is still delicious. The early mornings are fresh and fragrant. We manage to have breakfast at 7:30 except on Sundays when it is any time up to 10 a.m. And how one does appreciate the day of rest.

Malaria Laboratory, Tanga, October 1932

Nous y sommes at last. First impressions are that Tanga is a nice and pretty town. But it is much hotter than Oyster Bay, and far more mosquitos. On our journey here we stopped in Pangani, a small Arab town on the Indian Ocean not too far from Tanga. It was a lovely evening when we camped out among the palms and mango trees. Donald made a campfire with dried palm fronds and there was a bright moon. Pangani was such a charming place, I wish we were to live there. Such a wonderful shore fringed with huge palms backed by avenues of tall feathery casuarina trees and such delightful Arab houses.

Peggy's Family

Just as we arrived and settled in Tanga, we learned that Mother is back from her trip to Lourdes. My poor father is in great trouble over Dick. He is leaving the Army and going off somewhere abroad. He is convinced that he is of no use in the Army or to Clare and is better out of the way. I think our prayers must have been answered because in his last letter news about Dick was much better. He seems to have given up his dreadful resolutions of suicide and going abroad and I believe is doing his best to pull himself together. He is with Clare now and writes home that he is happier than he has been for years. Father is trying to arrange work for him in a garage, and Clare's father has given them the wherewithal to buy a house wherever they choose. I do hope that all will be well. I am awfully sorry for Clare over the whole thing.

Rosie and the children made quite a long stay at Dunstone lately. I am so thankful she was there with Father to cheer him up a little. To hear about Dick is not easy when you are ill and old, and it is not easy sometimes to feel that there is an Unseen Presence helping you to stand it.

November 17, 1932

I heard from Rosie today that Father is very seriously ill, and has day and night nurses. They say he is not in any pain or discomfort but is hardly conscious and very weak. Rosie says I could do nothing if I were there, as he would hardly know me. Rosie enclosed a letter written by Dick from Rendlesham Hall (the Hospital for Alcoholics where Dick has been under treatment for some time). The doctor says that he is the most promising hope of a complete cure of his manic-depression that he has had for a long time.

November 20, 1932

Father is dead. For his sake I am glad that he has gone. Life was very wretched for him. But I shall miss him badly. I am sure he now knows peace and I feel as if it were a message from him that all is well with him and not to grieve. I am so thankful I spent so much time with him when I was in England.

A little while before I left for Africa he told me that he felt he had made his peace with God and was ready to go as soon as his time should come. He told me of a vision he had in church. It was too sacred to ask him about, but he said, "You won't believe me of course, but for a moment I saw Heaven open to me, and I was allowed a glimpse of life beyond death."

If that weren't sad enough, I had a letter from Jessie Brown who is on her way to Nepal. She told me that Maharaja Chandra Shumshere Jung is dead. There had been two attempts on his life because he legitimized two of his illegitimate sons, thereby making two more possible successors. Jessie is going there to fit Nani with new splints.

Chapter 5

Malaria Research, 1932–1934; India and Nepal, 1935

by Peggy Lovett Wilson

We had been told that we were to do a malaria survey of Tanga, but Donald said that was ridiculous; we would do it in our spare time. What was really needed, he said, was to make a long-term study of malaria in an indigenous population limited to about 300–400 people, living in an area as far removed from all European medicine and health measures as possible. To this end we chose three villages 15 miles from Tanga. They were Mtakuja, Mgandi and Mwengere.

Donald describes our field situation [Wilson 1936, known socially as Donald, he used Bagster professionally to distinguish himself from three other Dr. Wilsons in Tanganyika]: "The only medical treatment available in the area was provided by an African dispenser, who was one of the staff of the Survey. With the exception of injections of bismuth sodium tartrate for yaws and syphilis, he gave no specific treatment of any kind for any disease to inhabitants of the selected villages. The people themselves were indifferent to treatment of any kind unless their diseases were very painful and would take no trouble to obtain it. They made spasmodic use of various barks and leaves for the treatment of fevers and other diseases.

"The food of the people consisted mainly of cassava, with various kinds of small beans; maize, sweet potatoes and millet are eaten to a small extent. Fat is obtained from coconut. Various kinds of green leaves are an adjunct to the main food. During their season many mangoes are eaten. Owing to the drought in 1933, the diet at that time was so reduced that obvious malnutrition resulted. The drought was later accompanied by locusts that were a most valuable addition to the diet.

"Infants are breastfed up to a year or longer but from the age of a few weeks breastfeeding is supplemented by starchy foods. Cattle are decreasing owing to East Coast Fever, trypanosomiasis and other diseases. Meat is a coveted luxury. Goats are a form of capital only drawn upon in emergency. In paid employment on sisal estates the men receive 12–15 shillings for six weeks work."

Muslim Hunting Story ["Moslem" has been changed to "Muslim" and "Muhammedanism" to "Islam" to reflect current cultural practice and usage.]

The people are Muslim, which has a strong bearing on this episode. We usually spend our weekends camping in the bush, often going out soon after dawn to shoot for the "pot." During the drought of 1933 the people of our villages were very poorly nourished indeed, and one weekend we decided to make a determined effort to get meat for them, plenty of meat so that they could dry it and it would last them quite a time. We took with us two Muslim trackers from one of our villages. In the distance we saw a herd of eland, great big antelopes, wonderfully good eating. We made a long and careful stalk, the last part on our stomachs, dragging our rifles up to an anthill. We rested our rifles on the top. Donald said, "I'll take the big bull and you shoot one of the cows." We fired simultaneously, and then all four of us ran up to where the herd had been.

There was the big bull shot through the heart. "Oh quick, quick," we said to the trackers, in Swahili, "quick, cut his throat." They made no move. "He's dead," they said, "It's no good." They were filled with gloom and kept saying, "Oh what bad luck, oh how terrible, and so on." I said, "Well I think I hit mine, let us look for a blood trail." We soon found it, and it led us about 20 yards to where we found the cow eland shot through the lungs just about to expire. Again we begged them to cut its throat (no Muslim will eat any creature that has not had its throat cut and the blood let out with the appropriate prayer while it dies), but they insisted that it was dead already and would not do it.

Then the moaning was renewed about it being the worst day's luck that anyone could ever imagine, and so on. Donald and I were pretty fed up, as after all, we had shot the animals in good style, and we were so greatly looking forward to giving all this splendid meat to the hungry villagers.

When the Prophet Muhammad made the rule it was a very sound one intended, presumably, to ensure that no one ate animals that had died from disease, but the poor silly mutts take it as literally as no doubt they always have, with no understanding of the reason. There we were, and not a soul in our villages got a taste even, and we had to go off to a Christian and to a pagan village, telling the people where the meat was so that they could collect it. It was a bitter disappointment to us for we had been so keenly looking forward to the pleasure it would have given in the villages to be presented with almost two tons of the best meat in Africa.

Much later, Donald shot a hartebeest for the people of Mwengere. This time it had its throat cut in true Islamic style before it died.

Research Methods and Findings

We spent 10 days of every month and sometimes more in the villages. We had a large sleeping and bathing tent, and a little banda (a grass-roofed hut) as sitting and dining room. Here we identified our mosquitoes and dissected out the salivary glands of the females to see whether they contained sporozoites that, when put into the bloodstream, develop into malaria parasites. We also dissected out the mosquitoes' stomachs to note the number that had the cysts on them that would contain the sporozoites, and make their way to the glands ready to infect the next person who was bitten. We took blood by finger prick from the entire population every two months for three years, and also examined each person's spleen to note the degree of enlargement caused by the infection. We stained the blood usually on return to our smart new laboratory in Tanga. We carefully examined the thick and the thin films, counting the parasites against the leukocytes [white blood cells] and noting which or how many of the four species of malaria parasites were present.

We found no infections in babies less than two months old. We used to wonder why, having no idea that they were protected against malaria and various other complaints by the antibodies that reached their bloodstream via the placenta from their immune mothers. This protection lasted only for a few weeks after birth and then began to wear off, and the babies changed from being fat, healthy, and placid into fretful, feverish, miserable little beings. After six months or more, the babies gradually began to develop their own immunity and if they survived this critical period, improvement began to be seen. From then onwards throughout life, every member of the community suffered from anemia in greater or lesser degree. This was not entirely due to malaria, although in infancy and young childhood it was the chief cause, but also later on was partly due to hookworm and bilharzia. A most important cause was lack of proper food. Donald said, "The final as well as the first impression of the inhabitants of our villages is their utter inability to make an adequate response to any stimulus; their quietness, their slowness and their poor physique."

In the mornings we worked in the nice friendly village and were rather helped by our large tin of peppermints, one of which went far towards consoling for a pricked finger. Sometimes I take the bloods and Donald examines the spleens, other times vice-versa. When we had finished we had our lunch under some thick bamboos: cold chicken, bread and butter, jam, and oranges.

I am very well, and except that my legs get swollen from the heat, I can still do a good day's work without being very tired, but I do feel the heat a great deal just now. (I was seven months in the family way). Also I seem to need a lot of sleep that Donald rather thinks is just laziness. (I was suffering from amoebic dysentery but it was not then diagnosed). We are writing in the tent, Donald sitting on his bed and I on my campstool. Flies buzzing around and subdued chatter outside where Gwebe the dispenser is treating the various patients who have come. We can't do much for most of them, what earthly use are two or three doses of medicine? Still they feel that something is being done for them. Our peppermints for the children are proving a great success but the adults feel that they should have them too.

Tanga

We are just back in Tanga again from the villages and very sticky it is. On Sunday afternoon the two Mission fathers had tea with us and we had dinner with them. They have a great many schools scattered about. The Mission Church is delightful, with big pillars of red stones stuck together with vivid grey cement. We went into the girls' school

Donald examining spleens of patients with the dispenser and local officials.

where an English nun presided. She had been teaching them folk dancing and the girls were quite good and obviously enjoyed it. Donald gave them a talk. The actual village we had been living in is a stronghold of Islam and the Fathers say that it has a strong atmosphere of evil about it. As Donald says, they possibly confuse evil with antagonism!

This evening Donald took it into his head to dig up a big buried stump on the edge of the tomato bed. With one of his violent blows he over-balanced and pitched forward through the supporting framework straight onto the precious plants. All the cherished little green tomatoes (at least six!) rolled *par terre.* We sorrowfully gathered them up and I am looking up green tomato chutney in the Olio recipe book.

As usual we have had a hectic week. Friday we were hard at it in the lab until 8 p.m. dissecting a batch of mosquitoes sent down from Moshi. Saturday a.m. the same. Then Donald and I went for a swim. When we returned, the Nicholls from Amani turned up for a drink. We rushed into evening clothes, and people arrived for a dinner of grapefruit, kidney soup, fillet of beef, golden cream, cheese fondue. Then we were off to dance at the Club and stayed until 2:30 a.m. when my feet refused to function anymore, ending up with a wild polka with Donald.

The *Hawkins,* Royal Navy cruiser, has been in Tanga this week. Mr. Longland, the PC [Provincial Commissioner] asked us to dine at the Tanga Hotel to meet the Admiral and his wife. It was a party of 16. The DO's wife acted as hostess. One afternoon Donald played a rugger [rugby match] against the Navy. It was a really hot afternoon and they started playing at 5 p.m. Donald had a very bad headache afterwards.

After guests for tea and for dinner, we finally got on board the cruiser about 10:15 p.m. There, with dancing on the quarterdeck and between the dances, some of the sailors gave performances with ventriloquism and guitars and an accordion, all great fun. Donald and the surgeon commander made friends while I made friends with another commander who knows my Fuller relations quite well. He showed me a lot of the ship and we had a great talk and altogether it was a very nice evening—about 200 Tanga people were on board.

Gombero

We often go to Gombero. One weekend we walked for three hours before breakfast and saw three buffalo, warthog, waterbuck, duiker and steinbok. We are going again next week with our rifles. I hope we shan't find the buffalo again; perhaps they'll have gone away. We are having a grand time here this week working, walking, and trying to shoot things. The total bag has been three green pigeons and two guinea fowl, all shot by Donald.

Donald has just had a nasty go of malaria. There are a great many infected mosquitos at Gombero now. He is better now, I am glad to say. We have had such a strenuous day. Up at six and two hours work before breakfast. The Milnes from Amani appeared mid-morning. Owing to that and other delays we were behind with the work and had to go back to the lab when they had gone. Home at last about 6 p.m. and poor Donald with an awful tummy ache due to the atebrin he has been taking. I am suffering from want of exercise. I miss the games and riding and mountain walks I used to have in Nepal. It would be heavenly if we could have horses here. There is no sensation to beat a good gallop.

We returned from five days at Gombero feeling much fitter. Half our troubles here are due to this sedentary life, sitting hunched up on a stool in the lab for hours on end. At Gombero we get a good walk every evening. Donald shot an oribi [small antelope] and a duiker so we had some delicious meat. The bush was simply lovely round Gombero, filled with delicious flower scents of gardenias and mimosa, and one very rich honey-like kind of scent. All the grass was new and bright green and there were lots of flowers about.

Servants

Our cook Benjamin continues to be a treasure and we are really fond of him. Little fat Kagundu, although he will tell lies and *won't* wash his clothes, is a perfect table servant and most intelligent for a 13-year-old. Simeon who cleans the car and runs messages is an amiable half-wit. The malaria staff are learning their work and we like them all.

Rice, upon whom we increasingly relied for the care of our home and family, and Benjamin were thrilled with their calendars at Christmas. They really are dears, both of them, and so is little Kiriof (otherwise Cleophas). What a daft name to give a native anyhow.

Rice laying out table at camp at Gombero under a large ficus tree.

We have been dreadfully worried about Benjamin lately. He had such an outbreak of drinking that we were afraid he would have to go. He was very ashamed of himself. I do so hope it won't happen again. Two nights he couldn't cook dinner; however, these last two days he's been quite himself again. We are going out to dinner this evening.

Rice and his wife Miriam made most of my costume for the fancy dress, mostly of colored grass mats. Tanga dances are dull though; stone floor and no supper, and I don't mind if I never go to another. Benjamin is trying quite hard not to drink, but his cooking is deteriorating. I hate the thought of the probable succession of idiots, rogues and incompetents who will follow him when we have to replace him.

Benjamin was dismissed in December. He expressed no regret at leaving us but surprisingly bicycled to Gombero to say goodbye. We were resting and didn't see him but Rice told us he was pretty drunk. Our new cook, Aidan, is a UMC Mission boy, very anxious to please. It will be a long time before he knows how to make the soufflés, creams and jellies that Benjamin excelled at, however.

Benjamin's wife had fits, whether epileptic or not we don't know, so he returned her to her own relations. It is their tribal custom that they may do so for any sufficient reason if married less than a year and no children. He put her in the train with some little presents for the journey and a chicken, and that was the end of it. As for Benjamin, we hear he is in prison in Tabora for having seriously injured a man.

Aidan has been trying harder lately but he has such elementary ideas of cleanliness. For instance, he thinks nothing of using the floor scrubbing brush to clean the forks!

Some of the UMCAs don't seem very particular about cleanliness, I must say, and Aidan has taken no trouble to learn to read and write, although our little clerk was to give him lessons at 6 d a time. Paid by us of course.

Christmas 1932

We're just back from our safari and shall not go away again till we go to Amani (East African Agricultural and Forestry Organization) Christmas Eve. We are going to take all our friends there a present of fish. I only hope we can get it there without it going bad. Mrs. Nowell, the Director's wife at Amani, had a Christmas tea party for the African women of the place for the first few years she was there and used to give them each a china cup and saucer or mug to take home. Alas, after the first time or two they began to look on it as a matter of course. Some of them actually hid the mug in their clothes so as to be able to get two! The day after the first party none of the men turned up to work and on being asked why, said that if the women had a party given for them, they could do the work as well. So after that, Mr. Nowell gave the men an ox for *their* party. We also had a marmalade making which was a great success. Every sort and kind of jar was pressed into service, even, I fear, some that were intended to hold mosquito larvae and not marmalade at all.

We simply love our Christmas presents. *So* thrilling opening them. The London book (H.V. Morton) is delightful, the hankies sweet, and as to the marvelous hamper—what excitement. Donald had to taste the cheese at once and pronounced it most fruity and excellent. Then he sneaked some almonds and raisins. The splendid variety of potted meat and fish delights us. So useful for sandwiches, toasties, savories, and they are luxuries we never allow ourselves. I was thinking last night how this time last year we were thankfully putting our chilly bodies into very hot water, and now putting our overheated flesh into water as it comes out of the cold tap, and even leaving it to stand in the bath all night to cool it a little more. Tomorrow blessed and beautiful Amani will welcome us again.

I have applied for the post of Assistant Entomologist to the Tanga Malaria Unit and shall be very disappointed if I don't get it, and rather surprised, as no Indian that they could appoint has my qualifications for the job.

Birth and Loss, January 1933

We had a hectic few days before I left [for Moshi]. We had friends with their two children from 12:30 until 7 p.m. and two more visitors during the day. The last left at 8:15 p.m. by which time we were pretty well worn out. Five minutes before starting for the station at 8 a.m., I had a violent nosebleed that only stopped in time to kiss Donald goodbye.

It was annoying when the aeroplane landed here in Moshi and then sailed off again carrying my letters from home, most tantalizing. I hope I shall have some good news for you this time next week.

The whole thing took about 12 hours and then a little baby girl was born dead. She was dark haired and small and very perfect. It became another occipito-presentation. Instead of forceps that were done for the first, in this delivery the agony that I went through before the analgesic, that was also amnesic, took effect was terrifying. The damage to the baby caused by the pushing against the hard scar tissue from the previous disastrous birth was enough to kill it. It was torn and damaged again as badly as in the time before.

Sunday, January 21, 1933. I wrote of my sorrow to Donald. "Donald my beloved, what can I say to you without indulging in an orgy of self-pity—I suppose Doctor Speirs will tell you about it all. You can't think how shamed and inadequate I feel. To have brought two children to the point of birth and then to have killed them in the act of birth is a soul-shaking thing.

"I feel like whining, Donald dear, and saying that life has hit me a bit too hard lately. We wanted Godfrey, I know, but all the same Sylvie was a surprisingly sweet little baby, dark-haired and small with beautifully formed features for such a tiny thing. And again the cot has been taken away and all the baby things gone and my arms feel empty. I should come back to you as soon as I possibly can—in 10 days if I can, and with you I shall find comfort. I am bitterly sorry for your disappointment, my dearest. You really were rather looking forward to it. I rest on your love, Peggy."

People here have been cheering me up so resolutely that I am quite tired. Ionides, who went on our honeymoon with us as white hunter, came to see me today. He is flying home tomorrow to get advice about his deafness. Too much firing of his heavy rifle, I am sure. Mrs. Speirs, the wife of the doctor, and others bring me flowers and fruit and books and sweets and cream, so kind. Donald arranged for me to have a special night nurse for the first week. Miss Eager, the hospital Sister, looked after me superbly by day.

If I had been the Queen herself I couldn't have been given more care. I wish our lab were here instead of Tanga. All the people are such dears and the flowers and fresh breezes are so delicious. I have just seen the mail plane appear in the sky and circle round against the hills before alighting at the aerodrome that I can see as a big stretch in the distance. I am to spend Saturday night at the Speirs's to get used to feeling up and about. I think Bobby Speirs blames himself, but feeling convinced that the forceps killed my first baby, he was determined not to interfere with nature this time. Oh, such a bad result.

What a lot of surprises Donald had for me to welcome me back. First a pneumatic front seat in the car, most comfortable, then all the excitement of the new house. A covered and painted humpty stool to put my feet up on, the old campstool re-covered and painted. Curtains he had machined! Pictures he had framed, and hung. How on earth he got it all done I can't think. He got a new lamp and made a shade for it, and he had arranged all my clothes in drawers and put out dressing table things. Our new house is nice. There is a lot of green grass, almost lawn round it and a well-grown hedge separates us from the road. We get far more breeze than in the last house. The bathroom is a symphony in white, grey and green.

I have started a little work in the lab but am taking things most easily, having breakfast in bed, etc. Our baby is buried quite near the hospital where she was born. There are white daisies planted on her grave and it is enclosed by a little fence, and the ground

round it cleared of brush. I am gathering strength every day. This morning on my way to the lab I ran out of petrol so had to leave the car by the side of the road and walk to the lab.

Dar es Salaam. European Hospital, March 16, 1933

I was operated on for appendicitis yesterday. I came from Tanga by aeroplane. It was a grand experience although I felt extremely sick. While travelling at 120 mph at 5,000 feet the pilot turned round (it was a tiny two seater) and said, "Have you got your ticket?" which struck me as very funny.

I have been given the Entomologist post. I must get very strong quickly as I am now a salaried Government official!

Returning to Gombero, we are not working at such high pressure now and quite often get a bit of a lie-down after lunch. I am strong now and able to cope with it. I can walk for two and a half hours before breakfast and be quite fresh after it. Tomorrow back to suburban civilization, but quite nice to have iced drinks, big baths, big beds, fish to eat and harbor to bathe in. We really do have a lovely life. I wouldn't change husbands with anybody I can think of, although he does call me a coot, a silly coot, or a bandicoot, 50 times a day.

Bumbuli

We went to Bumbuli and visited the Moravian Mission and the hospital. Herr Doktor Muller has 15 beds for Europeans and 120 for natives. He has a well-equipped operating theater, a training school where there are 12 African medical students under instruction and four nursing sisters. There is a large furniture workshop where they make very attractive articles of cedar, olive, ebony and other woods, including camphor. The religious work seems to be mainly carried on by Africans. Donald said that while it is nice for the local Europeans to have such a good hospital, it seems rather remote from missionary work.

Peggy having breakfast in the Bumbuli Hills, 1933.

Dr. Muller seems to have most of the attributes of a German, tremendous thoroughness, drive, dogmatism and preoccupation with the trees. They work in the loveliest of surroundings; a rocky hill rising behind them, and ridge and valley stretching away until they finally drop to the level plains in the distance. Beyond these plains, the Eastern Usambaras rise up equally abruptly to an escarpment that is sometimes smooth and rounded and sometimes deep forest. Whichever way you go from Bumbuli, the road creeps round the contours of the hills, dipping here and there to a sedge-covered bottom and then climbing up and up in the dark cool rainforest.

From the UK

To Donald's parents: Rosie tells me she has asked you if she may send some of my things to Muker. I expect you will quite like to have the lion and oryx (I had the sambhur skins made into presents for Donald—a suitcase, gun case, and cartridge bag). Rosie and Thomas had Mother and Nanny to live with them. Poor Thomas's future will be spent as a lone male in the midst of eight females. Indeed I am sorry for them, but as Rosie says, what is the alternative? She always seems to bear the brunt of our family difficulties.

Rosie has her hands even fuller than usual. Her two girls have whooping cough, Mother's nurse is in bed with flu and therefore Mother is in bed too. Mother returned from Lourdes much disappointed at not feeling any better. She says it was very foggy in the Channel and her boat had a slight collision with a cargo boat. Some of the passengers put lifebelts on, but she "sat quietly on the deck."

April 6, 1933, Donald has told you of this fresh blow of Dicky's death. He shot himself in a railway carriage in Madras.

Sisal Plantation

Day before yesterday we went to a sisal plantation 15 miles from here to investigate malaria among the 1,000 laborers. The manager is a Mr. Pritz. We took 200 bloods and examined and dissected mosquitos, looked for larval breeding places, and had a busy two days. Mr. Pritz believes in corporal punishment for natives and still has it done in cases where a man sticks a knife into another, for instance, and says that the natives themselves much prefer it to prison. He says the man jumps up and salutes afterwards feeling, "Well now that's all over."

Visitors

John Morris arrived. We took him to Amani. Colonel Boscawen came to lunch first. He and John gradually thawed to one another and discovered a lot of mutual friendships. We lunched Boscawen on soup and sandwiches and John on turkey and tongue sent by Donald's parents "and it finished as delicious rolls made by Peggy on Sunday." I can't resist quoting that; praise of my efforts is rare. We also took John to Pangani where we had a beautiful bathe and picnic lunch and tea. We hardly stopped talking for four days.

Yesterday we met the widow of the Antarctic explorer Wilson, Oriana, a naturalist. [Edward Adrian Wilson died in 1912 with Scott on the Terra Nova expedition, the first British expedition to the South Pole. He was a Wilson relative. His widow Oriana Wilson was a naturalist and humanitarian who was awarded the CBE, Commander of the Most Excellent Order of the British Empire.] A wonderful person. After being with us she stayed at the Mission at Handeni and sat on the floor of the Church all through the Good Friday and Easter services as the natives do. She couldn't understand a word.

Reg Moreau, a very keen ornithologist, stayed with us for Easter. He loved the camp. The forest was looking perfect: the new grass, the trees ... some scarlet-leaved and some copper like copper beeches. In places the ground was covered with lilies, white bell-shaped ones streaked with pink. There was a delicious scent of mimosa and there were little red velvet ticks on the ground. One night I heard a lion grunting away.

Moshi, January 1934

We have had a really splendid trip, and are both feeling so well and set up by it. At Usa we looked for larvae in people, pools, ditches, furrows and swamps. Next day to Arusha. After lunch with the Game Warden, Monty Moore, we drove a few miles up Meru Mountain along a grassy path. The people who live on Meru, the Waarush, are most wild looking. The men's hair and bodies are plastered with red mud and their sole garment is a sort of skin apron back and front, open at the sides. The women wear a skirt of hide and innumerable steel and copper necklaces, armlets and anklets that weigh them down so much that their gait is most ungainly. They were so curious about us that you might think they had never seen any Europeans before.

Tanga and Monk, February 1934

Donald has malaria again. He had a headache since Saturday and today his fever came out. He came to the lab early this morning but felt too ill to do anything, so I brought him home and he spent most of the day on the sofa drinking immense quantities of soda with grapefruit juice and Soda Bic. Meantime I have had the world's most hectic day. Nicholls brought us a lot more larvae from Amani that had to be sorted and dealt with and labeled. Newly hatched mosquitoes to mount, slides to examine, a medicine to make up, staff to supervise, indent to make out, jelly to make for invalid, and so on.

A week ago Donald saw a native with a minute baby monkey so he borrowed it to see if it had malaria. Finding it had, he brought it back here and took blood films from it, two hourly for 48 hours, with my somewhat unwilling help. We have therefore got its complete parasite cycle. It ended in our buying it from the native for 2 shillings. It is already quite tame and decidedly affectionate. It drinks a great deal of milk and its favorite food is cake.

Our little monkey is lost! I suppose he slipped out of the belt Donald made him.

I have had an exhausting afternoon examining spleens at the Baby Clinic. They nearly all screamed.

We now have another little monkey called Monk. He loved being in the lower branches of the trees eating little seeds and insects and sitting very peacefully on my shoulder. He loves company and hates to be left alone. He had such a lunch of cheese rinds today.

May 1934 Tanga's gay whirl has begun, starting with the Governor's visit. We had dinner with Baker and the McElderrys (now Acting Governor at Zanzibar). His Excellency arrived on Monday. Everyone went to meet him at the station, arriving in full panoply with sword and feathers and guard of honor. Next morning he visited our lab but was neither intelligent nor interested. However, we had dinner with him and Lady McMichael at the hotel. The dinner itself was quite perfect. Towards the end there was a most interesting discussion of closer union between Zanzibar and Tanganyika, the future of tribes like the Wachagga and the attitude of the Germans towards the British.

It is quite nice to be home again [in Tanga] (we had been to Moshi and Arusha). The garden boy had dug up the whole garden, and everything we had planted he had moved to somewhere else. He tries awfully hard, however. Hokelai is cooking very nicely.

The flowers at Arusha were lovely as ever. Such a bank of heliotrope in the hotel garden, smelling delicious, and beautiful peach and apricot colored gladioli, and violets. We went to Usa every day and walked over several of the planters' estates. The planters were all most helpful and anxious to do anything they were told that would lessen their malaria problems. We went to visit some nice people called Murray whose house is on a high hill overlooking Maasailand.

Then back to Tanga, and next day to Korogwe. We pitched camp on the other side of Korogwe, gathered firewood, supped off cold tongue and chocolate blancmange. Rice went up a tree to cut poles for mosquito nets. Our camp beds were shielded from the road by tall thick grasses and we went to sleep in the bright moonlight. Next evening we arrived in Arusha. The dust, the awful red brown dust of the road, had smothered us and our belongings, so as soon as we arrived we took possession of the bathrooms. Now I am sitting as close as I can to a nice wood fire in the hotel lounge and have had the usual thrill over the enormous roses and carnations.

Nairobi, Kenya, August 1934

There is such a queer strangeness about this place, Nairobi; you don't feel that you are in Africa nor yet quite in England. We arrived *very* dusty and dirty (the volcanic dust!). Donald was so thrilled at getting on to a tarmac road that we zoomed into Nairobi at 60 mph! I don't really much like the town. We have had to do a lot of shopping, and I have fallen for two frocks, one chosen by me, a blue and white chiffon with a little cape, and one chosen by Donald, an oyster colored elephant crepe, with silver beads on the bodice and cut on such slimming lines that it makes me look impossibly svelte.

Most of yesterday morning we spent in seeing the Government Laboratory and talking to those working there. Donald demonstrated our way of dissecting mosquitoes. Today we are going to see a native bush hospital.

At Kibaya in Maasailand on the way back we had quite a long talk with an old, rich and important Maasai chief. Although he must be worth quite £1,000 and is having three of his 50 sons educated (he also has 45 daughters), his clothing consisted of a brown blanket tied up on one shoulder. He talked Swahili very well, which *is* unusual for a Maasai. When the Germans passed through his country during the war, he was given the alarm just in time for him to drive his herds of cattle into hiding, but they took all his sheep and goats.

There is a beautifully kept grave near the Rest House of a young ADO named Spurwell, and on the rough grey tombstone is engraved after his name, "Killed by a buffalo at Kibaya. Only son of.... In God's keeping." A Union Jack flies over his grave and every year his mother sends a new flag. A lovely lonely place to be buried, quiet and cold.

A. wilsoni and Other News from Tanga

Quite a thrill awaited us on return. A letter from Miss Evans of the Liverpool School of Tropical Medicine to whom we had sent some mosquitos that puzzled us (caught as larvae on Geiglitz Estate and bred out). One is an entirely new species and another may be too. She is calling the new species *A. wilsoni.* We have now found the larva of *A. wilsoni* at Amani and have bred out several adults. Another rare species we found at Amani dies in Tanga warmth and we have not succeeded in getting a single adult. The last remaining larva I have put in the ice chest as a last hope and so far it is very lively.

We bred out our mysterious larva, and it turns out to be the previously unknown larva of a known adult, *A. machardyi.* As to the Report, the typist has gone sick with 60 pages left to do, so we are *very* harassed. I don't tire of work, I enjoy it immensely, but I often think how much nicer and more peaceful it would be to work for the natives but not with them or over them. The new microscope arrived and we don't like it at all.

Miss Evans is thrilled with our last consignment of larvae skins and mosquitos that we sent her. They included some very good series of *A. wilsoni* and another distinct new species. We haven't yet discovered the larva of the latter, but we have some larvae at the moment caught in a stream above Amani that do not fit with any description. We are eagerly looking forward to seeing the adult mosquito if we can persuade the larvae not to die until they have bred out first into pupae and then into adult mosquitos. They are a very delicate species indeed. This time we have them in an incubator over a large block of ice, renewed daily. Up to the present we have had 23 findings of *Plasmodium ovale,* which is the fourth and most recently discovered species of malaria. One case in a native has been reported from Kenya, but ours will make a new observation for Tanganyika.

Donald's trials are numerous as regards his assistants. Besides me who he always says is the most trying woman he ever met, no method at all, there is our Sanitary Superintendent who is sadly unreliable. He ought to check the Africans' work for us but in fact we have to check his as well.

I have had rather a nasty go of malaria. I still have one or two parasites in my blood. Poor Donald has had such a hectic week with looking after me and bookkeeping and doing double work at the lab. We had got on well with the mountain of slides until I went down, but find to our dismay that of the next batch, some 300 have been so badly stained that it trebles the work of examining them. Oh these Africans! Poor little Monk has malaria, too, but he is playful as ever. Donald made such a good nurse; you should have seen him sponging my face and hands with eau-de-Cologne.

Miss Evans proposes to honor me by calling our second new mosquito *A. lovettae*. (This happened for a short time but then was discovered to be similar to another. Sadly it has been decided now that *A. wilsoni* is a part of a previous species so it has been deleted, but at the time, it was fantastic.)

Gombero, October 1934

We are at our nice camp again, sitting outside after dinner but very shivery as the thermometer says 68F. Donald has embarked us on an enormous program of work for the month we are to be here. Besides our ordinary job of taking 350 blood films, we are taking 200 extra to count their reticulocytes. A whole lot of leucocyte counts, temperature takings, stool examination, parasite incubations, lib estimations, and dear knows what else. So far the victims have not complained, and I hope that the hookworm treatment they are soon to have will compensate them a bit for their inconveniences. Monk thinks this a heavenly place; he is loose all the time. He started carrying his ball up the trees with him, but dropped it every few minutes and had to come down and fetch it. He sleeps high up on a little branch.

I must hurry and finish as the boy who has brought our mail is waiting to start back on his 23-mile bicycle ride to Tanga. We had one expedition into the bush. Our guides got us back late to the car and then we lost our way and got stuck in heavy ground riddled with holes made by elephants' feet and didn't get out until dark. Then we had a most trying drive through thick bush, not a vestige of a track, with Donald sort of feeling his way through the tree trunks with the car. We were glad to get to camp at last.

We have broken the back of the month's work now.

Saturday simultaneously the Paynes and Bakers arrived to lunch. Later we had a rest, Donald being sadly disturbed by Monk who scolded and chattered at the Payne's dog unceasingly. Every now and then Donald threw a boot at Monk. Monk lost himself for the whole day today. I went for a stroll this evening and heard little sounds behind, and there was Monk coming after me as hard as he could get over the ground and jumped into my arms and oof-oofed with delight for quite five minutes.

The whole Territory has been shocked to the core by an awful tragedy at Malangali [Secondary School near Iringa]. Apparently the pupils of the school were being treated with shark oil, an inexpensive substitute for cod liver oil. The container got mixed up with one containing cattle dip, with 33 of the girls dead of arsenic poisoning, 25 very ill, and Saint Clair Wallington, in charge of the school, also very ill as she took a dose to show the pupils they were making a fuss about nothing.

Life is entirely colored now by the Report and will be for the next two months. Figures, percentages, tables, graphs, checking and re-checking. We are at home in Tanga again.

It *is* very perturbing news that Italy has mobilized on the Austrian frontier. I do so hope there isn't going to be a war. It is altogether too much like the situation of this time 20 years ago.

Christmas 1934

Christmas was all so perfect, with a warm, clear breeze. We were out of bed soon after sunrise and into the cool, clear sea. We swam about until the sun was too hot. Donald dived from the coral heights. We spent all morning lying in a cool recess of the rocks in complete shade and cool breezes, or we went paddling at low tide in hot water and found mauve and pink lumps of coral, sea slugs, sea urchins with bright blue and mauve decorations, and one really wonderful starfish. It was cafe-au-lait color decorated with brilliant scarlet in lines and points. All evening we bathed again.

Our dinner table was most festive with your [Donald's parents] good things. Our lovely food was mostly what you sent: the cake, pudding, foie gras, dessert, all the best possible. The turkey, alas, had been dead a little too long, but it held together until it got on to the table. Our friends the Feeleys were with us.

Nani

I heard from General Krishna of Nani's death. She had broncho-pneumonia and collapsed quite suddenly. I feel it too deeply to say much. He wrote such a wonderful letter, full of thought for *my* grief. [The Nepal-Bihar earthquake, magnitude 8.0, occurred January 15, 1934. Among the worst earthquakes in the region's history, it destroyed the Krishna home. Sylvie Emmanuel believes that Nani's exposure to the elements affected her delicate health.] We felt rather tired and depressed, so Donald suggested going on board a Union Castle boat after dinner.

My dear Nani will be a great loss to everyone who knew her. I have never met anyone of her age so charming, so unselfish and so thoughtful for others, not to speak of her gaiety and her braveness in pain of which she had only too much in her 13 years of life. Her parents could ill afford to lose her, but they left absolutely nothing undone that could make her life happier. I think I was greatly privileged to have been able to spend those three years with her. If her life had been spared, however, I am afraid she would never have survived the damp cold of England—General Krishna is to go to England next November as Minister at the new Nepalese Legation in London.

Return to India and Nepal

This bombshell about our going to India will be a shock to you, but Donald wouldn't tell you until it was all settled. At the beginning of the tour, applications were invited from medical officers who wished to do research work on grants from the Carnegie fund. Several people sent in their names from here, Donald among them. He was told that no more funds were available, and a long time passed until he was finally told that the Colonial Office agreed to his doing a three-month tour of India to study their research on malaria. I shall have to pay for myself, however, and we sail for India January 31, 1935. We shall see a fine lot of India, Bombay, Karachi, Hyderabad, Kasauli Assam and Calcutta. Donald is thrilled, too, in his quiet way. It is rather an honor his being chosen.

Aboard Ship to Bombay, January 1935

I am just beginning to recover from the dazed rush of leaving, but still sleep most of the time, to Donald's annoyance. Our ship is the S.S. *Karanja*, and we have nearly arrived at Bombay. I was very sick for most of the voyage, not that it was rough, but because of the baby that is on the way.

The first class passengers consist of the Indian ex–High Commissioner for Indian affairs in South Africa and his family. All are very nice. The Indian women all play deck tennis; a few years ago they used to stay put in their cabins for the entire voyage.

Karnaul to Kasauli

I am sitting on a stone step dressed in tweeds in brilliant sunshine, cold clear air, looking across to Simla and a long, jagged line of snow mountains, faintly pink. Colonel and Mrs. Sinton were kindness itself at Karnaul. Our train left at midnight and arrived at Kalka at 6 a.m. It was pouring with rain. Our newly engaged servant joined the train at Amballa. An English-speaking laboratory assistant met us and saw about our luggage. At Kalka we were shown over the malaria and the research institutes where they make all the sera and vaccine 9 for cholera, typhoid, tetanus, snakebite and so on. An enormous organization, apparently magnificently, if expensively, run. All done by Indians with a Colonel Taylor at the head.

When we arrived at Kasauli the wet and the intense cold simply overpowered us. No cars are allowed in Kasauli. Things are carted about on mules with red, white, and blue bead-trimmed harness. We are going to lunch and spend the afternoon with Major and Mrs. Covell. He is head of the Pasteur Institute here. Tuesday we dine with Major and Mrs. Wats, Indians; he is the malaria engineer.

Delhi, March 1935

The Spears gave us a very good time in Delhi. (T.G.P. Spear is the distinguished author of *The Nabobs*, *Master of Bengal*, and *Twilight of the Moghuls*.) He showed Donald a lot of Moghul buildings and even got him to go to the top of the Kuth Minar. All these old buildings are surrounded by beautiful gardens, great stretches of smooth green lawns, shady trees and flowerbeds blazing with color.

Donald observed, "New Delhi must be one of the most splendid pieces of modern planning and beautiful in the world (built by Sir Edwin Lutyens), but it seems to be difficult to justify in the face of the grinding poverty of the masses. All around it are tremendous anopheline breeding places about which nothing is done. The comment of an American here was that as the Government moved to Simla for the malaria season, it didn't matter."

We left Delhi and had a boat trip on the sacred Ganges in the morning. John Lowe lunched with us today. He will shortly be India's leading leprosy worker. Our servant with overmuch zeal unpacks all our boxes at every fresh place if we don't think of telling him not to. Annoying because we have to pack up again ourselves.

Calcutta, Travelling by Rail, March 1935

Our time in Calcutta was spoilt by my getting bacillary dysentery. However, bacteriophage cured me. We have learnt much about malaria control by anti-larval measures. Tomorrow we shall be in the Singhbhum Hills. Mr. Senior White is taking us on an expedition on the Bengal-Nagpur Railway. Our saloons are shunted off on to sidings at any interesting place and then hitched on to any convenient luggage or passenger train to go on to our next stop. In the intervals of trains and to save walking we go on the railway line in a trolley with a seat on it. Resting in the afternoon is a problem as one's bed is so hot, but Donald had a brainwave and sprinkled water all over the sheets and we had a nice cool rest.

We had one little adventure on the trip. Going along the line in our railway trolley we suddenly saw a train coming towards us on the same line. We sprang out of our trolley and ran down the line waving to the driver to stop. He equally urgently waved us to get our trolley off the line, which we could not do. Finally he braked, but not in time and sadly damaged the trolley.

That evening the wretched station master and his wife came and begged Senior White not to report him but Senior White said he must report him as owing to his mistake we might easily have been killed. But it was very miserable with the wife on her knees crying and the husband almost doing the same.

On Sunday we had to catch the 7 a.m. train to see a rural area that is being reclaimed by means of larval control, quininisation, and general health propaganda by an Indian Society with some help from Government. The whole area is covered with ruins of houses overgrown by jungle, deserted on account of malaria, and the population reduced from 40,000 to 2,000 in the last 60 years. Dr. Sur took us and the workers had staged various little demonstrations for us. We went from place to place with two Indian doctors, all four packed into a little covered carriage drawn by two ponies the size of Shetlands that were continuously and unmercifully beaten by their horrid little driver until we protested vigorously.

Riyang

We are staying with the manager of the chief cinchona plantation. He and his wife are very pleasant and have provided us with the most wonderful food and have the nicest house surrounded by rose trees. We came down from Shillong; I loved Shillong, ornamental pools and beautiful lilies, and spent the day seeing malaria control at Gauhati on the Brahmaputra. Then we crossed the river again and set off in the night train and had dinner on the ferry. We had to get out at 3 a.m. and spent the rest of the night in the station waiting room at Lalmanihat. Then on to Parbatipur.

Sikkim, April 1935

We took a week's local leave and went to Sikkim. ("Writing about travels is nearly always tedious," says Malcolm Muggeridge, "travelling being like war and fornication, exciting but not interesting") [Thomas Malcolm Muggeridge, English journalist and satirist, 1903–1990]. We arrived at Siliguri, then set off in a funny little railway into the forest of the Terai, creeping along the valley of the Teesta, on the one side a sheer drop of a few hundred feet to a wide fast running river, and the other, mountains rise straight up 3,000 or 4,000 feet covered with high forest.

At Mungpoo we saw great stocks of cinchona and different processes in the separation of the alkaloids from the bark. Then up to Kalimpong for lunch with Dr. Graham, Moderator of the Church of Scotland, and saw a little of his Homes for Anglo-Indian children (600 children). He is the most charming saintly old man you could wish to meet and his work magnificent. The homes and schools are perched on the crest 4,000 feet above the Teesta Valley.

After lunch we went to see the weekly market at Gangtok at which the various Nepali and Bhutanese tribes and Tibetans and some Chinese meet. Their clothes are colorful and sometimes astonishing; the Tibetans have a partiality for a trilby on top of their long full Chinese coats and Russian leather boots. A lot of monks in purple robes, other men in blue ones, the women in various colored long gowns and a blouse of a different color, the married ones with a striped multi-colored apron over all.

We arrived at Gangtok to find a very dirty Rest House but we dined well off kippers and tea and tinned fruit. Our [servant] Jon is very good at this sort of thing. Gangtok seems absurdly civilized, with electric light, even street lighting, some tarmac roads, and a fine hospital. I imagined it would be a tiny primitive little place. There are wonderful views of Kangchenjunga. The Maharaja and Maharani are both away but we saw their house. You couldn't call it a palace. It is rather like a French country house.

Karponang, 9,000 feet

The Rest House is built of wood and has an outer verandah as well as the inner walls and is perched on rocky slopes with a valley 1,000 feet below. We are about 12 miles from the Bhutanese border. We came up most of the way on ponies and walked when we felt stiff. It is a narrow hill road. In addition to two men with the ponies, we have four porters. Although misty, we had grand views down the valleys behind us and Gangtok looked a little pimple down below.

On the way up today we met two trains of pack mules and donkeys bringing down

Peggy in jodhpurs at Kanchenjunga (Nepal), 1935.

wool from Tibet. Also two yaks that have fine long horns and white front and stern and such long wooly side curtains that they look like funny old ladies muffled up for a walk on a winter's day. We also saw their new Buddhist temple, completely painted inside with the most vivid colors, red predominating, and frescoes of the life of Buddha. It was illuminating to see a monk copying out books, quite beautifully with a bamboo sharpened like a quill.

It is quite like a winter's evening at home. We are sitting by an open fireplace with an enormous log burning, a lamp on a little table between us, still in our jodhpurs because we haven't anything else. The ground outside and the mountainsides are white with hail that is also lying on the roof of the kitchen just opposite. Have just had tea and buttered toast. The two Sikkimese syces and the Rest House chowkidar all insisted on helping us to make the beds when we arrived and lovingly smoothed the pillows and sheets with their (probably) never washed hands, but somehow one didn't mind, they were so cheery and so eager to help. In an interval of the storm that had been going on since our arrival, we went outside and chatted a little with the syces, and watched a mule and pony train coming down the road from Bhutan, each animal heavily loaded with bundles of wool covered with a powdering of snow, their neck bells all tinkling.

We decided to go on the next day to the Chungo Rest House after a night of storm. We breakfasted at about 10,000 feet, very cold it was, with hail lying about us but a few glimmers of sun. After breakfast we climbed on up, mostly on our ponies, to a bungalow at 12,500 feet. Halfway up it was snowing briskly and then the sun came out. Icicles hung from the edges of the rocks.

When we arrived at Chungo there was thick snow everywhere and we looked down to a frozen lake covered with snow. We climbed another 500 feet to the crest of the ridge. We had come up the road that Younghusband made on the 1904 expedition into Tibet [British invasion of Tibet, or the Younghusband expedition, December 1903–September 1904].

Donald said, "I was done to the wide, but Peggy to my intense annoyance was hardly even breathing deeply." As the temperature was at freezing point in our bedroom we had a huge fire and slept together in a small bed under six blankets. How the syces who slept out on the verandah managed I just don't know, but they were perfectly [agreeable] next morning as if they had had the best night possible.

The next day was brilliantly clear and we came down in the day back to Gangtok. For the first time it was really clear and we had grand views down those enormous valleys. As we came to the crest overlooking Gangtok we saw Kangchenjunga trailing a wreath of cloud into the wind.

British Legation Kathmandu, Nepal, April 1935

What a thrill to write from this address again. We had two very good strong ponies for our journey. Donald's impressions of Nepal follow. "We are staying in a very comfortable house, Colonel and Mrs. Smith, Legation Surgeon and his wife, very kindly put us up. Although everything is supposed to be more dried up than it has ever been before, all the trees are very green with new young leaves. We were met by one of the Legation Escorts at each stage, and for the hill section, two of the Maharaja's hill ponies, a havildar with a gold peaked hat, and three people to look after the ponies.

Last year's earthquake did enormous damage. The roads are terribly dusty and there are dozens of lorries about, mostly carrying timber and bricks for the reconstruction. In Paten, where we went yesterday, there are still piles of debris lying about and building going on everywhere.

"It was interesting to see the piles of brick, broken pots etc., being rolled into the new roadways, and so to see the material for future excavation being actually prepared. I have never seen a place with so many temples; down the tiniest side street you are liable to come upon an attractive little temple with dwellings grouped around it, and most houses seem to have some little religious niche on their walls spattered with red ochre.

"We were very lucky that there was a wedding party at the Singha Durbar, to which all the Europeans were invited. We arrived in a chain of motorcars, eating the dust of the Minister's car in front, and were received by the Maharaja on the steps. We then went upstairs into the hall of glass candelabra and stood about very formally talking to the various Generals, all dressed in black long coats and white tight fitting trousers. A military band played outside and there was Indian music inside.

"After a bit, the King was led in by the Maharaja as if he were blind, and took his seat quite alone on a silver throne. We all went up and bowed and shook hands, but he continued to sit without speaking. When he took his leave in about half an hour, there was the same performance and he suddenly realised who Peggy was. Meanwhile we managed to get in quite a lot of talk and I was introduced to many. They all seemed genuinely pleased to see Peggy again.

"Nepal is at present a hive of activity, the whole place a mass of bricks, old or new. Many of the temples have been sufficiently repaired. Others, of which there were no drawings, cannot be reconstructed. There is a lovely old square in Bhatgaon in which you can hardly imagine that any destruction had taken place. Many houses have the loveliest and most delicate carved windows and balconies, and where they have to be reconstructed, the windows are being replaced so that the effect is not lost.

"On Monday there was a Durbar. First, we saw the arrival of the Maharaja at the Legation in full panoply of carriage and four outriders in scarlet. Then we went to the Durbar Hall in the middle of the town. Inside were all the Generals in full ceremonials and the King upon his throne. We were received by the Maharaja and then went up into the gallery. Then the Minister, Colonel Bailey (no longer called Envoy), and Colonel Smith arrived and were led up to the King by the Maharaja and shook hands with him and the more notable Generals. The King and Maharaja then removed their enormous headdresses with a sigh of relief and we were presented to the King. As we took our leave of the Maharaja, Donald was presented with a kukri and portrait of the Maharaja and Peggy with a brooch and a box of ivory and rhino hide.

"Meanwhile in the square there was a band playing and a regiment of lancers all massed together and dressed in scarlet. Around this solid phalanx of red, brilliant in the sunshine, were massed a few thousand people with two great pyramids, one of men and the other of women, grouped on the several tiers of the steps of two old temples. All around were the frame of brick buildings with their old tiled roofs throwing dark shadows over the moving people below.

"We went back to the Legation for tea with the Baileys who are delightful and most interesting people. He is very keen on birds and butterflies, has a cine camera, and a fund of experience of northern India and Tibet. We had an interesting morning at one of the temples and had a long talk with the Lama, a Chinese, known as the Chini Lama. He speaks English very well. My chief regret has been not to see more of the people. None of the lower classes speak anything but Nepali and there was no opportunity of meeting the others except at the two formal meetings. True, Peggy managed a good bit of chat on those occasions.

"We spent Sunday at Godavari. Going up and coming down, to and from Nepal, we had to have an enormous train of attendants: eight coolies for our stuff, two syces to look after the ponies, a sowar to look after the syces, a sepoy from the Legation to guard us, and a havildar to keep an eye on us.

"I found it difficult to decide whether it was worse going up or down the hills; the gradients are appalling and the surfaces worse. We passed a motorcar being carried up by 65 coolies. The motor ride down to the end of the railway is pretty terrifying as the drivers all come down the hills out of gear. It is also very noisy as they hoot at everything that comes in sight."

Peggy observes: In a way I was not sorry to leave Nepal. I don't feel I belong there now and it is all so changed. The peace has gone and it all feels unsettled and restless, largely owing to the reconstruction activities that keep the whole place in a continual cloud of dust. Donald saw it at its worst.

We rode past what was General Krishna's palace and is now a mountain of bricks. The spirit of Nani seemed to be with me in some of the places we had often visited together. At least they were filled with memories of her adorable self.

On the journey down to Sisagarhi we firmly abandoned our escort and climbed down the steep hillside to a shady bank of a rippling stream full of grey rocks. We enjoyed our lunch there immensely. We got to Raxaul at 6:15, as our little chuff chuff train was an hour late. The Mission doctor and nurse were to have dinner with us, and as it had still to be cooked by Jon, it was very late and they would not have anything to drink or smoke to help us pass the time. Next day our train was at 5 p.m. We crossed the Ganges by steamer and spent a depressing hot and dusty evening at Patna, sleeping until 4 a.m. on tables under a fan in the Ladies and Gents waiting rooms. My rest was disturbed by an Indian lady who prowled about, conversed with the raucous voiced old ayah, and switched the lights on and off continuously.

Udaipur, May 1935

We found a cable here telling us that Donald's father had had a stroke, but we don't know anymore yet. No paralysis, we are glad to hear.

My great friends from Nepal days put us up—Freddy and Marjorie Loftus Tottenham were then stationed in Udaipur, Freddy with his company of Gurkhas. More than any other place I have been to in the East, Udaipur is filled with the glamour of the Orient. This is not the best time of year to see it as it is very hot and dusty and flies are legion. But forgetting these disadvantages, there are exquisitely beautiful lakes surrounded by hills and trees, marble palaces perfectly reflected in the still water, islands with marble summer pavilions and temples gleaming cool and white. An absolute dream of beauty.

Last night the Runcimans, padre and wife, gave a delightful supper picnic on one of the islands and we had it on the flat roof of one of the pavilions in the full moonlight. In the evenings we go and bathe in a large square tank in part of the palace gardens surrounded by mango trees and pots of flowers. In the middle of the tank is a marble cupola-shaped fountain, and there are fountains all round the sides of the tank as well. It is what is known as the Slave Girls' Garden. Tomorrow, Colonel Beetharn, the Resident, is giving a cold supper picnic at the bathing pool. We shall bathe first. It is too hot to go out in the daytime.

We dined with a member of the ruling family and it was a grand success, including seven of eleven Rajput nobles and us English. They were dressed in white coats and shirts and tightly fitting white jodhpurs, looking very smart and cool. They received us in the garden and dinner was at a large table on the lawn. Before dinner we women were taken indoors to meet some of the noble ladies who were not dining with us. An elaborate and well-cooked dinner was served and our host and his family were most friendly. His eldest son has done a shooting trip in Tanganyika so we had a lot in common.

I sat between the Raja and dear old Brigadier Shuttleworth. At the end, our host, in a long and rather halting speech, told how he had visited England and seen with his own eyes how thousands of loyal subjects gathered to cheer their Majesties when they went out in horse carriage and how kind and good they were to their subjects. Very loyal and patriotic and then asked us to drink to their Majesties' health. Then there was a presentation to Colonel Hogg, the Residency Surgeon, of an engraved silver salver saying that he had by his loyal and devoted skill saved His Highness's life from pneumonia last January. Then we all went to sit in the drawing room part of the lawn, and about 11 p.m. we left.

In the Suez Canal, S.S. *Maloja,* June 1935

This is such a peaceful Sunday evening, the ship is quiet and the sun is setting over the Arabian Desert. A week today we hope to be with my parents-in-law at Muker in Yorkshire parish. We seriously considered whether Donald should fly from India, but concluded that it would not save much time, as he would have had to come right up north again from Madras by train. We are alternatively hoping for and dreading more news.

Alas, we received a radio message to say that Donald's father had died. He was buried in Muker churchyard. We needed to get home as fast as possible to be with Donald's poor mother, so we flew from France and then drove up to Yorkshire as fast as possible. We found her utterly beaten down and almost continually in tears, although she did her very best to bear up. Oh dear, it was a dreadfully sad time, so different from the joyful homecoming we and they had pictured so often in our letters. Both Donald and I felt that if we had got home sooner and if they hadn't both worked so hard to have everything, especially the garden, looking nice for our arrival, he might not have died. Well, it was a dreadfully sad summer.

Chapter 6

Sylvie and Angela and War, 1935–1945

by Peggy Lovett Wilson and Sylvie Wilson Emmanuel

In September we went to London for the birth of our third child. Sir Charles Reid, a quite famous New Zealand obstetrician, large and reassuring, was to look after me. To my great delight he decided to do a Caesarian section at the Chelsea Women's Hospital. So on 17 September 1935, Sylvie was born. Such a lovely baby with a lot of red-gold hair. Donald saw her before I did, and said, "She's got a lot of hair of a most astonishing colour!" I was ecstatically happy and Donald hardly less so.

When I left hospital we divided the time between Muker and Church Stretton to be with Rosie and Thomas. Donald was with his mother at Muker. Although she did not very much want to, we decided that she must go back with us to East Africa. She missed her husband so painfully that it did not really matter to her where she lived.

Sylvie: I had golden hair like my mother's mother, and a good little baby I was. My grandfather had died several months before, so when I was born there was great happiness. My parents were in England for a few months and then they brought my grandmother Sylvie back to Moshi with them, as she had no other close relations. She didn't really want to go back to Switzerland, and she adored her son, and here was this little grandchild, her namesake. My mother loved her very much. She called her "Little Mother," or "L.M." Reading her letters makes it obvious they were very fond of each other. In November my parents returned to Tanganyika with me and my grandmother, and we lived in Moshi for the first years of my life.

Donald's mother suffered badly from the heat on the voyage and also in Tanga, where we stayed for a day or two on arrival. Donald had chosen some frocks for her at the Army and Navy, very pretty chiffon and georgette, very unsuitable for the heat, and very difficult to get into, but he had done his best. I had a difficult time on board ship as Sylvie had whooping cough. Mercifully she had it lightly.

We then went to live first at Old Moshi in an old German bungalow where, at the end of the Kaiser's War [World War I] the local Peace Treaty had been signed by [South African General] Smuts and [Prussian General] von Lettow-Vorbeck. The rooms were huge and the building was infested with rats and bats. Still it was very attractive and the garden had flowering shrubs, pomegranates and lychee trees. Donald's mother had a nice room facing east. She always had breakfast in bed and would get up leisurely when she felt well enough and had finished her devotional reading for the morning. Donald was seldom home as he had been told to do a survey of labor on sisal estates, but he often came back for a day. As he had the car, we lived a very quiet life. We could not even get to Moshi three or four miles away.

Old Moshi was on the lower slopes of Kilimanjaro and the climate was delightful. The nights were always cool. We took little walks after tea, quite little ones, as there was no level ground. I would carry Sylvie on one arm and L.M., or Little Mother as we called Donald's mother, took the other. I also carried a campstool for her to rest at frequent intervals. After three months, when Donald finished his survey, we moved down to a bungalow in Moshi and used another bungalow next to it as our laboratory.

Donald reluctantly became Health Officer for the Northern Province, so then I had a bench and a microscope in the Health Office. One small excitement happened about then. On examining a blood film from an adult African who was a patient in the Native Hospital I saw that he had parasites, the like of which I had never seen before. The parasied red cells were very greatly enlarged, and had the impression of considerable distension and thinning. The parasites occupied only a small part of the cell and were very solid and compact.

The stippling of the parasitized cells resembled that of *Plasmodium vivax.* I asked the hospital for more blood films but by then, to my great chagrin, the patient had been given an anti-malarial. Donald and I made camera lucida drawings of the parasites and Donald sent them and the slides to London to a Laboratory meeting of the Royal Society of Tropical Medicine where they created great interest. However, the final decision was that it must be an aberrant form of *P. vivax.* In all the thousands of bloods I examined subsequently I never saw the like again.

When Sylvie was about nine months old, Donald wanted me to go with him on safari in Maasailand and to leave Sylvie in charge of her grandmother L.M. It was a good safari and all went well. I was invited into the house of a Maasai woman who lived there with her two daughters. She spoke some Swahili. One had to stoop down to enter the mud and wattle house that was dark and windowless, the only light coming through the door when it was open.

As all the houses in a Maasai manyatta are infested with flies, the darkness does keep the dwellings fairly fly free. A high thorn fence to keep lions out encloses all the cattle, as well as the houses of the particular manyatta. I was given a little stool to sit on and introduced to the teenage daughters who were nice friendly girls. I was given a kibuyu (gourd) of milk to drink. This really put me in difficulty for I greatly dislike plain milk and I knew that their gourds are washed out with cows' urine. However, to my great surprise, the milk tasted neither of urine nor of wood smoke and I managed to drink most of it.

Then my hostess said in Swahili, "And what is a child like you doing on safari?" As

I was then about 38 years old I thought she must be joking, but she was quite serious. I had on my double terai that hid my greying hair and of course did look much younger than my age.

L.M. quite enjoyed living with us in Moshi. She sewed, embroidered, and took great delight in her grandchild, and well she might, for Sylvie was an angelic child. L.M. was pleased to find that she really enjoyed our little parties and meeting our friends. She was surprised that none of them was ever seen to be the worse for drink that she unhappily anticipated. We all had one or two drinks on social occasions but when we were alone we hardly used any alcohol at all.

Sylvie was about a year old when we took L.M. to see a nun dentist at the Roman Catholic Mission at Kilema, on the lower slopes of Kilimanjaro. When we were leaving she dropped her handbag and I noticed that her speech was slurred. Donald made the best time possible back to Moshi but by the time we got to the hospital she was deeply unconscious and she died the next day.

Donald wrote to friends and relations in England to tell them of his mother Sylvie Wilson's death in Moshi: "The funeral was on the evening of October 27, 1936. The service was first held at the little English church in Moshi at which all who knew her were present. The two hymns we sang were 'The King of Love my Shepherd is,' and 'Praise my soul, the King of Heaven,' and the Twenty-third Psalm was read. The Reverend W.A. Cross, the English chaplain, gave an address.

"We took her body up to the Lutheran Mission above old Moshi at Kidia, some 5,000 feet up the mountainside. The German pastor, Dr. Gutmann, with whom she had been great friends, gladly acceded to our request and had made a grave in an angle of the church (just like my father's grave in Muker in Yorkshire). The mission children sang two hymns in KiChagga, and Dr. Gutmann gave a most beautiful address in KiChagga explaining to the people how her life had been spent and why they were glad to give her body a resting place in their mission. There, at sunset, we left her in a grave filled with flowers, with the snows above and that tremendous stretch of plain growing purple at our feet.

"We are glad that my mother came back with us for these ten months. She had been increasingly fit to enjoy the beauties around us and such little adventures as we were able to arrange for her. Her passing was much as we had always asked for her. In these small communities the sense of a family comes out very strongly when one is taken, and we have had very many expressions of sympathy and appreciation; but the one who has missed her most is our head boy, Rice, who seems to have felt her loss almost as if it had been his own mother."

Little Mother and Donald's father were both the most saintly people it was possible to imagine, and the most loving and charming.

Soon afterwards we were on safari in the hills and Sylvie developed malaria. We had a terrible job to force the poor child to swallow the horrible-tasting mepacrine. It was a cold windy evening and our bedroom was a banda with walls that came up only to about four feet six inches. Nothing would do but Sylvie must have a bath, so against my better judgment, she did in our canvas safari bath and took no harm.

On another trip she was bitten on the thumb by a scorpion, luckily a very small one. However, a bite from even a small one must be extremely painful and we had no

Rice with Sylvie, 1937.

local anesthetic with us. She cried for a long time and it was not until I removed the strapping from her thumb that she put it into her mouth and went to sleep.

We were due to go home on leave in 1938 but we had to find somewhere to live as Muker Vicarage was no longer available to us and my home, Dunstone, was sold after my father's death. We arranged to rent a house at Corsham, Wilts, for about six months.

Sylvie was nearly three and was a most lovely child. Friends of ours said, "Do you mean to say that those two produced that beautiful child?" and a male guest said, "I really can't take my eyes off that child, she is an absolute picture." And so she was, with her red-gold hair, rose leaf skin, and big greenish eyes with long up-curling deep gold lashes, until she caught impetigo on her face from a playmate in the second class part of the British India ship. All we had to treat it with was *Lotio nigra*, a weak mercury preparation. I had to try and remove the scabs that covered her poor little face. It was very hot in the Red Sea with a following wind and high humidity, so that her septic sores were in the best possible conditions for spreading and worsening. Her father and I were in despair.

We decided to land at Genoa and go straight up into the hills in Switzerland. We did the last part on a little mountain railway and then climbed up a steep path to the pension where Donald had arranged for us to stay. Oh, the cool air and the wild flowers and the mountains and the views! In a week Sylvie's skin, except for some staining from the scars, was quite cured and the staining disappeared very soon too. We had a

Peggy and Sylvie in Switzerland, 1938.

charming time and Donald enjoyed talking French with the locals and drinking wine with them in the evenings in the bar of our small pension. There was no bathroom. I bathed Sylvie in a small wooden washtub, much to her delight. We were all sorry to leave that enchanting place.

Arriving in England, we paid visits to friends and relations and engaged a nurse for Sylvie and the expected new baby. We also engaged a cook at £8 a month and a house parlor maid at £6 a month. When staying with Rosie and Thomas we visited my mother's house at Church Stretton, not a very nice house and she always regretted the loss of Dunstone. She couldn't see why Rosie and she couldn't live in a re-purchased Dunstone, and Minnie, their servant, look after Thomas.

At the end of September Donald and I went to Amsterdam for the Tropical Medicine and Malaria Conference. I attended all the lectures at which Swellengrebel took the Chair. I remember that Bruce-Chwatt was very vocal and he had a great deal to comment on, to argue about, and to hold forth upon. We did a lot of sightseeing in that delightful town. We were all invited to a banquet in the Rijksmuseum. Before dining we went for a tour of the Museum and saw Rembrandt's famous "The Night Watch." The painting was magnificent and the banquet lasted for three hours. We sat with the Senior Whites and much enjoyed ourselves. He especially was such good company and most amusing.

When we returned to England we settled in at Dicketts Corsham, a mock Tudor, pleasant, but very cold house until it was time for me to go to London for another Caesarian operation. This produced another baby girl whom we named Angela Katherine Bagster. A splendid strong little baby with, from the very first, a most determined will of her own.

Sylvie: I had one sister, Angela, who was also born in England. She was three years younger than me, and we had very different personalities. My first, most vivid memory is in England in 1939 when my parents bought Spa House. I remember the daisies on the lawn.

In January 1939, Donald was informed that if war broke out, as then seemed practically inevitable, he should join the Tanganyika Field Ambulance with the rank of Captain. Meantime we were to do a venereal disease survey among the Maasai. I dreaded having to do this because I foresaw endless difficulties, particularly in the refusal by the women to be examined. However, when we had only begun to get our mobile laboratory together everything was changed because World War II had begun.

We were up at Lushoto, staying at the Lawns' when one evening we heard Hitler's raucous voice on the wireless assuring the world of Germany's strength and splendor and justifying their need for *Lebensraum* that would necessitate their conquest of most of Europe.

Meantime at Lushoto the District Commissioner wanted to know the military strength of the British—what we possessed in the way of rifles and guns and how many of us could use them if need arose. This anticipated a possible invasion of Tanganyika by the Italians if they first managed to conquer Kenya and come down our way. We didn't take this possibility very seriously, although before we said goodbye, Donald told me that if this did happen I was to take my rifle and the children and give Rice Mweso (our wonderful servant) my shotgun and all go into the nearby coffee bushes and await developments.

All the German settlers and planters in Tanganyika were rounded up and driven off in lorries to concentration camps. It is hard to know what else to call the camps but I believe that although there was often discomfort and sometimes downright hardship, there was no cruelty and perhaps occasionally some consideration; the Von Kalcksteins were allowed to take their cattle and their piano with them. None made any resistance when they were taken, hardly any objection in fact. They were all given a bit of notice to make arrangements about their animals, servants and belongings, but there was to be no argument. Each lorry was in the charge of a responsible and usually kindly Briton. Many in fact were friends and neighbors of these Germans. One of the internees got left behind by his lorry when he had got out, and he ran after the lorry shouting for it to wait for him. Camps were set up in various places such as Oldeani. A number were sent to South Africa where in winter they suffered badly from the cold. Poor inoffensive Mr. deLuigi got pneumonia and died.

Donald's last day was partly spent in buying necessities for use in camping or bivouacking. He and his fellow medical officer friend were together and Tom Austin, who had become a major, was in command.

Sylvie: I remember the whole family going to Arusha when my father left and saying goodbye sadly, as I loved him very much.

We said goodbye in the New Arusha Hotel and then I, with Sylvie and Angela, set off unhappily back to Moshi. The Medical Department had no idea what to do with the left-behind wives so we just returned to the bungalows we were living in at the time and continued to live in them. I felt sure that I should be contacted by the DMS [Director of Medical Services] with a view to doing some essential war work. I thought they would probably ask me to take over a hospital that I didn't feel very happy at the thought of doing, but I was prepared to do my best and I felt that if someone was available to do most of the surgery I could manage the medical cases. So I waited and for weeks nothing happened.

Well, as the MOH and two white Sanitary Superintendents had been "taken on the strength" as you might say, I wrote to the DMS offering to do my best on a part-time basis to replace them. I wired Donald to tell him of my offer and had a most discouraging reply, strongly advising me against it and saying that much of it was entirely unsuitable work for a woman.

However, the DMS (our friend Dr. R. Scott) wrote to me quite surprised and pleased and immediately appointed me temporary Medical Officer of Health of the Northern Province at a salary comparable to that of a starting-from-scratch MOH working half-time. I cared little or nothing about the salary and in fact I would have done it for nothing.

However, while it did last I was quite busy, seeing to the anti-mosquito measures, inspecting latrines in Moshi, rat proofing grain stores and go-downs, and inspecting the meat, the milk, and the schools. Every month I went to Arusha for ten days or so, taking the children with me. I was the Executive Officer for the Township Authority in both Moshi and Arusha. I had to be concerned with plans regarding additions to buildings and the proper permission to be obtained for doing such work. I took Sylvie to a little day school in Moshi and Rice looked after Angela.

Sylvie: I remember one of the times my mother had to go to Arusha and I went with her. It was during the rains and although chains had been put on the car, we still slid down the hill to the bridge over the Kikafu River into a right turn onto the bridge. We were very muddy when we arrived in Arusha and our hostess said, "Would you like to have a bath?"

When I was five, we lived in Moshi just after my father had gone off to the war. I went to Mrs. Renton's school. The building is actually still there in Moshi. Mrs. Renton was a very large lady. I remember the stories and I remember a slide. I used to take a marmite sandwich and orange juice in a Heinz tomato ketchup bottle.

Just before my fifth birthday my mother wrote to my father, "When I said goodnight to Sylvie this evening and said it was her last night of being four years old I asked if she'd had a happy year. She at once said, "No. No, I haven't." I wanted her to tell me why, and she said, "It's this horrid war! When will it ever stop? I can't forget how I want my daddy back." She does miss you. Another time she even prayed that Hitler would die.

One time Rice got relapsing fever and I could find no one to look after Angela in the mornings and look after both of them when I was working. Finally dear kind Mrs. Salter offered to look after Angela in the mornings until Rice recovered. I was practically in tears when I threw myself on her mercy.

It was very difficult to know what to do about the latrines of the Indian houses in

Moshi town, especially in the street known as Block F. The latrines were almost always full to overflowing and there was no space in the little back yards to dig other pits, but somehow space had to be found.

During this time I had a lovely big bungalow with enormous rooms. The garden had been quite neglected but I had no time to do anything about it. My job lasted for only a very few months and then the MOH was released from the Army and one of the Sanitary Superintendents as well. The bungalow was needed. Donald wrote at the time when I was having to leave Moshi before going to Monduli, "We are all very angry about the latest Tanganyika Government effort about wives, namely, that they may be turned out of their houses if possible with four weeks notice," and may "apply for assistance up to 5 shillings a day" from a public assistance committee or the Treasury. We all feel that the Government is trying to write us off as a bad debt.

"I have enjoyed your ginger cake, it provided my breakfast yesterday. And the fudge, I regret to say, is nearly finished. This is a demoralizing existence (waiting for a possible Italian move into Northern Kenya). I must admit to a changed opinion of the Kenya Regiment. They have put up an extraordinarily good showing on this outfit."

Just then Mr. Page-Jones, DC [District Commissioner] of Maasailand, offered me the DO's bungalow at Monduli until a DO should be appointed. I was overjoyed. Monduli was at nearly 5,000 feet and I knew the climate would be delightful and so good for the children.

We moved, settling into the nice bungalow, and lived there at Monduli for the next 18 months. We were quite close to the Page-Jones's and I walked over most evenings to listen to the BBC news. How miserable and depressing and awful it always was. We had nothing but reverses and defeats and the Germans were everywhere victorious, and conquered and annexed country after country in Europe.

Sylvie: After the war started, there was no longer a house in Moshi for my mother, myself and my sister. So we went to a funny little house in Monduli. I enjoyed it. A little mud house was made for me that I liked because it was my special place. I still have the pink blanket I had for my "bed." In Monduli there was no school so I used my imagination and played with invisible friends. I think I was probably a little prig. My mother said once when we had visitors (I was six or seven), I said, "Mummy, aren't you going to ask them if they'd like some tea?"

We ate anything that was offered us and, being English, we had breakfast of bacon and eggs. We certainly drank a lot of milk because my mother was aware that she had never been made to drink milk and that was why she had the deformed pelvis. I didn't mind that. One thing that my sister and I liked so much was ice cream. At some stage during the war, my mother came and said, "Oh, they said they're not going to be selling cream any longer." I said in horror, "But how will we have ice cream then?" To this day I think I eat ice cream slowly because my sister and I would eat so slowly that the adults would leave and then we could pick up our bowls and lick them.

I lost our wonderful servant Rice through my own fault by showing him how the war was going on the map. It never occurred to me that he or anyone could have doubts about the ultimate victory of the Allies, but alas, he had grave doubts and decided to make off to Nyasaland to look after his family and his cattle. I was extremely sad to say goodbye to him but after all, his family and affairs came before ours.

My mother wrote about the servants they had early in their married life, how they came and went and some were good and some were bad. A very special one called Rice was from Nyasaland. My mother was doing medical officer health work in Moshi, and had to go over to Arusha for several days. Because there had been some bad flu epidemic there, she didn't want to take my sister and myself. So I went up to stay with friends but my sister was left in Moshi with Ricey for five days. My sister had a problem with her eye, so he pushed her up in the pram to the hospital to have her eyes treated. My mother never wanted to have an ayah.

I had no official work to do, so Page-Jones asked me to work in his office as a temporary voluntary ADO [Assistant District Officer]. I enjoyed drafting and answering letters to the various departments. Once he asked me to make out indents [requisitions] for stores for eleven dispensaries, some of them new ones, for a year, and work out the prices of all the drugs and equipment ordered from the catalogues, taking into account the recent price rises. It was quite a job. Donald said in a letter, "Yes, I am amused that you have joined the Administration. I shouldn't think Page-Jones will be able to put up with you for long."

I went most days to the Monduli dispensary to see any patients that the very intelligent and competent Dispenser William Marijuani wished to consult me about. He did a fine job rescuing the airmen who crashed in the Valencia plain in south Maasailand. The survivors walked until they found a Maasai Boma and there the Maasai gave them water and milk, and killed a sheep for them, and built them a shelter for the night. The Maasai Moran went off to Kibia for help and got there in record time. William the Dispenser got together food and medicines and a stretcher and porters and set off on the six-hour walk back to them. Then he dressed their burns. Two were very badly burnt; he bandaged them and cooked them a meal and started back with them to Kibia. The South Africans were so impressed and so grateful for all the help the Africans had given them that they gave all the money they had with them to be divided among the helpers. The experience of collecting the bits of charred remains of others burned to death shook William badly and no wonder. But he knows we are all proud of him and I've assured him he will calm down in time.

There were some difficult cases that I couldn't diagnose, such as one man with glove and stocking anesthesia. Occasionally there were wounds from lion mauling. Anything that William and I could not cope with we sent to hospital in Arusha. There was a great deal of venereal disease among the Maasai and on rare occasions a man would come in suffering from stricture of the urethra and inability to pass urine.

I was afraid of having to try and catheterize such a case, not then knowing that one could empty the bladder by means of a large hypodermic syringe into the bladder through the abdominal wall. However, sitting the patient in a hot bath and telling him to urinate into the water often worked. "Dear Madam, patient has passed all urine out into bath thank Madam" ran one note from William.

One day I was sent for urgently to Rasha Rasha, Frank Anderson's shamba, to see a man who had fallen off a tractor with cutting discs, possibly having gone to sleep in the sunshine. His legs were in a terrible state, calf muscles sheared off and hanging on one side, half the other foot sliced off through the metatarsal joints and only attached by skin, and a compound fracture of tibia and fibula sticking out. He was definitely a case for hospital.

I soaked dressings in acriflavine, had wood cut for splints, padded them, bandaged them and gave him morphia. When Frank came rushing to the spot, the patient was all ready for the journey to Arusha and seemingly comfortable. He gratefully drank the tea that Frank gave him and he never cried out or even groaned. Of course he must have been in shock. He did well and walked again in time.

One evening after dark I was asked to go to Rasha Rasha to see two unconscious laborers. I did lumbar punctures by the light of a hurricane lamp and instead of cerebro spinal fluid, thick pus dripped out. This was my first experience of meningococcal meningitis but fortunately M&B 693 (Sulphapyridine) was available in tablet form. Both men still had their swallowing reflex and William was very clever in administering the crushed up drug. We treated them with the top doses and next day both were conscious and both recovered.

A day or two later I was sent for to another estate, Laurence Albert Bennett's, to see an unconscious laborer. He was so restless that I failed at doing a lumbar puncture, so I took a blood film and went home to lunch. When I stained and examined the blood film I saw that he had cerebral malaria, so I went back and administered intravenous and intramuscular quinine and he too recovered.

Every month there was a Red Cross sale in Arusha and the Monduli ladies and I made a number of saleable goodies. Some of these were in aid of Greeks who were suffering so much in the war in Greece. One month I personally made a ginger cake, iced sponge cake, coffee cake, seed cake, fancy biscuits, water biscuits, rich chocolate cake, Dundee cake, Malta cake, and 17 pounds of fudge. As the Monduli ladies either had no car or were unable to drive, it fell to my lot to take all our produce to Arusha for the sale. Once I was rather in despair, for the road was so thick with mud that I kept on skidding round and facing in the wrong direction and my poor shamba boy simply could not get the chains onto my heavy Ford V8. However mercifully I met a car containing two members of the Legislative Council plus an efficient servant and between them they soon turned me round and sent me rejoicing on my way. In case I got into trouble on the way home, Page-Jones always told me to ring up from Arusha and say when I would be leaving.

One evening, walking back to my bungalow escorted by the nice Dutchman, Mr. van Emmanes, my little terrier ran off barking loudly. Mr. van Emmanes said he would see what he was barking at. He came back and said calmly, "It's a lion." I was surprised and slightly alarmed to think we had a lion so close to our houses. A night or so later, I was having a bath when a lion roared just outside the bungalow.

I leapt out of the bath and ran round the house shutting all the windows. A day or two later I was wakened about midnight by an African who said that a lion had got into the donkey stable and killed the Page-Jones's Muscat donkey and Memsahib said would I come and shoot the lion.

The few European men on the station were all on safari. So I put on a coat over my pajamas, took my rifle, filled my pockets with cartridges, and with my tongue cleaving to the roof of my mouth (yes, literally), walked over to the Page-Jones's house. Joan said all she wanted me to do was to drive up to the donkey stable and shoot the lion through the windscreen. In those days the windscreens of some cars were made to open.

I woke up the cook and gave him my shotgun and told him not to do anything unless I said so. Then I drove up facing the stable and had to make quite a noise maneuvering the car up to it, and faced an empty stable except for the dead donkey and a bloodstained hole in the wire door. So I went home to bed.

Sylvie: Sometimes we heard wild animals. We must have heard lions occasionally because my mother always said that I went on sucking my thumb until I was eight, when we moved to Nairobi. Then I was no longer afraid of anything at night.

Soon after, we heard that an ADO had been appointed and would be arriving almost immediately with his wife. Page-Jones was still on safari but as I had only been given the bungalow until an ADO was appointed I began to pack my belongings with all speed. I wondered where best to go and decided I had better go to Nairobi. I was all ready for departure when Page-Jones returned. "What are you doing?" he said. When I told him, he said I must not think of going, that they wanted me to stay (how heart-warming that was) and that he would arrange that I should have Mr. van Emmanes' house for a rent of £1 monthly and that van Emmanes would be happy to live in the Rest House rent-free.

I felt rather dreadful about this but it appeared that van Emmanes really did not mind, so all my belongings were moved 50 yards and unpacked again. Our new abode was very small but adequate. The only thing I did not like was that the loo was at some little distance and if one needed to go there after dark one could not help wondering if one would meet a lion.

Donald was able to come for an occasional brief leave. He had the rank of major and was then largely concerned with advising on and inspecting staging posts as far down as Broken Hill and Lusaka with the object of protecting from malaria the South African troops who drove up in trucks, lorries and cars in a steady stream from South Africa. On one of his visits I told him that if he had an affair with any woman while we were separated, I should not blame him but should regard it as a physiological necessity. I never asked him whether he had ever taken advantage of my remarkably broad-minded permission, but I am pretty sure he did.

I did very little shooting in those days but occasionally when I had unexpected guests, and nothing much to offer them, I coasted down to the plains to save petrol and shot a couple of sitting kwale. What would Dick have thought of that! During the week's safari when he went with us in 1930, I remember we saw a fine fat Spurwing goose sitting on the ground. "Oh do shoot it," I begged him, "we do so need it for dinner tomorrow."

"What! Shoot a sitting bird," he said, horrified, "Of course not." He took a great deal of trouble to get the reluctant goose into the air and then he only winged it with his first shot. However, he did kill it with his second.

In the autumn of 1942, Donald wrote that he was then in charge of all anti-malarial work dealing with our forces in East Africa. His Headquarters were to be in Nairobi and I was to pack up our belongings and come, as he had rented a house from the American Charge d'Affaires. So I sent our heavy luggage by train, said goodbye to all our kind friends in Monduli, and with Sylvie and Angela, then aged seven and four, drove up to Nairobi. The road, although then all-weather, was very rough in places, covered with knobbly stones or sand and in many parts very corrugated. Also there were

Peggy and Sylvie with the Ford V8.

many drifts that held a lot of water in the rains but were all right in the dry. They were very steep and the tail of a heavily loaded car always caught on the upgrade.

Sylvie: I can still remember going up to Nairobi, Mummy loading the car. The journey wasn't dangerous but it was certainly challenging, a woman with two young children driving, managing on her own. There would have been one of the servants as well, probably it was Sefu, who was with us for many years. He was a nice chap.

When we arrived in Nairobi and turned at right angles out of Riverside into the private drive of our magnificent abode, I misjudged the turn and came to rest ignominiously stuck across the culvert! Donald called the staff to lift the car out of its precarious position and was amazingly good tempered about it. We had the lovely house for six months. It was double-storied and outside there was a garden with terraces, a tennis court, and a small ornamental pool. We thought it was wonderful. We had it for £25 a month, which seemed big money. Sylvie was so happy to go to school. She was altogether very happy there and stopped sucking her thumb.

When we went to Nairobi I finally started going to school. Mrs. Smith owned the little school. Old Smithy could be quite a fierce old lady and we spent our time doing sums and parsing [sentences] on the blackboard. She'd say, "Pump, pump, pump! Hammer, hammer, hammer! That's how I have to get it in all your heads." By the end of the morning there was time to do a bit of history or something else. But I liked it. Mrs. Smith also tried to teach me piano. I never practiced, so not surprisingly, I was no good. I was the sort of golden knight because I was a good student. We had a play at Christmas. I was

Left–right: Angela, Abdallah's daughter May, and Sylvie.

one of the fairies—I remember this lovely sort of mauve carpet of jacaranda flowers. I was perfectly happy there.

A number of Greek children who were much older were there and one from a family we knew later. We used to call him "Mucky Tomatoes" because his name was Makondonatos. We're now great friends.

If father was home, he wanted me to learn French. So at breakfast he would say, "We're going to speak French." I would just sit there and say, "Je ne comprend pas." If a child has no reason to learn a language, she doesn't have any desire to.

Sefu was the gardener for many years, and from when we were in Nairobi there was Abdallah, the cook, who was quite short. He had a wife and children there. We have a photograph of his little girl and Angela and me. He was a good cook. We had a little wood burning Dover stove.

Our first house in Nairobi was lovely. But we were only there for about six or eight months. It had been the residence of one of the American Embassy people. It was double-storied with a garden and a little fountain, near the arboretum. They'd left a few things behind, including a gollywog, a black doll with wooly hair all sticking out. Robertson's Jam used to have a little gollywog on the label. You're not allowed to use the word gollywog now; it was very racist, I'm sure. But I had Golly for a long time and loved him.

Then we moved to another house on the other side of Nairobi where we stayed for the rest of the war, until 1946. That house had a lovely garden that went right down to the river. The other side of the river was a native reserve, as it was called then, with a eucalyptus plantation, located near St. Helen's, my primary school. I would walk back home in the afternoon on my own, a good mile, if my mother was still working. I was 9 or 10 years old.

Donald soon found work for me examining all the many blood films he had brought back from Somalia, Ethiopia and Kenya. To begin with, I worked in a room functioning as a lab in the Town Hall. I was often asked to instruct members of Army, Navy and Air Force in the rudiments of malariology including some very simple parasitology and entomology. My pupils were mostly of a low educational standard. One day one of them said to me, "Was you ever a proper doctor?" I pretended not to understand him but he asked again, "Well was you? Did you look after ill people like a doctor does?" I assured him that I had. "Coo," he said, "you must a been one of the first!"

Early in 1942, Geoffrey Milne, a famous soil chemist friend from Amani, died. Kathleen Milne had to leave Amani and couldn't get back to England. Her two boys were at prep school in Kenya. Donald and I decided to offer them a home with us, and they lived in the two-room rest house of the house we rented on Marlborough Estate after our tenancy of the magnificent house in Riverside Drive came to an end.

Donald was very seldom at home. His commitments on malaria control round camps, staging posts and Italian POW camps, took him all over East Africa, as well as to Madagascar, Mauritius, Mozambique, the Sudan, and S. Rhodesia. He was Officer Cadets Units, 2nd Mobile Malaria Section.

My days were quite full. After breakfast I took Sylvie to her day school, dropped Kathleen Milne at the Meteorological Office where she worked in Nairobi, then I went to the Military Malaria Unit where I worked until midday. Then I did some quick shopping, mostly buying food for the family and for our two dogs Patsy and Fanny, a pointer and a smooth haired fox terrier. I then collected Sylvie and took her home to lunch. Angela went to a boarding school at Turi. She was very young, but there was no one to look after her at home. Mrs. Lavers, the headmistress, was fond of "that little scamp," as she referred to her. Angela began to learn to ride there; I think she was happy and made some good friends.

By then we had hired as our cook Abdallah Saidi Ndope. He cooked for us for 18 years, was our faithful friend, never grumbled no matter what he was asked to do.

Donald's staff included some very remarkable young men. Among his non-commissioned officers at that time were an entomologist, Kay Hocking, an ornithologist, Williams, a zoologist, a coffee research entomologist, and a paleontologist. As soon as possible Donald got them all put up to ranks of captain and major. I had known several of them slightly before the war but I got to know them very well when they were all members of "our" unit. Donald Gordon Macinnes was my very special friend but I was fond of them all.

Occasionally, Donald asked me to spend up to a couple of months at Taveta to carry out experiments on the repellant (to mosquitos) properties of different ointments and lotions with a view to their use by the troops in Burma. One of our Africans would sit with part of one shin bared, (they took it in two hour shifts). He had a hurricane lamp by his side and a test tube in his hand ready to catch such insects as alighted on him. I spent one night in a small wooden hut, the walls of which were impregnated with DDT. Mosquitos had been allowed entry earlier, and the door and window shut. I spent a horrible, although very busy night. The DDT stimulated and irritated the mosquitos and they bit savagely. We learned something, albeit at my expense. Then I worked in a tent impregnated with DDT and with 6 or 8 Africans sleeping in it as bait. Mosquitos were allowed entry, then all canvas was carefully closed so that none could leave or enter. After an hour I with a helper began catching with test tubes. Then the procedure was repeated, opening tent flaps, waiting, catching. And afterwards noting numbers, sexes, fed or unfed, and species. It added up to a very busy night, and I seldom even lay down on the camp bed that was there for me. Then I had to see about meals and stores to feed such officers as were there with me. They liked substantial food like six-cup pudding and when hungry enough, they would eat, but not appreciate, soya links. Gordon Macinnes had his shotgun and was a very good shot so he often contributed to the commissariat. I enjoyed my times there very much indeed. It could be terribly hot in the middle of the day but one didn't mind.

I slept in a long banda of wattle and daub with walls halfway up to the roof and no door, only an open space. One night I was in bed and Gordon, passing by, came in to say good night. "You look almost beautiful," he said, as he kissed me, "and incredibly young." I liked sleeping there almost out of doors and hearing all the animal noises so close.

One afternoon Colonel Grogan came and had tea with me, he of the famous Cape to Cairo walk to win his bride. He had a big sisal estate near Taveta where we were working. Homer's Camp, as it was called, was on his land; in fact he owned all the land round about. Chatting about my work he said, "When I get an attack of malaria I always take 2,000 grains of quinine." I gasped. "Colonel Grogan, you can't mean that," I said.

"But I do and it cures me and I have no more trouble." [Colonel Ewart Scott Grogan was the first person documented to walk the length of Africa, from Cape Town to Cairo, to prove his character and win the hand in marriage of Gertrude Watt. Sylvie added: *When his wife died, he started in 1947 a big children's hospital in Nairobi in her memory, Gertrude's Garden Children's Hospital.*]

At that time we had begun to use atebrin, later to become mepacrine, both prophylactically and curatively, and huge and prolonged doses of quinine were of the past. Colonel Grogan was a fine and splendid man, tall, upright and strong at seventy, with very blue eyes.

When I was at Taveta, Mrs. Milne kindly looked after Sylvie. On one visit to Taveta I was there at the beginning of the rains, and my companion was a young man just out of Officers' Cadets Training Unit. The irregularity of the whole set-up, and especially my presence there, worried him dreadfully. Over and over again I assured him that, as Colonel Wilson was the Officer in Charge of the Unit, he had nothing to fear, even if some unexpected senior officer should suddenly appear. "But it is my responsibility and I should get all the blame," he wailed, "and the whole thing—the whole situation is so irregular."

I saw his point and I did think it was rather too bad of Donald to have put him in such a position to work under my direction, totally unofficially and a civilian at that. I had been twice asked to take a commission but I refused each time, as I was afraid of being sent where I could not quickly get back to the children if they should need me.

The rains made everything very difficult because the young Officers' Cadets Training Unit and I were at first in tents and nobody warned me about getting a trench dug round the tent. The first morning after the heavy rain old Juma waded in with my early tea and saw my suitcase bobbing about on the waters. "Oh pole, Mama, pole sana," he said over and over. I don't know how or where he slept.

Taxi Lewis was District Commissioner for Taveta then and he and Doris were marvelously good to me and to any of Donald's staff who happened to be staying there. About 1943 I made friends with Ronald Reisch who was staying there after being stationed for a long time in the Northern Frontier District at Wajir, as he could not get permission to be released and join up, and thought that he would then be nearer the war. This was surprising; although a fanatic in many ways he was totally unmartial by nature. He wanted some advice about quartan parasites.

Donald knew so many people in the Services and we gave small dinners about twice a week. After dinner we sometimes took them to dance at the Four Hundred that was above the Kenya Fish where there was a good Hungarian band consisting of a woman pianist and a violinist and a drummer. Sometimes we dined at the Nairobi Club or the Muthaiga Club. Once or twice Donald asked me to go to Jinja in Uganda and collect blood films from the Italian POW camp. On one occasion Ronald Reisch drove me, as he had never been to Uganda. He had a terrible attack of hay fever while we were there so it was not such fun as it might have been.

We were also concerned with malaria control at Kisumu where at one time Donald had an air-spraying program. I have never seen so many *A. gambiae* larvae as there were at the beginning of the rains on the flat grasslands round Kisumu in the shallow warm rainwater. One day, when the air spraying was in progress I told the pilot of the Baltimore bomber that had been adapted for spray work, how much I should like to go on a run. I was strapped into a seat in the glass nose and there seemed to be solid walls of instruments. I didn't enjoy myself much because I could hear a continuous blurred talking on my intercom and I thought the pilot was perhaps telling me to do something with one of the instruments. What a relief when the pilot's voice came through asking if I was enjoying my little trip! Donald was cross with me for going up.

Coming back to Nairobi from Kisumu one time, I was travelling with Gordon Macinnes. He suggested we stop at Songhor where he wanted to look for fossils. We found fossil snails that he said were Miocene period, anything between 2 and 10 million years old. Our various journeys were very interesting for me as he was a mine of information, not only on paleontological matters but also on the formation of mountains and volcanoes, and the changing nature of the Kenya countryside over the years. He is dead now, and Ronald Reisch is dead too. I missed them both for a long time.

I couldn't help enjoying those war years although always at the back of my mind was the knowledge of the terrible suffering that was going on in so many parts of the world and the longing to hear that Hitler's evil power was totally destroyed. Donald occasionally took some local leave but almost always it was connected in some way with the work; taking the opportunity to see how a control was getting on; to discuss this and that with the local District Commissioner; or to meet the local Medical Officer and discuss his malaria problems. But the main object of those local leaves was to do some trout fishing on Kenya's lovely rivers.

Sylvie: When I was a child during the war, my father had no desire ever to go to the sea for holidays. Two years living in Tanga had been enough. So we went trout fishing.

We had fishing holidays up in the hills after Christmas. When we were living in Kenya, we'd go up to a river where we'd spend a night at a rest house, then we'd walk down to the river and camp for several days. We'd take a tent and a canvas bath. Water was heated up at night. Whoever had the first bath didn't have much water but it was really hot. The last person to get in, coming one after another, had more water but not so hot.

Driving to these rivers required a lot of organizing. The back seat of the Ford V8 would be taken out and bedding bags put there. Then there was the tent, the camp beds, the wooden box of plates and cutlery, the 20 gallon tin for heating water or using as an oven.

My father would fish, my mother would fish, I would fish a bit, and Angela would play. Faithful Abdallah, our cook, would come as well. We'd catch trout that he cooked. He had a four-gallon tin that was used like an oven for cooking bread. He was an amazing person, Abdallah. He'd worked for us in Nairobi and he worked for my parents after that when they went to Muheza and Amani; he was very much a part of the family.

The children enjoyed paddling in the streams and doing a little mild fishing and the fun of camping either in tents or in the various fishing huts where we stayed for 5 shillings a head per night. We all saw a tremendous deal of the country and had picnics every day, fried our trout, or rather Abdallah did, in the evenings. We had a lovely time in most ways but we never did what the poor little dears would have liked to do most of all, to go to the coast. Donald disliked the coast. He had done no sea fishing, did not care for bathing and never wanted to sunbathe. The truth was that we took something of a dislike to the coast after our tour in Tanga. Neither of us felt well or energetic in the heat and my chronic dysentery was always worse. So we went to the cool up-country trout streams instead.

In November 1945, Kathleen Milne went to England by ship with her two boys. My life continued much the same with the same kind of work. I think it was in the previous year that Donald said to me "There are five majors coming to you for instruction tomorrow morning." Oh no! I said, tomorrow is Christmas Eve. "Sorry," he said, "but they are posted to Burma at short notice." I wailed and grumbled but of course I had to do it. I wonder if they took in or remembered anything of what I tried to teach them that morning.

Sylvie: Christmas to me as a child—the most important thing was the birth of Jesus. We went to the children's church in Nairobi, which was lovely because all the services were geared toward children. Occasionally when I was a little bit older I went with my father to the cathedral for Evensong.

But Christmas was also the Christmas tree. My father, being half Swiss, always reckoned children shouldn't help decorate; he would do it when we'd gone to bed. On one occasion when my parents had been out and they got back late, my father said, "Now I've got to cut a Christmas tree and then decorate it until I don't know what time!" We always had candles, not electric lights. I've carried on with that. It's always meant a lot.

I still remember one Christmas looking out and seeing the star and I was quite sure that was the star that had led the Wise Men to Jesus. Our stockings that we'd find on our beds early on Christmas morning were also very important. We didn't have big presents, partly because of the war. I just loved books. My father's aunt Theodora Wilson wrote quite a lot of children's books and I loved reading those. Books were my best present.

My father had come from a missionary family, but he didn't really talk about religion much, nor did my mother. But I was brought up to say prayers every night and that I always did. When I was eight, I prayed I would wake up in the morning. I'm not quite sure why I was so worried I might just die in the night!

When Donald was in Nairobi he had his own military vehicle and I had the use of our Ford V8. One morning in Nairobi Donald stopped my car and said he couldn't start his engine, and I must push his car with mine. The street was crowded with cars and trucks as usual. The pushing was successful and his engine started, but to my dismay I found that my front bumper was caught on his rear. I hooted violently and he stopped, luckily without stopping his engine. I got many disapproving looks from people who only saw a silly female who apparently had got her car tangled up with a Lt. Col's, inconveniencing him shockingly.

The war was over. Donald was made malariologist of Tanganyika. He decided he would first go to Muheza. I stayed on in Nairobi for the time being. Donald saw to it that I had plenty to do in the laboratory. I fetched Sylvie for her half days when she became a weekly boarder at the High School. I gardened and exercised the dogs. I went to join Donald for a week or so and tried to feel enthusiastic at the possible prospect of spending a tour at Muheza. Donald felt it would have many advantages as a base. The anopheline population all round was most satisfactory; it was easy and quite quick to get to Tanga, which was a not too bad shopping town. In the evenings Donald planned, measured, perpended, deciding where the various buildings should be.

Sylvie: After primary school I went to Kenya High School, a boarding school. I was very young, so my parents decided I shouldn't go straight away but wait until the second term, in April. They didn't realize what a mistake it was because all the other girls had gone the first term and already made their friends. I was somebody quite different. I had been to a day school, but a lot of them had been to boarding schools. They wore pyjamas, but I had nightdresses. I was different.

I hadn't done geometry—I remember sitting there in maths class with tears streaming down because I didn't know how to use a set square or a compass. Then there was PE and we hadn't had PE with Mrs. Smith. I didn't know how you did a double beat to use a springboard and jump over. But I must say the other girls were very nice and would say, "Sylvie's trying very hard," when the teacher got cross with me. The first term I cried myself to sleep.

There were only European children there, some of them English like me, with government backgrounds, some of them from farming families, also some Greek girls. They spoke Greek but we got on well together. Then there were the Afrikaans speaking girls. Well, there's a rather disgraceful little story. At the end of my first term I was to go on the train up to Uganda to meet my parents because it was my father's demobilization leave. When I got on to the train I realized I hadn't actually got much pocket money left. We were given sandwiches for lunch and supper that day, but there wasn't enough money to have both bedding on the train and breakfast. I thought I better have bedding because otherwise it would look very peculiar. Then they said that actually there weren't really enough bunks—we needed to share. Most of the other girls were going to Eldoret and Kitale, which is where the Afrikaans speaking girls left. And I said in horror, "But I can't share a bunk with one of those." Hmm, racist? Yes!

The next morning, I had no money left for breakfast, so when the other girls said, "Are you going to breakfast?" I said "Oh no, no, I'm not hungry," and I was starving hungry. I was sitting there by myself feeling very, very sad when one of the prefects came. I said, "I don't want any breakfast." Then the tears started rolling down. She found out what was wrong and took me along to have breakfast and paid for it.

Coming from Tanganyika, in spite of colour bars, there was a different attitude to Africans. In Kenya at that time, 1946 to 1949, I was shocked. Many of the girls didn't even know the words for "please" and "thank you" in Swahili. We weren't meant to talk to the servants at school.

In July 1946 we went up to Uganda for my father's demobilization leave. We were right near the Mountains of the Moon. We saw Pygmies and we boiled eggs in the hot springs there. Then we went to Lake Bunyonyi, which is beautiful with all the hills around. A leper colony was on one of the islands and another small island was a prison for lepers and then there was another island where the doctor who was in charge was living. We stayed with them for a short time. It was such an interesting climate because they were growing raspberries as well as bananas. And oh it was beautiful.

Then we were also near the Kasinga Channel. We stayed at the little hotel there where they sold souvenirs. I still have a table napkin ring made out of a hippo tooth.

Chapter 7

England, Muheza and Amani, 1945–1952

by Peggy Lovett Wilson and Sylvie Wilson Emmanuel

We had a last Christmas in our rented Nairobi bungalow, gave the dogs into the kind care of our great friends the Taxi Lewises, and after a final work safari to Uganda, departed for England.

Sylvie: In May 1947 we went to England as my father had six months' leave. We went on a chartered Dakota aeroplane [Douglas C-47 Skytrain] for a five-day trip. There was a huge weight allowance; I think it was 240 pounds each, including your own weight. So we arrived at the airport in Nairobi with trunks.

The first day we flew to Tabora in central Tanganyika. A lot of flights came up from South Africa and used Tabora. Then the second day we flew to Khartoum. Khartoum is so lovely, beside the Nile. We found it quite amusing staying in this hotel; if you used a bit of your Swahili—some words were Arabic anyway—people understood. The second night was near Tobruk, just outside the battlefield, and you could see a few rusty tanks. The next night it was Rome. My father said, "Right, we must go and see as much as we can." He hired a taxi and off we went to Saint Peter's and several other of the churches there. The next day we stopped at Marseilles to refuel, then finally landed in Croydon, just outside London. It was all very exciting. We had never seen sugar lumps, and although sugar was rationed, we children were so excited about sugar lumps, they gave us several.

When we arrived at the station, my father went to the third-class booking window. When I told him where first class was he said, "In England we travel third class."

It was the first time we had been home in eight years. We arrived just at the end of what had been an extremely hard winter. We first went to stay with our great friends the Ashley Turners and soon realized how difficult life in England still was, with ration books, clothing coupons, sweet coupons and so on. We never needed all the bread we were entitled to, and certainly not the sweets, but the tiny amounts of butter, cheese, and meat really surprised us. Potatoes then began to be in very short supply. However, it was so lovely to be in England again that we never thought to grumble. Everything tasted good and we had enough to eat.

When we left the Turners, we were still not able to get immediately into Spa House, so for a few days we went into the Lansdown Grove Hotel in Bath. It seemed very old fashioned and very stuffy as, by the beginning of May, summer had started in earnest. We only needed a sheet over us at night and the children said, "But Mummy, you never told us that England was just as hot as Jinja," where we had been just before leaving Uganda.

Sylvie: We had six months in England and went to Spa House. It had been let during the war, but there was a huge amount to do because all the curtains had blackout material on the inside, and everything was filthy. A lady called Mrs. Wooton lived in a cottage just down the road and we'd take down wheelbarrow loads of washing for her to do. It was a very hot summer with my father and my mother and me working in the garden a great deal. They got my sister a pony and so she was quite happy.

The garden was beautiful. There was a lot of crazy paving, a pond, a rockery, and a big lawn that had originally had stables. The original part of the house had the date 1629 scratched in the stone in the back, and the front part was later, Georgian. It was a lovely house. It was called Spa House as it had medicinal springs. We enjoyed making our visitors drink some of the horrible tasting water—very similar to Bath.

Finally the tenants got out and we were able to get into Spa House. It was a truly wonderful summer and Donald kept us hard at work from morning until night. We had to take up every carpet, lug it into the garden, and beat it until the clouds of dust began to lessen. I unpicked and removed all the blackout material from the curtains and they were then sent to be washed or cleaned. Washing, ironing, cooking, cleaning, there seemed no end to it.

Sylvie: I had my own room, a lovely, lovely room on the second floor. At that time in England they had double summertime; it got dark really late. It was bliss, nobody could see that I was reading until some ungodly hour of the night. There were a lot of books, the ones that my great aunt, Theodora Wilson Wilson, had written. She wrote children's books and a few adult ones and they were all there, as they had been given to my father. I really enjoyed all the books there.

When I first realized that whatever the four of us had for meals, I had to buy, prepare and cook, I was totally dismayed. It was so different from just telling Abdallah the quantities and then leaving him to get on with the mixing, beating, sieving, cooking the food. Sylvie, then age eleven, was wonderful. Always ready to make a chocolate blancmange, and always asking what else she could do to help before going off on any ploy of her own. Angela had a very happy, full time with a pony that I hired for her. Donald dug up the garden with a pick and the sweat of his brow, and lost pounds of weight.

A good many of our belongings had been stored in the loft. Donald decided that his workroom/study should be one of the attics on the third floor and that he must have his father's immensely heavy oak desk and Shannon files transported down the loft stairs, across the garden, and up three flights of stairs to said attic. I was not able to lift any heavy weight as my back would not stand it, and so the Herculean task was accomplished by himself and his two little girls. I cannot imagine how it was done without serious hurt to any of the three but it was. In spite of all the work, we did have a lovely summer.

Sylvie: When my paternal grandparents died in Muker, my father inherited all the furniture. That's partly why my parents wanted to buy a house in England. My grandfather's huge roll top desk was put in the loft at the cottage that also belonged to Spa House.

A few things came from my mother's family, including the grand piano. My maternal grandmother was Scottish. Her family were wealthy shipbuilders. Each daughter when 18 was given a diamond ring and a grand piano and my mother inherited them. When my mother died, my sister had the piano, and after she died, my brother-in-law was selling the house and none of her children wanted it. My daughter Sophia said, "Mum, couldn't I have it?" So we arranged for it to be shipped to Greece. The piano got to Athens and was due to be put on the ferry (the Samina*) to Naxos. Fortunately there was a lorry driver's strike and the piano didn't get put on the* Samina*, which sank just off the island of Paros and quite a lot of people were drowned. It was terrible, but the piano is now there in Naxos.*

Mr. and Mrs. Hucker had worked for us all through our leave and had been absolutely wonderful. Mr. Hucker was employed by the railway and worked mostly in Box Tunnel. He gave Spa House garden all his spare time. Mrs. Hucker worked for us in the house in the mornings, and cleaned and polished until the place shone like a new pin. The weather continued perfect until it was time for us to return to Tanganyika. The house was let again.

Sylvie: We stayed in England until November when we came back by sea on a ship called the Empire Windrush. We called it the Empire Windsock because it broke down in the Red Sea and it was hot! I can't say I enjoyed it very much. My father was trying to give me Latin lessons because I missed two terms of school. They didn't bother to send me to school in England.

While in England we made do with a hired secondhand Morris car. When we returned to Tanganyika Donald settled for a new Ford 10. It was a game little car but small and slightly top heavy—I cannot think why he bought it. We had a nice bungalow at Muheza and Abdallah came back to us, as well as our dear faithful Sefu for some of the tour. There was a great deal of work to do and a good deal of safari.

Sylvie: In Muheza we had a little house, not a particularly nice one, but it did feel like home because I had my room. The big joy was going to Tanga to swim in the sea. We'd go to the Conditorei Café, owned by a Swiss, where they had lovely little cakes, and we'd go to the grocer, Almeida and Menezes. My father would be shouting away at those poor people when they didn't bring things as quickly as he wanted.

The children had very dull holidays and it was usually uncomfortably hot but we went to Tanga sometimes to shop and to bathe. I did not look forward to having Muheza as headquarters with any pleasure. Our three white Field Officers were not entirely satisfactory.

Sylvie: Tanga was a small town in 1947 before the sisal boom. Still, quite big ships would come into the harbour. There was a swimming club in the bay. Tanga saw a lot of fighting in the First World War. There were still a lot of old German buildings. The Provincial Commissioner, for instance, was in the old German Boma; the hospital was German-built. It was just 25 miles away from Muheza where we were living.

My parents were travelling a great deal because of their work. Angela and I didn't travel with them because we were at school. A train on Tuesday and Friday afternoons from Muheza took us to Moshi where we spent the day with a friend of my parents, Mrs. Emslie. Then in the afternoon we would get the train, arrive in Voi in the evening, change trains, and arrive in Nairobi the next morning.

Returning to Muheza for school holidays was quite a journey. Although terms always ended on a Wednesday, we weren't allowed to leave on the Tuesday train but had to wait until Friday afternoon. We arrived at Voi very late and transferred to the train for Moshi. It stopped at Maktau early in the morning and all the first and second-class passengers got out and had breakfast—eggs and bacon. Then on to Moshi where I spent the day with kind Mrs. Emslie. Often she took me to swim in the icy cold swimming pool. Then in the afternoon onto the train, arriving in Muheza on Sunday morning. After a year or so, my parents discovered that we could get the train to Mombasa on a Wednesday afternoon when school finished and then fly from Mombasa to Tanga on Thursday morning. What a welcome change!

The holidays were really pretty dull; it was exciting to go to Tanga for swimming, but Muheza itself was hot and not very nice. One time I'd gone for a walk along the railway line. An African said, "Don't go further because there's a lion!" I thought pffff, why does he not want me to go ... rubbish, so I walked on as far as I wanted. I came home and said, "Daddy, there's this African who said don't go on further because there's a lion, how stupid." "Oh," he said, "I forgot to tell you. Yes, a lion's been seen."

In 1948 Donald went to America for two to three months, leaving me in charge of the Unit.

Sylvie: In a letter to my father dated April 4, 1948, I drew a caricature of him lecturing, with a caption: "Sirs, I am now going to read you a paper on malaria, that wonderful and most absorbing subject!"

I was being paid by Government. Some weeks prior to Donald's trip to America, we were on safari at Mwanza where Donald asked me to find out whether *A. funestus* were breeding on the edge of the lake. The Africans were loath to go into the water to search for larvae but as Donald had been assured by the MOH that there was no danger of bilharzia I told the Africans so and waded in with them. I have felt a mild grudge against our good friend Noel Chilton on this account. A few weeks after Donald's departure, I felt very unwell but could not discover the cause of my illness and tried to ignore it and carry on. I had in fact got bilharzia but could not diagnose it.

Donald and Peggy at Muheza, 1950.

I was deputized to do a bit for Donald now and then. For example, the town planner wanted him to advise on whether it would be suitable to build dwelling houses on a bit of land below Moshi where a number of springs surfaced. There was always a certain amount of anopheline breeding going on and it was very difficult to control. On hearing that I was acting for Donald, I was asked to go to Moshi. So I drove up, assessed the situation, and chose an alternative site for the new buildings. My proposals were adopted, but only in part; the area was designated an industrial area without living houses, and so it is until the present day.

Donald returned from America having had a most interesting and instructive time. Soon after his return he was asked to go and advise about a sharp malaria epidemic at Chunya [in Kenya]. He was too occupied with Administrative meetings in DSM and Nairobi so he asked me to fly down to Lindi [near the border of Mozambique] and investigate and deal with the problem. He thought three days would be enough. I was put up very kindly by the Medical Officer and his wife and we then started on as busy a three days as I have ever had. I checked up on records of hospital fever cases that had occurred recently. I took a number of blood films while the doctor examined the same number of spleens. I set men to mosquito catching in the native houses; I walked over the ground assessing larval breeding. I found very heavy infections of *p. falciparum* in the blood films. The spleen rate was as high in adults as in children.

But here came the great surprise. Hardly any adult anophelines were found in houses. Again to my surprise, no *A. qambiae* larvae were found in breeding places. These breeding places consisted of shallow sandy runnels, and numerous larvae were breeding in them. But when I came to look at them I found that they were all *A. pretoriensis.* And here, because I had to do the whole survey in such a short time, I missed finding out for certain about the vector causing the epidemic. I felt sure that *A. pretoriensis* was the cause and that the infections had occurred in outdoor biting.

I told the MO and I carefully showed him how to dissect out the anopheles' salivary glands and how to recognize sporozoites in the glands. Meantime I went round the one or two local garages and begged all their waste diesel oil and showed the mosquito boys how to apply it. I thereby spoiled all the pretty little sandy trickles, killed the larvae in them, and stopped the epidemic. Such a pity I could not have stayed longer.

As it was, a week or so after I got home, I heard from the MO who said that a number of the mosquitoes had been caught biting out of doors, that he had dissected them, and that two had considerable numbers of what he was sure from my description were sporozoites. I wanted to publish this interesting finding, the first record of *A. pretoriensis* as a vector causing an epidemic in Tanganyika Territory. But Donald wouldn't have it! He said nobody would believe the MO's findings; that if I had seen them myself it would have been different, but as it was, it must remain non-proven. I was very disappointed.

I flew up from Lindi to Nairobi and found that Donald had booked us in at the Norfolk and had arranged a dinner party at the Club for that evening. The next evening we dined at the Muthaiga Club with Doris and Taxi Lewis and Colonel Grogan.

Our next visit to Dar es Salaam I went to see Dr. Williamson about my insides. The laboratory found I had the intestinal form of bilharzia. It was decided that I should be treated with intramuscular stibophen in Tanga Hospital. A week after leaving there I was as bad as ever.

I loved Amani itself, the cool green forested stillness, the little trickling springs falling into small pools of clear water edged with begonias; and shaded banks covered with maidenhair fern under the tall forest trees. This was untouched rainforest that had survived from time immemorial. There were many tree ferns, huge long lianas, and many epiphytes on the trees.

It was always hard to go back to Muheza which, as our ex-sergeant Field Officer said was "limited, very limited." Now and then we heard a lion not very far off at dusk. But the best thing about weekend evenings and nights was the really marvelous drumming. I have never heard the like. It often went on all night, one, two or three drummers, blending their complex rhythms with syncopation hour after hour. I often went to sleep on Saturday night to the sound of those drums and woke about 7 a.m. to hear them still going strong. The dancers stamped and shuffled all through the hot night sustained by copious draughts of *pombe* [beer]. Occasionally we went to watch the dancing.

Some weekends we went for little expeditions. Once to Pangani along the old road from Muheza taking David and Roger Phipps, the sons of our entomologist. What a road! In places the Ford 10 just managed to straddle the deep clefts caused by the last heavy rain. We took a picnic lunch and had a lovely day in and out of the sea. On the way home we found the road blocked by a lorry with presumably a broken back axle. The driver was not there. It was impossible to get past.

We tried ineffectively to dig out the bank but it was hopeless. So we settled that Sylvie and the boys should walk the two or three miles to Muheza, and Angela and I would wait with the car. The time seemed endless and we were dreadfully bitten by mosquitos. At last we heard a car and Donald with two or three *watu* [people] arrived. After one glance at the lorry they simply pushed it off the boxes on which it was propped and shoved it to the side of the road.

Sylvie: Several times we went with my parents to Pangani from Muheza. One time Mummy drove us. It was just 25 miles. The road must have been a bit better than it is now to drive in that little Ford 10 that my father bought in 1947. We'd take our camp beds and mosquito nets and put them up among the trees by this great big beach and have supper. It was so exciting—the sea, the sea. Swimming was such fun. Trout fishing holidays were lovely, but this was different.

My mother would go with my sister when I was at school in England. There was even a cinema in the little village. It was one of the slave trade portals where slaves were sent to Zanzibar. A lot of the remnants, lovely old Arab buildings, have fallen into disrepair.

Once we went on a fishing trip up into the Pares. We thought it would be quite a walk but we didn't know that after having climbed about 1,800 feet in the car we should have to descend on foot the same distance and then climb it again starting from the other side of the chasm. The sun was very hot in the late afternoon and Sylvie was almost crying with tiredness. Angela however, then only 6 years old, cheered us and pulled us up in turn on some of the steeper parts of the path. It was a very impressive show of strength. Even after getting to the top we had quite a walk along the level before getting to the camp. I remember nothing about the fishing!

Sylvie: I remember tickling a trout! But I couldn't catch it.

When it was time to leave, Donald had to walk back all that way to get the car and then drive it down to the bottom of the hill. The children and I clambered down the path and at the bottom had an unpleasant two-mile walk in deep sand with the sun pouring down. At last we arrived at the Lund's lovely big cool house at Makanya on a sisal estate; how kind Mrs. Lund was. We were at once given delicious lime drinks with lumps of ice in them, and shown to a bedroom and bathroom. Once we were clean, our clothes dried in no time in the very dry atmosphere. I remember the delectable cold tomato soup at lunch. I am afraid that we were never able to return that splendid hospitality.

Sylvie: We went for fishing holidays twice on Kilimanjaro. One time, we'd heard that leopards were around. I slept in a camp bed between my parents and Angela slept in the car because we were also taking a puppy down for a friend. In the afternoon my mother had gone fishing and she suddenly saw a leopard quite close and was just thrilled to bits. On our way back my father decided to return by an old road. We came to a drift that our car couldn't manage until we had built up the drift and removed most of the luggage. As we foraged for sticks, etc., for the drift I kept wondering if I would meet a rhino around the next bend!

On West Kilimanjaro one time we were going up to one of the rivers, quite high up a perilous path. A great pool was under a big waterfall and a lot of fish. I was standing there fishing and singing and I found that I would catch a little fish when I was singing, "All people that on earth do dwell." By the end of the first verse I had landed my little fish.

Another time we went quite near where we're living now, up from Machame, and stayed in the government rest house. We walked down a steep path to the river to fish. The fishing was good because the British had stocked all the rivers. Lower down there were rainbow trout, higher up, brown trout. There was a guard in those days on the river—you paid a small amount to fish.

At the end of the holidays I took Sylvie and Angela to get the evening train for Nairobi. From there, Angela had to go on up the line to Turi. It was always a very sad evening for they were miserable and cried and I felt a hard-hearted wretch to be sending them away from home. Sylvie was at the High School in Nairobi. I think they probably cheered up fairly quickly after the train started with the prospect of dinner in the restaurant car—that they always enjoyed.

Sylvie: When I returned to school after we had been in England in 1947, a girl called Griselda Worthington came to the Kenya High School. She and I became great friends and we're friends to this day. We were at Cambridge together and we've kept up although she's in Australia. That made life quite different and I enjoyed school very much.

I was at the Kenya High School until 1949. My last years, 1948, 1949, were very happy because my friend Griselda and I did all sorts of stupid things. We played lacrosse on the lawn outside the Governor's state house. Griselda and I would "lose" the ball, so we'd spend most of the game hunting the ball so we didn't have to play. I was hopeless at games.

At a hotel in Nairobi we swam on Saturday mornings. Saturday afternoons I'd go horseback riding, Sundays, we'd go to the cathedral for Evensong. Later that last year at the high school, other girls were going to the dances with the boys' school, the Prince of Wales, but I was too young. My parents certainly didn't think I should be going to dances, so I didn't. But the prefects and older girls who went would save up little cakes and bring them back for us. Sometimes we'd go down to the cinema to see films.

We'd escape sometimes from games that we didn't want to play because we were the first year in some prefab dormitories. It was quite easy to make our way behind them where nobody would see where you were and you could just do what you felt like. We had midnight feasts occasionally. The staff may have had an idea. I can still remember for a dare eating sweetened condensed milk with anchovies. I can imagine nothing more disgusting!

I struggled on with maths. Biology was all right, but because I'd missed out on several terms, I really had no science at all. I'm completely ignorant with chemistry and physics, but I seem to have managed without them.

I especially liked the history teacher, an eccentric Irish lady. I went on to study history basically because of Miss McTavish. She made it interesting, her stories and her slant on everything, not just straight facts and dates. She was very Irish with a rich sense of humor.

We had a geography teacher, poor Miss Anderson. I remember when she was telling us about the earth going round the sun, we pretended not to understand and made her walk round and round the desk.

Then we had Latin. We had a good teacher but I didn't like it. Both Griselda and I knew that we had to get a credit in school certificate in Latin, because in those days you had to have Latin if you wanted to go to Oxford or Cambridge. So we just learned off our Livy or Virgil by heart. In fact, we did pass.

Later, when I went to Cheltenham, the teachers asked about Latin. I said, "I'm hopeless," and the teacher said, "I see you got a credit." I said, "We just learned everything off by heart." So she gave me a test and said, "Yes, you're right."

We had scripture lessons. Our teacher was Mrs. Bewes, whose husband was well known at the cathedral. Their son, Peter Bewes, was later a very well known surgeon at KCMC [Kilimanjaro Christian Medical College in Moshi] and his brother has written hymns that we sing now. Most of the children didn't really want to do much scripture and I did want to learn it. I felt sorry for Mrs. Bewes and I didn't like her to be made fun of or teased.

Once when Peter Bewes was at KCMC, I was bitten by a bushbaby that had come into the house to attack our tame bushbaby. I managed to separate them but the next day thought that I should see a doctor. Peter Bewes wrote in my file, "Bitten by irate wild bushbaby defending its territory!"

My father was certainly very low church. There is a letter in which my grandfather, in 1921, wrote to my father. "As to theatre, we want you to feel that our conscience is not necessarily yours, and that you will not grieve us should you feel led to see any special and refined drama. But we have given up our own desires for Christ's and our work's sake. I am confident that you will not misunderstand my object in writing this and that we are not bursting with desire for you to become a 'play goer.'"

My father would take me to the cathedral on Sunday evening and my mother took us to the children's church and when we were in Nairobi we said our prayers. But there wasn't really much talk of religion or faith. There was definitely the ethos in the family, how you treat people well. At Muheza, for instance, a man who was working for my father had malaria and later got TB. When I was in England he'd written to me and I'd written to him. He replied, "Thank you really for your letter that I received in the month of May. I beg excuse for delaying to answer your letter, and that was made a special to wait my progress after some months of treatment. Now my health is improving better and gives me hope that I will be able to leave the sanatorium in August.... Madame I missed to meet your father but so long I live I will never forget him how he love me, not for my work but by personally he love me indeed...." *Your faithful F.M. Mrope*

Sadly, Mr. Mrope died quite soon afterwards.

Angela wrote before her birthday saying how much she would love to have a pet, "only please not something like a grasshopper." So on our next visit to Nairobi with the car we brought Fanny back from the Lewises and from then on, she was Angela's dog.

Donald had very little Government money to spend on putting up any new buildings but he erected a fine guesthouse, doing it as cheaply as possible. There was no glass in the windows, but it was mosquito proofed with double doors opening outwards and wooden shutters. In the cool weather it could be extremely chilly and visiting workers found they had to wear jerseys and thick coats in the evenings. However, in hot weather it was excellent. The water supply was something of a problem. All the water for all purposes came from a stream that ran past the hospital. However, well boiled and filtered it was perfectly safe and was very nice to drink.

In 1949 we had guests for our last Christmas at Muheza: Gordon Covell, Paul Russell, Pampana and Swellengrebel. I made all the traditional Christmas foods. It was very hot and it would have been more sensible and much kinder to serve cold chicken and jelly or something equally innocuous. The result was that most people had upset tummies except for Donald and the children. However we much enjoyed their visit, Donald especially, and the new guesthouse came in very useful.

In 1950 we had another U.K. leave. We arrived in bitterly cold weather. Donald stoked up the old boiler that provided us with central heating. A rather temperamental little stove heated the water. I was terrified of being left with it when Donald was away as I never mastered the stoking and the dampers and never got the water really hot as Donald did.

Sylvie: I left Kenya High School in 1949. I could have continued there but my parents wanted me to go to England. They'd gone round and looked at schools. I think one of the reasons they chose Cheltenham Ladies College was because the uniform was green and that would go with my red hair better than the school with red uniforms!

We went to England in February on a flying boat, one of the last flights before they were discontinued. We started from Lake Naivasha in Kenya, refueled at Khartoum, and at Alexandria spent the night in a nice hotel. The next day it flew to Augusta in Sicily and we spent a night, then to England and landed at Southampton.

The flying boat had an upstairs and a downstairs. There was a table where the four of us sat. One thing I didn't like on the plane was the airhostess's strong Elizabeth Arden Bluegrass scent. But it was such fun, and so beautiful; as you took off you whooshed up through the waves. I'll never forget it.

In the spring Donald got hold of a technician who agreed to come out from Bath every day to give me intravenous injections of antimony tartrate. He was very skilled and never put a drop outside the vein. It is a very toxic drug causing coughing and vomiting, shoulder pains and arthritis. At the end of three weeks I had had the right amount and to my joy it cured my horrible *S. mansoni* [schistosomiasis].

Soon afterwards I went into a London Nursing Home for a general repair operation by Sir Charles Reid. Very painful afterwards but a very necessary procedure. The fees at the Nursing Home were £35 a week, which seemed a tremendous lot of money. The nursing was excellent and the food really superb, so I enjoyed my convalescence.

Donald and I went to a Buckingham Palace Garden Party, summer of 1950, for which I bought a gold corded silk suit and a large black hat. Donald hired morning clothes from Austin Reed. We also went with Sylvie to the Palace to see Donald get his OBE (the Order of the British Empire). Sylvie started at Cheltenham Ladies College.

We bought a new car, a magnificent Humber Super Snipe. In August I drove it up to Scotland with Sylvie and Angela, my sister Rosie, and her daughter Pom. We did it leisurely, staying a night in Kendal and visiting some of Donald's relations. It was lovely hot summer weather and the Yorkshire moors looked superb. We had tea at Tan Hill, the highest inn in England, and we went to Muker to see Donald's father's grave and the window in the church that was given as a memorial to him. It was a very expensive trip because of all the lunches and teas that we had. It never occurred to me to buy cheap foods and have picnics.

When we arrived in Glasgow I had difficulty finding our hotel as the tramlines were very confusing. We got to the hotel eventually, the quaintest, most delightfully period one imaginable, where the chambermaids were elderly and comfortable looking with long streamers to their caps. The loos were on built up thrones and the baths were extremely "period." However, the water was hot.

The next day we visited my Aunt Maggie, a lovely little old lady with snow white hair and the bluest of eyes, wearing a satin and lace bed jacket. We visited our other Scottish relations in their lovely homes at Craigallian and Dougalston. Craigallian was where my uncles had lived and I remembered going for holidays there and fishing in the lake. Then we set off homeward. Pom was a very great help; she did a lot of the driving. We needed petrol and at a filling station I said grandly, "Fill her up, please." The tank held sixteen gallons and we had to empty our pockets to the last penny to pay for it.

Sylvie: I went to Cheltenham Ladies College, in Gloucestershire, for my last three years of school. It was so different from the Kenya High School and I am sure I would never have got into Cambridge if I had not been there.

There were good teachers and many extra-curricular activities. I enjoyed the Cotswolds Club very much; you had to pass an exam to get in. We visited old churches and castles and learned about their history. We attended very good concerts. One was very aware of the school's history, founded in 1863. There was a poem:

Miss Buss and Miss Beale,
Cupid's darts do not feel.
How different from us,
Miss Beale and Miss Buss.

Miss Beale had founded the Ladies' College and Miss Buss the North London Collegiate School. My Lovett grandfather had been to the Boys' College and according to my mother, he was once found near the Ladies' College by Miss Beale who led him back by the ear to the Boys' College!

I took History, French and Latin. There was a wonderful library. We all spent many hours there. I was hopeless at games. The first year I had to play cricket but I couldn't hit the ball or throw it more than halfway up the pitch so thank goodness I was able to give that up.

I enjoyed riding in the autumn and winter very much as we used to go up in the hills outside the town and you felt free and away from all the rules and restrictions. One of these was that you were not allowed to go onto the High Street. Once, I had gone bicycling with a friend and the only way to get back to school without a long detour was to go a short way on the high street. The next morning at Assembly the Head Mistress said, "Two girls were seen on the high street. Would you own up?" So we went up and explained what had happened and we were excused and not punished. But some old spy had noticed us.

Another thing I'll never forget really hurt me. I loved Charles Morgan's books. He was coming to Cheltenham to give a talk and I went with others. That day, instead of my hair being down, I'd tied it into a ponytail. The head mistress saw me and summoned me to take it down in front of everyone. To be humiliated in that way in a public place, I couldn't enjoy the talk after that. I remember going to the housemistress. She was so nice about it. She thought it was so stupid. I had no great love for the head mistress. I made good friends and several of them were at Cambridge when I went there.

Angela returned with us to Tanganyika and went to Limuru Girls' School. Arrived once again in Muheza, it seemed possible that we might not be going to live there after all. Amani and all its buildings were available and Donald was given the chance of having it as his headquarters for the East Africa Malaria Institute, as EAAFRO [East Africa Agricultural and Forestry Research Organization] was moving to Kenya.

In about 1898 the Germans who first colonized Tanganyika created an Agricultural Research Station at Amani. It seemed a very suitable place, about 3,000 feet up in the Western Usambara Mountains, on the edge of primeval rain forest, with an average rainfall of about 60 inches. The road that they built was laterite surfaced and rocky in places with eleven hairpin bends, no retaining walls, and many steep drops to several hundred feet. It ran through the forest for most of the way and there were many charming little streams and small waterfalls. Pink and red balsams edged the road. The last 1,800 feet rose steeply so that the climate of Amani was much cooler and fresher than would be anticipated from its very moderate altitude.

The views over the neighboring forested ridges were most attractive and bracken grew on the open slopes. Once arrived at the top, one saw that the forest had been cleared; there were surfaced narrow roads, the banks of which were all clothed with maidenhair fern. The Germans with their usual thoroughness experimented in planting every kind of useful medicinal and ornamental plants, shrubs, and trees. They built excellent spacious laboratories, good bungalows and a Power Station on the Sigi River 400 feet below the summit. The local tribe was the Wazigua. They did not apparently object at all to the establishment of the Research Station.

The Germans had travelled far and wide to collect plants for Amani. The range and variety was amazing. As to the trees, they brought many cypresses, araucarias, junipers, flowering and other eucalyptus, camphor, Persian lilac, many varieties of bamboo, including the giant *Dendrocalamus giganteus*. Many varieties of palms, several cassias, and trees bearing flowers with the most delicious scent such as *Michelia Champaca.* All the varieties of coffee, tea bushes grown for seed, the cocoa bean, the Paraguay tea *Yerba de Mat,* and then so many creepers, the clerodendrum [glorybower, bag flower and bleeding-heart], the vanilla orchid, and rare trees like spice trees and breadfruit trees. It was a horticulturist's paradise.

In World War I the Germans made a great deal of quinine from the Amani cinchona trees. They also made many other articles of medical and food value: 10,000 pounds of chocolate and cocoa, 10,000 cakes of soap, tooth powder, 300 bottles of castor oil. The Germans collected their plant treasures as cuttings, as seeds, and as rooted plants, from China, the Philippines, the East Indies, India, Ceylon, Australia, the West Indies, and South America, and they brought them to Amani where very many of them flourished.

Anyone who wishes to know the complete list of all that was planted or grew at Amani could find it in what they called *The Amani Bible,* of which there were only three copies, drawn up in the first place by Peter Greenway when he was the botanist at Amani. One may still be in the Amani library. I borrowed a copy and typed it out.

There were 700 acres in all belonging to the Research Station, on which were constructed the staff houses, the double-storeyed stone Boma where the director lived, the laboratories, the post office, and some other buildings such as stores, workshops, etc.

After the First War this was all taken over by the British, together with a hundred zebu cattle that provided manure for the plantations. In 1950 the East African Agricultural Research and Forestry Organizations decided to move to Muguga near Nairobi to be nearer the center of things, as it was thought that Amani was too difficult of access and too limited to allow for expansion. So the whole place, after being considered and rejected as a site for a secondary school or a police headquarters, was offered to Donald as a possible Malaria Research Institute. His reactions were very mixed. He had grown used to the idea of having Muheza as his center, and had been most interested and enthusiastic in the planning of it. Now he was being offered this really splendid place with its lovely climate, delectable views, excellent buildings, all self-contained, with three lovely villages for the upkeep of which he would be responsible. Everything pertaining to this upkeep was to be found on the premises. Under the control of the maintenance superintendent, who wished to continue working at Amani, were the carpenter, plumber, painter, vehicle mechanic, gardener, and under them quite an army of minions. Many of them had worked on the place for years, a few of the old ones since German days. One or two were very exceptional people. Mwindadi Simba had had responsible work on the plantations for many years and knew the botanical name of every tree and shrub in the place.

My parents moved to Amani after I left for school in England. We'd go up to Amani from Muheza sometimes for a day when it was still the EAAFRO before it moved to Kenya. An African there named Mwindadi knew about plants. My mother tried to propagate ones that she felt were in danger of dying off. Amani was ideal for the Malaria Institute; it was a bit higher, cooler, healthier than Muheza. There were more buildings with laboratories.

Malaria research would continue in Muheza, but staff would live up at Amani. From Muheza to Amani was about 22 miles. The first bit of road was quite flat. Then you came to the Sigi River. In German times a branch of the train went from Muheza to Sigi. From Sigi you went up through nine hairpin bends, right up to Amani. Further down was a plantation with mangosteens [tropical evergreen from Indonesia], cinnamon, and cinchona. The forest at Amani was beautiful. Then there was a big lake, made by a dam that my father cleared because it had a lot of quarter weed [Lamb's Quarters]. My parents lived in a wonderful big house called the Boma. My mother's letters expressed great joy that they were finally in Amani.

At the end of the first year at Cheltenham I went to Amani for the holidays. That was a lovely holiday. The government paid for one trip for a child every tour, in the two and a half years. So in 1951, my fare was paid. Going for the summer holidays was a big excitement. But when I arrived, my mother said, "I put you in the spare room, darling." I had no room of my own! She didn't realize what that meant to me. That is why Spa House meant so much. There, I had my own room.

Looking back on it I realize how Donald's heart must have sunk at the thought of taking on all this. All he really wanted was to be let alone to get on with the job of research into all aspects of malaria, and if he accepted Amani he would be unendingly distracted from his purpose. He asked me what I thought about it, but alas for him, the odds were for me too heavily weighted in favor of taking it. Perhaps selfishly, I loved everything about the place. So he agreed to take it and early in 1950 we moved up there, keeping Muheza as a Field Station.

The staff increased rapidly with entomologist Mic Gillies, Field Officer Michael Christie, junior Field Officers such as Gerry Shute and Gerald lvebbe. Amani became the East Africa Institute of Malaria and Vector-borne Diseases. As Donald was the director, we lived in the splendid German-built double-storeyed stone Boma with its big garden and its lovely views of hill and forest, and about 30 miles away as the crow flies, the sea. And so began for me, nine years of pure delight.

It was all so *lush.* The greenhouses, the cool, the paths through the forest, the ferns which grew in such profusion; everywhere the eye was rested and refreshed. EAAFRO had dammed up a meandering stream, making a small lake surrounded by grass and flowering shrubs, Persian Lilac, *Medinilla magnifica* [showy medinilla, rose grape, the Philippine orchid] with its splendid panicles of rose-pink flowers and masses of yellow and red cannas. Where the stream emerged from the lake it ran over rocks and rippled its way downhill. And just there was the Fern House containing the lovely *Selaginella glauce* [spikemoss or arborvitae ferns], and various Philodendrons and Anthuriums. It had been recently neglected in the preoccupation of moving to Nairobi. However, I joyfully took it over with the help of Mwindadi and an African laborer that Donald had allowed me to have. There was a little succulent garden outside, and in the shade at the edge of the stream were African violets. There was a punt on the lake and sometimes in the evening I would paddle it out to the top end of the lake. Once I saw a brilliant blue kingfisher sitting on a partly submerged tree branch banging a little fish on it over and over again before swallowing it.

From our house, the Boma, as it was always known, i.e., the seat of Government, all the roads and paths, except one, led downhill. One that I had occasion to use very frequently went past the cinchona trees, past the cowsheds and to a garden, always known as the Bustani. Here the EAAFRO had propagated shrubs and trees of many kinds for sale. I tried to carry on this small business and fulfill and dispatch the orders, but until I got some experience, I sold plants too soon before they had developed a proper root system. Any money I made in this and other ways on the estate I handed over to the funds for running the place.

The Boma was the nicest house imaginable. There was a porch at the front covered with golden shower *(Bignonia venusta)* and quite a large entrance hall. This was rather dark and gloomy because there was so much wood—the staircase, a tall settle, and a gate legged table on which I always had a large vase of flowers. Donald decided to paint some of it a Georgian green, which lightened it a great deal. The big sitting room had an open fireplace in which we burned logs for much of the year, a big dining room with French windows opened on to stone steps down to the lawn, and a study-library. There were two bathrooms, one up and one down stairs, three good bedrooms, and a long upstairs room with glass windows along one side, always known as the signal box. The servants lived in the village, three minutes walk down the hill.

In the village were the meat market and a small dispensary. The Amani Post Office and Donald's office were quite close to the Boma. The laboratories were more or less on the same level and staff houses dotted here and there. Everyone had a garden and a bit of green lawn. There was a guesthouse where people from outside could stay by appointment. It was known as the Zoo and housed the bachelor staff. The small Anglican Church was quite a walk away downhill, as was the Power Station to generate our electricity from the steeply falling stream. The highest and most isolated dwelling was Forest House.

Donald lecturing at Amani.

When we first went to Amani an EAAFRO officer named Nicholls lived there. A month or two after our arrival he was going through an emotional crisis and drinking heavily. One evening the girl secretary came to the Boma and begged Donald to find out if something had happened to Nick. We set off in the car. There was a brilliant light near the Fern House and Donald said that some Africans must be having an *ngoma*. Then he said, "No, my God, it's the truck burning." And so it was and Nick was in it, dead.

One evening I was hurrying up to get things ready for Donald's safari the next day when I slipped on the mossy path and fell, hurting my back and breaking my left wrist. Donald set it for me and next day had to depart. There was no very expert orthopedist available and I saw that my wrist was in a very bad position. When Donald returned we decided that I must go to Nairobi. Mr. Braimbridge did an open repair, a beautiful job making it as good as new. The Worthingtons at Muguga [Griselda's parents] kindly asked me to stay until I was able to get back to Amani.

About then, something had to be settled about the Amani cattle, all those no-account zebus. The African veterinary assistant, Mningereza, was in charge of them and there were four milker-herdsmen. They were herded all over the station wherever there was the most grass, milked twice a day by hand and shut up at night. Until I learned something about their management it was a very poor show.

Donald said soon after we got to Amani, "Who is going to be responsible for the cattle if we accept EAAFRO's offer to keep them on?" "Oh one of the Field Officers," I answered quite gaily. "But I can't spare one of the Field Officers," said Donald. "Aren't you prepared to do it?" I really thought he was in fun. I had never had anything to do with cattle and I did not want to do it. However after a few acid words from Donald to the effect that I never wanted to do anything to be helpful, I gave in and said I would do my best.

Mningereza was very good. He saw to the weighing of the milk and the recording of the amounts and the measuring out of it to the customers, the European and the African staff, those who could pay for it. I let the Africans have it at 50 cents a pint and the whites at 60. The local Sikhs who ran a Saw Mill were the biggest customers, taking two gallons a day.

The calves were dreadfully mismanaged both by EAAFRO over the years and by me. To have enough milk to supply all who wanted it the calves were only let suckle when there was hardly any left. As an EAAFRO officer said, they mostly lived on a diet of good fresh air. So over a long period they were literally half starved. And the calf paddock was much too small and they all suffered from worms and were always having to be dosed with phenothiazine. Mningereza took a blood film from every animal once or twice monthly to look for trypanosomes. If positive, the animal was thrown and injected with dimidium bromide intravenously.

These cows gave so little milk that we decided to try and upgrade the herd. Tanga Dairy bred and sold both bulls and grade heifers of Boran or Friesian or Guernsey blood with the Zebu. So from time to time I, and occasionally Donald with me, purchased one or two grade heifers and a grade bull. Obviously there was no point in breeding better calves if one was not going to feed them properly, so I began to buy calf-rearing foods such as Unga Cream Equivalent. The "dry" herd was kept at Kwamkoro a few miles away through the forest. Now and then I visited this herd in the little Ford 10.

It was quite a job to bring a bull up from Tanga in a truck. A special retaining chamber had to be constructed with pieces of wood and the animal had to be held very firmly to avoid damage caused by bumps on the road and too fast cornering on the hairpin bends. One or two of the new bulls were less quiet and docile than the Zebu and would jump out of their paddock to chase after the cows that were being driven up the road to pasture. Nobody, especially mothers with their children, cared to meet the herd coming round a corner on the narrow road.

Finally, Donald took a hand. He said that paddocks must be chosen and enclosed, must be planted up with Kikuyu grass, must be used in rotation and changed when the grass was sufficiently grazed down, and the herd must remain outdoors at night. It was all entirely successful and the milk yield went up.

On February 6, 1952, we were doing our mock A level high school exams. At the end of one exam the teacher looked very solemn and said, "I've got some bad news to tell you." What had happened? People didn't cheat on anything there. The news was that the king had died. Some of the students were from really rather posh places (and knew the royal family). I was sharing a room at one stage with a girl who used to refer to Buck House (Buckingham Palace).

Angela had a wonderful view of Princess Elizabeth and the Duke when they were in Nairobi before they had to rush back to England. She wasn't yet the queen.

My mother had a feeling that something wasn't really quite right and persuaded my father that I should go home at Easter, 1952, just before the higher-level exams. The teachers all thought this was a very bad idea. But in fact it was very important because I was missing my parents so much, yet saying to myself, it's okay, I can cope.

Returning to Cheltenham an extra term in the autumn was required before taking exams for Oxford and Cambridge. I only tried the Cambridge exam because my father had been there and that's where I wanted to go. I didn't get a place initially. I got a waiting place. So I stayed on at school and those were the two best terms I've ever had because the teacher said—there were just a few of us—"What do you want to do? Which history would you like?" We hadn't done much eighteenth-century history, yes please. "What else?" German, I hadn't ever done German. So we started two terms of German.

July 21, 1952. Mummy wrote, "I'm 55 today. It's an unpleasant thought because each succeeding year I seem to have done less and less. I fear I shall never accomplish anything that's really worthwhile but just pad along with routine work indefinitely."

Chapter 8

The Coronation, Amani and Cambridge, 1953–1955

by Peggy Lovett Wilson and Sylvie Wilson Emmanuel

In 1953 we went on leave to the U.K. It was a very cold spring and summer, but we all had the thrill of going to the Coronation of Queen Elizabeth. We were in the Colonial Office stand facing the Abbey. On that day there was also the great thrill of hearing the news of the successful Everest climb. It was a bitterly cold day.

Sylvie: My father had four lottery tickets for the Colonial Office stand, so we were able to go as a family and watch the coronation. It was wonderful, something to remember. We were waiting for the train and saw the newspaper saying that Mount Everest had just been climbed. I thought that was all so exciting, and I was jumping up and down, and my sister said, "Really Sylvie, behave yourself!" She was rather shocked at my light-heartedness.

This was the description of Coronation Day, June 2, 1953, written at school by my sister, Angela.

A Day I Will Never Forget, by Angela Wilson

We, Mummy, Daddy, Sylvie, and I got up at half past four on the bitter morning of the coronation. We cooked our breakfast, on a "put a shilling-in-the-slot stove." It was lovely and warming and consisted of eggs, bacon and coffee.

We set out to the underground station nearest us, the sky still dark. We got onto our train with not much trouble and squashed, and we got out where we had to change trains and we were simply carried along the platform by the crowd, but we managed to buy a paper. And at the top were the marvelous words, "Everest conquered." It made us forget about the squash to have such a lovely thing to begin what was to be such a grand day.

We were practically carried on to the train by the crowds. We got off at St. James's with the crowds, but when we got into the street, there seemed to be hardly anyone. We held our coats around us because it was bitterly cold and set off to our stands. There were policemen everywhere. I wondered how there could be any left anywhere else in England. As we got nearer to our stand, there were people lying, sitting, and standing, some sound asleep, but all were wet.

We found our Colonial Office stand and went up to our seats. There were Boy Scouts selling beautiful programs. There were cushions that we could have and there was a man going round with hot cups of tea that everyone was buying to warm themselves up. There were marches playing on the radio that was booming out to keep us awake until about seven o'clock.

People started arriving at the Abbey about half past seven. We were opposite where the peers and peeresses went in and so we had a marvelous view. People like Miss Fisher arrived first [Niece of the Archbishop of Canterbury and headmistress of Limuru Girls' School where Angela was enrolled].

Everyone was very smart, but most people certainly weren't dressed for the weather. Some didn't even have a fur cape. It was pouring with rain but we were under the shelter of the Colonial Office stand. It was great fun looking at all the people's clothes, and soon after eight, the peers or peeresses started arriving and they looked marvelous in their lovely red robes and white and red coronets. One peer's coronet fell off in the wet under the car and the peer's pageboy had to bend down without getting muddy and pick it up. There were roars from the crowd.

The prime ministers started arriving in their carriages. The less important ones, first of all, with their bodyguards. The Prime Minister of Canada came with all the Mounties around him and they looked simply lovely, the beautiful black horses and the red-coated Mounties on top. The Queen of Tonga came next with her great arm waving to everybody. I'm sure I've never seen such a tremendous woman in my life. She smiled at us all.

It stopped raining for a while and the Sultan of Zanzibar seemed very small after the Queen of Tonga, but it was nice to see him. Winston Churchill came along about last holding his fingers up in a VE to us all. He didn't put on his robe until he got out of his carriage. Then, the best of all, the royal family started arriving, headed by the Gloucesters. The two little Gloucesters looked sweet all dressed up. The Kents came next. The Duchess looked lovely, but the Duke looked so young and inexperienced.

Princess Royal and Princess Margaret and the Queen Mother arrived next with a lot of Royal Horse Guards behind and in front of them. They certainly looked fine. The door under the annex was opened by two Beefeaters and the lesser royals entered. But then came the great moment when the Queen and the Duke arrived in their lovely golden coach. Seeing them arriving, I had to blink my eyes because it was so like a fairy tale and I couldn't believe it was real.

The Queen looked lovely, but so small and young to be undergoing such a great event. They disappeared into the Abbey and the doors were closed. The band of the Royal Marines had been playing "God Save the Queen" and stopped.

Below us, in front, were a few RAF, to the right of them was the Royal Marines Band, and to the left were the Grenadier Guards. It was pouring rain again and the hair of their busbys was right over their eyes. All the rest of the way we could see was lined by the Royal Marines, all soaking wet.

We listened to part of the service over the radio, but then all the troops started marching past and on to the top of our road. They looked glorious, hundreds of them, everyone in time. The KAR got a big roar [the King's African Rifles from Kenya].

We had some lunch and as we came up, hymns were being sung in the Abbey and all the stands joined in. Soon afterwards, people started coming out of the Abbey and the bells started ringing.

The Queen's coach came out first and as it was still pouring, the horses were skidding all over the road, but the site was as fine as ever. The Queen with all her bodyguard of the Royal Horse Guards left first, then everyone else, one after the other.

The Queen of Tonga didn't bother about the rain and got soaking wet. When at last everyone had gone, it was about five o'clock. Just as we got out of our stands, the fly-past started. The planes went over in wonderful formation.

We had dinner with friends and then were driven to the South Bank to see the glorious fireworks. They changed into all the different colors as they went into the sky. I've never seen so many colors. It was a cold night, but somehow the fireworks seemed to warm us. At about 11:30, we set off to go back down the mall, but the crowds were so dense, we couldn't get through, but we still saw the lovely illuminations.

As we turned round, the Queen and the Duke came out onto the balcony at Buckingham Palace for the last time and then we went back to our flat through the pouring rain. That was the end of the most glorious day in my life.

Peggy: Back at Amani I usually had a number of blood slides to examine, collected during our safaris in Tanganyika, Zanzibar, Kenya and Uganda. There were two or more courses a year for Europeans or Africans, two or three men perhaps from each territory; but when it was specifically a WHO [World Health Organization] course, men were sent to us from such wide apart places as Somalia, Ghana, Nigeria. I lectured and demonstrated on elementary parasitology and entomology.

At the beginning of a course we always gave a drinks party with little eats and invited all our staff. I was very impressed at one of these parties when a tall bearded Nigerian said *sotto voce* to one of the staff standing next to him, "The lady next to you has an empty glass." Such quiet sophisticated good manners were something one hadn't encountered.

This reminds me of an incident in London on our last leave. I was to meet a Nigerian at our hotel, the Royal Court,

Peggy at Amani.

and I didn't want to risk a possible embarrassment for him so I asked Reception, "Is there a colour bar in this hotel?" "I am afraid not, Madam," came the answer, "but there is an American Bar at the end of the passage."

Sylvie: The summer term of 1953 continued to be very enjoyable. We didn't even have to wear school uniforms most of the time. I was allowed to go to a dance at Marlborough, the boy's college where my "brothers"—my guardian's twin boys—were in school. It was great fun. On the last day of the term the names of the new college prefects were announced and I was one of them. But just then there was a letter for me. I opened it and it said my "waiting place" was now a definite place at Cambridge for October! I said, "Oh, fantastic!"

My father said, "You are so young, you should really wait another year." I didn't want to. My friends were going up. In a way I'd waited another year because of having this extra term. So I said, "No, I want to go." In many ways he was right, because I was too young. I would have benefited from being a bit older. I was just 18 and I was the youngest of the year. I was the youngest when I went to high school, the youngest at Cheltenham and at Girton. But that's the way the cookie crumbled. So I got ready to go up to Cambridge in October and started three wonderful years.

In 1954, at the end of my first year at Cambridge, I went to Tanganyika for the long vacation. When I arrived, a Royal Navy cruiser was in Tanga harbour. There weren't many girls around so we had a great time with the young officers—picnics and swimming and a dinner on the cruiser. The captain wrote a poem (maybe he adapted it to wherever they went).

At the end of the vacation my parents arranged that a friend and I have a couple of days in Cyprus and then Istanbul. They had been there the year before for a conference when there were celebrations marking 500 years since the Ottomans defeated the Byzantines. So Vivienne and I had an unforgettable few days. We were even taken up to the outside balcony of Santa Sophia. I had not read much Byzantine history and so was not very upset that the greatest church had been turned into a mosque. All the Turks were very friendly and we were well taken care of.

My father wrote to me in September 1954 when I was on the way to Constantinople: "I do hope that your trip is proving a success. As you can guess, you took a large piece of my heart away with you. I would like to carry on a little further with what I tried to say to you last week before you are so far away that these cannot be said without risk.

"I would like to ask you to ask yourself whether you're making the most of this opportunity of becoming a citizen not merely of no mean city, but of the world. I know that you're of a body and you're only young once. But had you gone to Cambridge a little older you would have had no doubt of this being an opportunity quite unique of developing your mind and spirit.

"You will have opportunities and plenty of developing other things later and I cannot help fearing that you may come to have regrets later on. I'm not, repeat not, thinking in terms of academic distinction nor trying to persuade or suggest that you become a one-sided scholar, but nonetheless do not try to take refuge behind some persuasion that you're not a scholar or have a first class brain.

"You have undoubtedly got a good mind, even if only a woman. And I have again wondered whether you have sought to integrate your spiritual life with your mental life and whether in fact there is not some danger that you should even unconsciously keep your spiritual lodestar for an illumination of the physical growth alone.

"I'm well aware how unacceptable this sort of parental exaltation can be. And yet my dearest Sylvie, I've asked you to ask yourself some questions and if you do that I'm content to leave the rest to your splendid and dear character. We've had tremendous joy from your stay with us. As if there were not enough on hand, today Angela has broken her clavicle falling off Paris her pony and so I've had to throw my weight about getting her to hospital and Brainbridge's attention. The poor child was very upset at not being able to go to the Nakuru show, where she would have been jumping and taking part on her pony."

Peggy: I was quite busy with hostess duties most of my time at Amani. In 1955 we had a total of 42 houseguests over the year, and very many people came to lunch. Abdallah was a splendid cook and how we managed with just a stove was incredible, especially since the firewood was often a bit damp with such a high rainfall. He usually got it dry in the oven somehow or other.

I wrote to Sylvie: "The lovely grapefruit spoons from you and Angela made our silver wedding anniversary much more silvery. We're delighted with them and now look forward to the grapefruit season to use them. We hadn't meant to have a party and wrote to the Gils to put them off coming, as Daddy couldn't get up any enthusiasm, and various people we would have asked were not available. So I didn't tell anybody. But Angela must have because she left the spoons with the Cullens to send over and everyone wrote notes and the Christies gave us a charming silver spoon and a twig of Joseph's thorn from Glastonbury.

"There was a huge notice on Daddy's office door with 'Happy Anniversary' on it and a vase of flowers on his desk. So we felt that the least we could do would be a drinks party and sent a notice round that all would be welcome. We were 24. I put a lot of roses and other flowers in the sitting room, and there were cashew nuts and chips, tuna fish on bread and butter, anchovies on toast, red cocktail onions speared onto bits of cheese, cheese biscuits, and little sausages. They drank our health and it was all great fun. I wore my favorite dress, the pink flowered brocade."

I was always greatly preoccupied with food—for ourselves, our guests, our dog and cat, my fifty or so chickens, my dozen or so ducks, and my hundred or so cattle. I had large bills at the Tanganyika Farmers Association for various poultry foods, and coconut cake, cottonseed, rice polishings, bran and mineral bricks for the cattle. Occasionally I bought a little pig that was fattened largely on sweet potatoes and avocado pears and then slaughtered; it was eagerly bought by the European staff.

There were so many avocado trees at Amani of different kinds, including a few of the enormous ones. Initially the Africans didn't eat them, but all the animals and poultry loved them. I used to take huge kikapus [baskets] down to Tanga to give away. I could have sold them for the benefit of the station but I never thought of it. However the idea of picking and selling wineberries was put into my head. The wineberry is the Japanese raspberry. I had a regular order to sell to the Tanga Grocery and made quite a few shillings for Station funds. I ordered vegetable seeds either from Kirchhoffs or Suttons and had a flourishing vegetable garden. Peas did wonderfully. When I grew Alderman peas, they reached such a height that Abdallah had to use the kitchen steps to pick them.

Angela on her horse Paris at the Nakuru show, another year.

Mohammed brought my early tea at 6:45 a.m. and I often got up then and walked down to the cowsheds to see the milking. After tea in the afternoon, which we usually had on the grass terrace outside the dining room steps, Donald would ask me what I would like to do that evening. I would have a mad idea of saying that I should like to be driven to Tanga and go to the pictures, but I always settled for walking down to the new cattle pasture, or perhaps to the lake or the Fern House. Or I would work in the garden until dark and Donald would say, "Come in now, it's getting dark," and we would bathe and change and have a drink and then supper. Donald would often go back to his office and perhaps we would have coffee taken over there. There would be a fire in the sitting room for about half the year, and if it was moonlight, the view from the big windows was perfectly beautiful, looking over the forested ridges, over to the rhino horn Magamba and away to the shine of the moon on the sea. I could not bear to draw the curtains.

Occasionally we had the dinner table carried outside and had dinner by moonlight. But the table was so heavy that I hated telling the servants to carry it down the steps and out onto the lawn. It was an old German table and could seat 12.

In January 1956, Peggy wrote to Sylvie: "Amani is quite a different place with Daddy away. It and everyone in it sinks back peacefully into a leisured dream. There's an air of Sabbath calm and peace that is restful. I am glad he's gone away for this fortnight. It will do him heaps of good because he just can't keep on working the same way as he does here."

Sylvie: When I started at Cheltenham, my first Christmas holidays I spent with my aunt, my mother's sister Rosie. I was fond of my aunt. She and my mother were utterly different. My mother had gone on to become a doctor. My aunt stayed quietly in England

and married a clergyman. She had two daughters, as did my mother, and in the same way, her daughters were completely different from one another. I spent some holidays with Aunt Rosie when I was at school in England and later at university, and we enjoyed lovely walks. I also spent holidays with our Swiss cousins. If it was the Christmas holidays we went skiing. Also very good for my French!

When I was at Cambridge, I got to know the Scottish relations, and they were really so kind to me. In the spring I went to visit my guardians, Uncle Ashley and Aunt Margaret. Ashley had been the secretary of the Student Christian Movement. My father had known him from when he was at Birmingham. They invited me for the Easter holidays. It's been such a very special relationship, because Uncle Ashley, who was a vicar, did a great deal for my spiritual world. My Aunt Margaret was a doctor and I loved her. They had four children, two sets of twins. The two younger boys were 18 months older than me and they were at Cambridge when I was. I was introduced as their sister at Cambridge.

I read history at Cambridge and we had wonderful tutors. I was at Girton [a college within Cambridge University], which in those days was women only. Because I was a late admission, I wasn't able to have a room in college my first year. I was staying outside with people who were very kind. If I was back late, Mrs. Garner would have left me some hot milk. It was a bit different the other two years I was in college. There was a lot of socializing, I must admit. In the whole of University, there was one woman to nine men. Most of the men had done their national service, so they were actually a bit older than us.

I was involved with the Student Christian Movement [SCM]. Once Archbishop Ramsey from York, who was later the Archbishop of Canterbury, came and I was at his first talk. He looked around and said, "I feel green looking at you. I'm green with envy. Here you are young and you've got everything ahead of you." I'll never forget it.

The SCM had a mission in Kent at the end of the summer when you could meet people picking hops. I joined the Hopping Mission for a couple of years. It was where the people from the docks went. Women and their children would pick hops in September. A lot of them had little huts that they used for their infrequent holidays. So we went to Kent and we'd pick hops. We weren't really missionizing much but the idea was the example we would set. The second time I went, a woman was obviously about to give birth. We said, "Surely she should go into the hospital," but the midwife said, "Oh no, she's all right." She started labour that evening and they said, "Well, you. Cut the cord." I was 21. I hadn't a clue about what happened when a baby was born. I didn't know what to do, so I cut it. There weren't even any medical students there.

Later that next year I was practice teaching down in Bermondsey. One of the docker's families had asked me down one evening. I thought, wow, it would be rather dangerous in the East End of London. I'll take my umbrella, put on flat shoes, and then I can run, if necessary. I got to the underground and the closer I got, the friendlier the people became. By the time I actually arrived at the Jefferies' I was feeling so ashamed of what I'd been thinking.

Behind the houses and the laboratories of Amani a hill rose up 700 feet. It was called Bomoli, and in German times, the staff of Amani would be pushed up to the summit on their mono wheels and perhaps have a cheery beer-drinking session. It was a steep climb up in places on foot through forests of imported trees, junipers and cypresses, a camphor plantation, dense thickets of blackberries as are found also on Kilimanjaro, and semi-giant heather about seven feet high.

Once a year, at the time of the warm weather and a full moon, we gave a barbecue up there. Everything had to be carried up, including the glasses and drinks. Donald organized the charcoal and the fire for the barbecue beforehand so that it was all ready. The guests had no way of arriving but on foot, however no one refused on account of the 700-foot climb. Once or twice there were accounts of frightening growls from the forest on the return journey, which was about 11 p.m. But the view from the ridge where we had our supper was glorious. To the west there was the aftermath of the setting sun, and to the east the big silver moon was rising up as it seemed out of the sea on which it later cast a shimmering pathway.

We had barbecued steak, liver, and sausages to eat, and I had made American barbecue biscuits and a rather fierce sauce, and afterwards, apple tarts made with tinned apples. There was beer and sherry and squashes to drink. There were usually about 15 of us.

In spite of the many cases of trypanosomiasis in 1959, the milk for the year amounted to 3,768.5 gallons. At the end of the infection season every animal was injected with antrycide pro-salt. This prevented further infection for the rest of the year. On advice from Mr. Graham of Tanga Dairy a supply of TRILK was ordered and also a Rose-Miller aluminum calf feeder with a rubber teat. Bull calves were castrated as soon as possible after birth. At one time I had a good deal of worry about horn damage to people or other cattle. So I got Mgereza to saw the horn from a dead beast up to the quick. This proved to be about one inch from the tip. This was carried out on all the sharp horned cows and also the bull, and the ends filed smooth.

Christmas was always very busy and very gay. Angela was home from school. We might go to Nairobi on the way home from some work safari and there we could buy goodies and presents. But for special eats like crystallized fruits and Elvas Plums and such, I sent home to the Army and Navy. There were always one or two special trips to Tanga for groceries and for the great bags of boiled sweets. Donald chose the tree. We had plenty at Amani and unlimited greenery for decorations and plenty of helpers to cut it and bring it to the porch. We invited the Locks, our great friends from the Sisal Research Station at Ngomeni, almost every year to spend Christmas with us.

Donald and Angela saw to the decoration of the tree with real candles. Abdallah usually coped splendidly with Christmas dinner, but one dreadful year he returned to cook the dinner at 7 p.m. The dinner, or rather the turkey, was ruined, having been at least two hours short on cooking time.

On Christmas morning all the estate children were brought by their mothers to a rendezvous in the village where I presented each child with a 6 oz. bag of large, brightly colored sweets. Angela and I had previously weighed them. Then the Honorable and Mrs. Douglas Gourlay always invited us and our guests to a pre-lunch drinks party. On Boxing Day or New Year's Day we gave a tea party for all the senior African craftsmen and some of the laboratory assistants. Several of the station ladies and I made delectable sandwiches, scones and cakes. We waited on them ourselves as the guests included our servants. After tea there were games and competitions and the favorite contest of winning a 5 shilling note on a darts board hung on a tree. It was quite difficult as one had

Peggy and Donald at Amani, giving out sweets to children of Amani employees at Christmas.

to stand at increasing distances from the board and hit the note each of the three tries one was allowed.

For the first year or two, we held our yearly supper and dance on Boxing Day, but I found it such an effort on top of Christmas, that we changed it to New Year's Eve. We invited all the European staff and members of the Amani Club and our friends and acquaintances from the neighboring tea estates. We had a fine cold supper of turkey and ham and salads and cold sweets; trifle, made properly with egg custard and cream and various creams and jellies; wine cup made by Donald and quite potent other drinks, and coffee.

We danced in the signal box to the gramophone and great fun it all was. Donald arranged the mistletoe bough over the front door and kissed every girl as she came in, some more fondly than others. Angela, at one of the dances when she was 16, looked quite charmingly pretty in a long dress, with her shining hair smoothly parted in the middle and her peach-like complexion. I remember Sylvie when about the same age at the Muthaiga Club when we were dining there, and Colonel Grogan compared her to an English rose.

Every week the Station truck driven by little Paulo went down the hill to Tanga, mostly on Station business but occasionally a member of the staff would go down in it. Coming back after dark there was the chance of seeing a leopard on the road or a serval cat dazzled by the lights. Once I saw a leopard try and leap from the road up the steep bank on one side. He fell back into the road but succeeded on his second attempt. But usually we went down in our own cars. Very often one had to go straight to the garage to get the damage repaired that occurred on the way down, i.e., loose nuts or bolts, broken spring or cross-member.

Once when I had gone down in our Humber Snipe, the Greek chief mechanic said to someone who later repeated it to me, "That little lady's got guts," a great compliment. If the weather seemed all right after I left Tanga, I would sometimes stop at Ngomeni and call in on the Locks for a chat and a drink.

Donald was always cross when I got home, always asking why I was so late. One day I asked him why. To my great surprise he said, "But didn't you think I might be anxious?" I was very touched but still thought that his concern was for the car rather than for me.

One day we went down together, but my pleasure was short-lived when he said he was collecting a new car for the Station and would I rather drive it back or ours. It was in the rains and I chose ours. What a drive! The PWD [Public Works Department] had put so much earth on the road, especially on the hairpin bends, that I stuck repeatedly and kept on having to hoot at Donald to stop and help me. I will say he was quite good-tempered about it, and if contemptuous of my inefficiency, concealed it nobly.

Early in 1956, coming back up the grassy slope from our evening walk, we talked about our coming leave. Donald said I had better go home a month or two before him and go to hospital so that they could find out what was wrong with me. I was surprised but I certainly was making heavy weather of the hill. He said he had noticed for some time that I wasn't well so I had better do something about it or I should get no more sympathy from him. I didn't know I had been getting any!

I went into the Tropical Diseases Hospital and after three weeks I was still undiagnosed. I had a vague lump in my tum and Alan Woodruffe, I think, wondered if it was cancer. I cheerfully agreed to be operated on but Donald came home then and said he wanted me to be operated on by Naunton Morgan at St. Mark's Hospital. I am afraid the surgeon at the Tropical Diseases Hospital must have been rather hurt, but anyhow, I went to St. Mark's. Cyril Garnham, Edward Cullinan and Alan Woodruffe were all there to see what the lump was and to everyone's surprise it turned out to be an amoeboma, legacy of my long ago amoebic dysentery. It had in the course of time become sealed off, so no wonder no one could ever find any cysts. When it was unsealed and most of my colon cut off and discarded I had dysentery in real earnest. Courses of emetin and entovan and diiodohydroxiquinoline had no effect and for years I had the most intractable diarrhea. Opium in various forms controlled it to a certain extent.

Both Sylvie and Angela were at home as it was summer vacation for both of them. Later Sylvie and I went on a little motor trip via Glastonbury, where I managed to get to the top of the Tor, then Lyme Regis, and then Seaton, where we stayed a night or two.

Sylvie: At the end of my second year in Cambridge, I didn't go home but had another wonderful long vacation. There was a month at Cambridge—called the Long Vac term—where one was working without the pressure of lectures and tutorials. Then five of us rented a barge and had a week on the canals near Stoke-on-Trent. We became very good at opening and closing the locks, though when there were three together, we finally had to get help. We caused a lot of amusement to any young men around.

Bicycling in Holland 1955, left–right: Sylvie, Isabel, Kate, Patience.

For our next adventure, four of us from Girton went cycling in Holland, staying at Youth Hostels. The family with whom I had lodged in Cambridge my first year gave us £5 and said, "You must go to the Five Flies in Amsterdam and eat smoked eel." I had an introduction to Professor Swellengrebel who knew my parents from malaria conferences. So I went to see him and I said, "We have been told that we should go to eat at the Five Flies." He said, "I am afraid that I can't come with you but my secretary will come." His secretary was delightful and paid the bill. The money we had wouldn't have paid for a drink for the four of us! We had all tidied ourselves up and parked our bicycles outside. But we had smoked eel thanks to Professor Swellengrebel, and very delicious it was.

The next excitement was going to Scotland. I first stayed with the Scottish relations at the magnificent Craigallian where my mother had stayed as a child with the ship owner uncles. It was just outside Glasgow. Then we went up to Colquhonnie where they went for grouse shooting. I managed to keep my mouth shut at a dinner party when a young man was complaining about all the "very ordinary people" who were being accepted at Cambridge.

From there I went up north and met Griselda and her parents who had come up from England in their old Rolls Royce with their boxer dog. Dr. Worthington had rented one of the old railway coaches at Strome Ferry near the island of Skye. We were lucky with the weather but even so the sea was quite chilly when we swam before breakfast every day!

And then, I had managed to get on to a British Council course in Edinburgh. When it suited me I was an African student and that is how I was able to go on this "crème de la crème" of courses, which was during the Edinburgh Festival. We went to concerts, operas and exhibitions. The Royal Edinburgh Military Tattoo at Edinburgh Castle, with all the military bands and pipers with their bagpipes was an evening to be remembered.

There was a very interesting mix of students on the course—Swiss, Australians, West Indians, and Africans. At a party I danced with an African for the first time. I hadn't been brought up to consider doing that, but I just danced.

After that amazing three months, it was back to work at Cambridge for my last year. After university I wanted to come back to Tanganyika. When I was about fourteen we were driving up to Nairobi and near Longido where there had been a lot of fighting during the First World War I suddenly said, "I know what I want to do. I am going to write a history of German East Africa." But during my years at Cambridge I realised that I wasn't a research student. So I thought of other options. One possibility was working among ex–Mau Mau women—not very suitable for a young graduate. In the end I decided on teaching. I went up to London for an interview at the Colonial Office. I thought it was quite obvious that I wanted to teach for a time and then get married. That did not go down well with the large lady interviewing me! But what is the point of pretending that one wants to spend the next forty years teaching?

CHAPTER 9

Amani, Machame, Nic Emmanuel and Mwanza, 1957–1959

by Peggy Lovett Wilson and Sylvie Wilson Emmanuel

We returned to our lovely Amani in the autumn and welcomed the usual stream of guests. At long last, hot water came out of the bathroom taps. Donald had an outside wood-burning boiler fitted and Mohammed no longer had to carry buckets of hot water up to the top bathroom. It was a huge improvement. I had always felt sorry for Mohammed having to do it.

We had brought a new car from home, a Humber Hawk, the successor to the Snipe that was sold to Sylvie, then teaching at Machame.

Sylvie: My father taught me to drive up at Amani on those little roads and little bridges that often didn't have sides. No wonder my mother was terrified when I was learning to drive. It was in that great big Humber Super Snipe. My father said I could buy it for £100 because they'd got another car. I took the driving test in Moshi. The examiner was a rather stout Irish police officer. I did the first part and then had to reverse around in a figure eight. He looked at the car and said, "I'll do it first," and at the end of it he said, "I think we'll leave that bit out for you!" It was obviously a bit too difficult. But he passed me so I got my driving license. I had that car for some time in Machame and then in Mwanza.

During my third year at Cambridge I went to the Colonial Office. My father wrote that he had been working behind the scenes as well; "...you made a very favorable impression on the Colonial Office lady at your interview. I've seen her letter and you can definitely have a job in African education. Carry on through the Colonial Office and if you find you're not getting what you want then you can communicate directly with Kenya. I have spoken with the deputy director but I suggest you don't do the latter without communicating with me and telling me what you propose to say. He mentioned the possibility of going for a year or so to one of the schools and then an administrative appointment. There seem to be no objections to getting mixed up in the community development ... but we shall see."

Honestly, it's just incredible, using your influence and going through the back door!

I was appointed as a teacher in the Colonial Service but I didn't know where I would be sent. First, I was to do the postgraduate diploma of education in London, but I would be paid while I did that. A friend and I rented a basement flat from people we knew in Chelsea. Patience had been at Cheltenham and Cambridge and she was going to be working at the BBC. So that year, 1956 to 1957, I was in London.

I was practice teaching in Bermondsey, in the east end of London, where I learned a great deal about how to teach. It was south of the river where people were very deprived, the setting for Jennifer Lee's Call the Midwife, *and it was fascinating. I was there just at the time she is writing about.*

I learned to teach having a class of eight year olds. The classroom had a large piece of plywood against the wall. I gave the children work and then some would finish earlier and start going behind the wood. I'd say, "Come out," still waiting for the others to finish. One particular afternoon, I went into the staff room in tears because the children were just everywhere. The next day, the teacher came in and said, "Do you like having Miss Wilson?" and they said, "Yeah."

"Well," she said, "You must sit down while she's teaching." From then on, I never waited for the slow ones to finish, because otherwise, everyone was jumping up. I learned a great deal, and the teachers were so supportive, they were really good. That was the primary.

The secondary teaching was in Essex, where I was able to live with Uncle Ashley and Aunt Margaret. I was at a grammar school where the history teacher was very helpful and imaginative. We did funny things, like being knights, and dancing. "What was all that thumping?" We were having a battle, students carrying other students and being "knights in armour." It was really most enjoyable.

So then I passed my Postgraduate Diploma and I still remember that last exam. I put my pen down and I said, "I am never going to do another exam." I never had any desire to go on studying.

Teaching at Machame

In September 1957, I was told that I was going to teach at Machame Girls' School near Moshi. All the other teachers were coming by ship, but I wanted to go by air so I could spend a little time with my parents. I was the only one going to Machame, but one was going to Tabora Girls' School, the top Girls' School. One was going to the girl's school at Mwanza. There were several men, one whose wife later became one of my greatest friends.

I spent a few days with my parents, then sent a telegram to the school to say that I was arriving on the Wednesday morning train. I got to Moshi and nobody was there to meet me. So I left my luggage and went up to the Education Office. I didn't realize that the road to Machame was bad then, and the school lorry only came down on Saturday to collect mail, etc. It was not the day for the lorry, and they hadn't got the telegram saying when I was arriving. But the chief education officer said he'd drive me up to the school. At the school, everyone said, "Do you mean to say you went to the Provincial Education Officer? "I said, "Yes. Why not?"

PE class at Machame with Kilimanjaro in the background, 1958.

There was a mixed bag of teachers. The English teachers and the African ones really had very little contact. The African teachers were admittedly not as well educated. Among the English ones, I was pretty horrified by the one I was staying with, because she seemed to be so racist. She was a rather old-fashioned domestic science teacher who had been there several years. Machame was just at the point of changing from Standard Six to starting Standards Nine and Ten, which is why a graduate teacher like me and another were brought in.

One of the teachers, Bridget, became a great friend. We had similar backgrounds and she had been at Tabora Girls' School before coming to Machame. We were fairly isolated since the school lorry only went down on Wednesdays and Saturday. But Bridget and I used to go down to musical evenings every month. People had records and that was fun. We would go down to church on Sunday morning, usually for the early service, and some very kind people would invite us back for breakfast afterwards. Bridget and I did some exciting things for the girls. For instance on Guy Fawkes Day we bought fireworks and for a surprise for the girls, we had a little fireworks display and then dancing. It was great fun and rather unlike most of the other things they did.

We also went on lovely expeditions. We drove in Bridget's car round the mountain to see where we could camp. We asked at the West Kilimanjaro farms and they said, "Why don't you go farther up? There's an abandoned cattle shed you could sleep in." We couldn't actually get into it, so we just slept outside. We hadn't got a tent. And the stars! Luckily no elephants came very close to us.

After several weeks I was given a house to stay in as the previous teacher had left. She was an artist and left the place in quite a mess. After she'd left, other teachers helped themselves to bits of furniture they liked. There was a great dearth of furniture, so after a week or so I said, "I need to go down to the Public Works Department and get more things." Again, the teachers were amazed that I would have the nerve to approach public officials. So I went down and, being quite attractive and persuasive, there was no problem getting more furniture.

No one had been in the house for a while, and the garden was a complete mess. I hired a servant who never worked for anyone before, so I had to train him. My first night there was September 29, 1957, and I'd never actually slept in a house on my own before. I had my Bible Fellowship notes and I saw it was the feast of Saint Michael and all angels. I thought, that's all right then, Saint Michael and all angels, that's fine. Now I am not scared.

I started teaching English and history. I was even teaching art for a bit and singing. There was no piano, but the girls were so musical—you started singing a song and they would pick it up and then add different parts. The pronunciation was a problem. One of the songs they knew was Cock Robin. They would sing, "All the bards of the"—it's not "bards," it's "birds"—but could we ever get them to sing "birds"? A few years later, when our son Gregory went to kindergarten, he had a lot of little Indian friends, and he came back singing, "All the bards..." and I said, "What did you say?"

The students were mostly Chagga, and most were boarders. It was quite difficult to get them to answer questions because at their previous schools, if you answered incorrectly you were beaten. To break this down, to get them to say, "I don't know" was difficult. I was so pleased because one girl was really thinking and asking questions. It was quite a challenge but several have been so very complimentary on how they enjoyed my lessons. Because their English wasn't good, I'd read them bits out of When We Were Very Young *[A.A. Milne], poems like that, or anything that could bring them out.*

There were quite a lot of rules. We had to inspect their dormitories. It really upset me that on Saturday mornings they had to bring their clothes out and you had to check that they'd all put their knickers out to be washed. I thought this was so humiliating. I really loathed it. Then they had to keep the area outside the dormitories tidy. I found one of the girls cutting the grass with a razor blade. I said, "For goodness sake, just leave it if you can't find anything else to do it with."

Machame Girls' School was on its own, as there were no boys' schools around. The first headmistress luckily got married and left. Then we had another one who liked to keep us busy on school holidays. She reckoned that as we were colonial servants we needed to be kept busy. She would get us to do all sorts of jobs that we considered not really for teachers, like painting. So like naughty children we just tried to avoid her and skip round the back where she couldn't see us—it was pathetic.

Once, when my mother was visiting, the girls came and said, "Oh, there's a baby in the hedge." We went to have a look and there was a tiny dead baby. One of the girls had had it. So my mother and the science teacher did a post mortem. *In fact, the baby had been born dead, and the girl continued on at school. Usually the girl would have had to leave the school. Whether she'd been raped or whatever had happened, it always would have been her fault. But she went on and was able to finish school.*

Peggy: In February, Donald had occasion to go to Moshi and decided to go by train. He asked me to go to Muheza Station with him and take our Hawk home to Amani afterwards. It was dark and I was going up through the forest when suddenly, round a corner, I came face to face with an elephant. It really surprised me, as I had never heard of anyone meeting an elephant on that road. I stopped, but kept the engine running and the lights on.

I was really scared. The elephant seemed to ponder for a minute or two and then began to descend the steep bank on the right hand side of the road. Oh good, now I can go, I thought, but the noise of my revving up must have seemed to him like a growling challenge and in a trice he had leapt back onto the road, threw up his head and trumpeted. It is a very frightening noise when one is all alone on a narrow road. Still, there was nothing to be done but sit and wait again. That time I waited quite a bit until all the leaves disturbed by his passage stopped quivering. When the forest was quiet, I went on up the road.

At last, in 1958 I had a small laboratory to myself. Normally I didn't need one and in any case I had my own microscope. I became interested in the demonstration of anopheline chromosomes that Mic Gillies and Michael Christie tried to encourage me in learning. The object of the work was to try and make good enough squash-stained preparations from larval salivary glands to identify and map the bands on the chromosomes. The arrangement of these bands, it was hoped, might have a connection with a resistance to particular larvicides. I made some quite good preparations and the bands showed up fairly well, but I could never manage, even taking the utmost pains, to map more than a few of the bands on each chromosome arm. Then I ran into difficulties over making permanent preparations. Michael Christie suggested photographing them. We fixed my camera over the eyepiece of the microscope and got hopeful photos. Then on a visit Cyril Garnham saw them and told Donald he ought to get me a proper camera for use with a microscope, which he did, although he thought it a lot of nonsense.

I did take some pretty good photographs and developed and printed and enlarged them myself, but I still never got a clear and definite picture of all five chromosome arms. So I really wasted two years which would have been better spent in photographing malaria parasites. Donald was right as usual. He said it was too difficult.

Late in the year we went to visit Rhodesia [now Zimbabwe]. We stayed with our great friends the Alec Ramseys for most of the time. They lived in a bungalow 12 miles from Salisbury with TV, a garden, and two servants. I think Helen Ramsay disliked their servants and there was no friendly relationship such as we always had with ours. We saw quite a lot of Rhodesia. Besides Salisbury, which is a clean, quite attractive town, especially with all the jacaranda trees in flower, we visited [Cecil] Rhodes' grave in the Matopos; Bulawayo, hot, dusty; and Umtali. But we didn't take to the country. Something about the atmosphere or perhaps the knowledge that we had taken the country by a trick against Lobengula [Lobengula Khumalo (1845–1894), last king of Northern Ndebele people]. We were not sorry to leave.

For some time I had been worrying about Angela's future and felt she must be trained for some profession. With her consent I arranged for her to do a course in physiotherapy. I had no idea how much it had all changed since I became a trained masseuse. She tried for a time but she found the work too difficult as she hadn't studied the necessary subjects in school, and changed over to nursing training at the Middlesex Hospital. She did this for a year. Meantime Sylvie was teaching at Machame.

Sylvie: Meeting Nic

There was a tennis court up at Machame where I was teaching. Various people would come up and play tennis but some unattached young men would come up to inspect the latest teachers. Nic was one who had come up to play tennis with the previous headmistress, who'd been very good to him and given him a lot of books. That's how I met him, this tall, very good-looking Greek. He was ten years older than me but very different from many of the young men I'd met before. I'd been fond of someone in England, but that petered out after I met Nic.

We were fairly isolated up there because at that time, the road from Machame down was rough, and during the rains you had to have chains on.

One time during the rains, I'd asked the school driver what the road was like. "Oh," he said, "It's fine." So I started off in the Humber Super Snipe and it was not fine and I went down a bit and then swoosh—slid across the road. It was such a big car that I couldn't put the chains on by myself. Luckily a very nice young African stopped, and I felt so sorry for him because he was wearing a white pullover, but he helped me put on the chains. Then, when I got to the main road I had to take them off because you couldn't drive on tarmac with your chains on. Bridget and I would walk down to the big green on days when we weren't going out and look at the outside world, as we called it.

That Christmas of 1957, I had malaria. I was the only teacher at the school as everybody else had gone off on holiday. I was feeling so sick, I thought, "What would happen if I died?" Then I went to see my parents at Amani.

One of the extra jobs at school was seeing girls who came to the sick bay. I had no desire to take this on but was told, "Come on, your parents are doctors, of course you can do this." I discovered that the previous teacher in charge just gave sulfa drugs to anyone with a high temperature. I thought that was thoroughly bad medicine. So the next time I went home, I said, "Mummy, please teach me how to examine blood slides as there is a microscope at school." For the next girl who had a temperature, I took a blood slide and it was positive, so I treated her for malaria and she was fine. Girls from down the mountain often came back to school with malaria. At that time it was very rare at Machame.

Then one awful afternoon I came down and heard, "Miss Wilson, Miss Wilson, come. Indeshawawa, her eye, her eye." Indeshawawa was a rather quarrelsome girl. I came in and, at the end of the dining hall, I could see this girl wearing a pale orange dress with blood all down it. I thought, "Oh my goodness, what has happened?" It was not actually her eye; she'd been having a fight with somebody and she'd cut herself. I thought it was a deep cut and took her to Machame Hospital. A German doctor there said, "Oh, okay," and he just dressed it. I couldn't help thinking if she'd been a European I'm quite sure he would have put a stitch in it. Anyway, she survived.

There was the Mission hospital in Machame. But if they were really sick, we'd take them down to Moshi to the government hospital. There was the African hospital and the

European hospital. The European hospital was later called Kibo hospital and the African, Mawenzi, and as you can understand, Kibo was higher and Mwenzi was a bit lower. Yes, get those distinctions right!

Quite often after teaching I would take my fishing rod and go off down to the river and catch a trout for my supper. It was about a half hour walk. At that time a lot of the rivers on the mountain had been stocked with trout and scouts actually patrolled the river, so it was possible to catch a fish. In Moshi there was a Fishing Club and an annual competition. When the District Commissioner heard that I was catching fish, at the next fishing competition he said that if that girl catches one fish, I will catch a lot. So he went up there but didn't catch any fish. Nic had gone 'round to West Kilimanjaro and that year he got the prize for most fish.

Nic and the Vespa

When I was at Machame, my friend Pauline worked in the telephone exchange in Moshi. She had a difficult home life and two young brothers whom she helped care for. Pauline was English but had been born in America when her father was working there. Pauline really wanted to go to England where she felt she could get work. She hadn't had much education. The only thing she had was this Vespa that I presumed she had saved up for. She was my great friend and very fond of one of Nic's good friends and we did things together. Nic said he would like to buy her Vespa and he gave her more money than it was perhaps worth, which gave her enough money to get a ticket to England.

She later moved to America and married Thomas Tusher, who became president of Levi's jeans and they have been quite successful internationally. She has published her own story, My Journey In and Out of Africa *[2005]. We've kept up during the years and occasionally manage to see each other.*

A few years ago she wanted to come to Tanzania and we said "Lovely!" One of her brothers was in South Africa and came up to meet her. I took her around Moshi to see where they used to live. We went over to West Kilimanjaro because she had had great friends over there. The second evening we were sitting on the veranda and she said, "I want to tell you the real reason why I've come." She looked at Nic and said, "I wanted to come here and look you in the eye and say 'Thank you' for buying that Vespa, because that's what started me on the rest of my life."

Nic and Mwanza

I taught at Machame from 1957 to 1959. I had met Nic, my parents had met him, and it was obvious that we were quite fond of each other. I must admit he did stay rather late at night sometimes. My parents thought I would marry someone who was in the administration or.... I was not to marry a Greek sisal grower!

When Nic did come down to Amani for a night, he was talking to my father about opera. He was obviously talking about Maria Callas, whereas my father was talking about Kathleen Ferrier. Nic was well educated in Greece, as were all of his family.

Left–right: Tom Tusher, Nic, Sylvie, Pauline Tusher near the Kenya Tanzania border.

My parents were not very enthusiastic about this new boyfriend. The Greeks on the whole were more peasant people. My parents had known some Greeks in Tanga, but many of them spoke virtually no English, so communication tended to be in Swahili.

This relationship wouldn't do at all for my parents. When it looked like things were getting a bit more involved, my father talked to the colonial education people in Dar es Salaam. "I think my daughter should be moved." So she was moved to Mwanza, on Lake Victoria, a long way away. The poor girl who was there of course didn't want to leave her friends but she had to come to Machame. I was sent to Mwanza because that would obviously break up this relationship and that would be that.

I was told that I was to go. At first I didn't realize that my father had orchestrated this move. I said, "Oh, that is mean to make me move!" and I think Mummy said, "Yes, dear I know." She came up to Moshi and I was going to drive the car down to Dodoma and put it on the train. My mother came as far as Arusha. I think she was aware by then that Nic was going to drive with me down to Dodoma. Dodoma is right in the middle of Tanzania—it's the capital now. So I packed up my things and sent my cat off on an aeroplane to Mwanza, and I left. We drove down and stayed the night, then put the car on the train to go from Dodoma up to Tabora and then up to Mwanza.

Bwiru Girls' School, like Machame, went up to Standard Ten. It was near Mwanza but right beside Lake Victoria. I was given the house where the poor girl who had been moved to Machame had lived. The teachers were all very friendly. The first day I was in the staff room asking a lot of questions. Then I said, "Where does the night watchman sleep?" There was a roar of laughter. I wondered why they were laughing until one teacher explained, "We can tell you have been here a long time because you can't see what's funny about your question." The night watchman always did sleep at work, of course.

I had my house and they said, "Oh there's a girl who can come and work for you." Laziest creature I've ever met. In Mwanza, in the evening, lake flies like tiny midges would come in through the mosquito netting. In the morning you'd find a great pile of them. I told this girl to sweep them up, and she said, "If you'd just shut all the windows, you wouldn't have any." She didn't last long. I had another servant called Dowdi who was very nice, but one sad, sad day he let my precious cat Jemima out in the evening; she wasn't meant to be let out, and a leopard ate her. Quite a few leopards were around. Another evening my kitten was inside near a window, looking out. Suddenly all his fur stood on end and he growled. I looked out and a leopard was in the garden just a few feet away.

Sylvie with Jemima at Mwanza, 1959.

I was put in charge of the food store. That was a very challenging job because, when the previous person found she had too much of some particular thing, she'd just throw it away, which seemed to me a terrible thing. It seemed to me better to cook the books. So you see, corruption was not merely now, it was then as well in a different sort of way.

Mwanza was quite a small town. The sad thing was that we didn't swim in the lake because we were afraid of getting bilharzia. My mother some years before had only once been in the lake collecting mosquito larvae and she got bilharzia, which in those days was a horrible disease and not so easy to cure.

In Mwanza, like in many towns in Tanganyika, there was a Greek baker and I used to go to get my bread and try out my little bits of Greek. I was determined to learn Greek.

After several months Nic decided he would come to visit me. He and his friend Costa drove over the Serengeti to see me for a lovely weekend. They had quite an adventure getting there. Costa was taking photographs; at one stage, they got back in the car and drove on for about a half hour when suddenly Costa realized they'd left one of his lenses behind and they had to drive back and collect it. Another time Nic flew out to visit. Mwanza seemed a long way from everywhere. You could get on the train from Dodoma, but it was a long journey. You could fly, but it depended on the weather because the little airstrip could be underwater during the rains.

Peggy: Our last full year at Amani was 1959. Donald was longing to retire. He had so many financial worries to do with the running of the Unit, with the High Commission, WHO, UNICEF, and the local Treasury, and also with inefficient secretaries and various staff problems. He just felt that he could not cope any longer. At last, after long searching and perpending, his successor was appointed, Dr. Gerry Pringle.

The cattle were at long last a really paying proposition, there was plenty of milk to sell, the calves were healthy, and the paddocks were in good shape. No longer were the cattle herded all over the station to wherever there was enough grass for them. A year or two previously the bull became unable to serve cows, and it appeared he was suffering from hematuria, possibly due to his having eaten bracken. Dr. Press, the WHO chemist then working at Amani, said that he might be able to decide this point, which could possibly influence the treatment, if he could have a catheter specimen of the bull's urine. I asked Donald who would do it, but I knew the answer beforehand.

"But what am I to use?" I almost wailed. No difficulty it seemed. I should use a stomach tube. So rather apprehensively I found one, boiled it and set off to the cowsheds where Mningereza and two of the milkers threw and roped the bull. I had no idea of a bull's urinary anatomy and therefore did not know what a vet told me later, that the tube would have to turn a corner to enter the bladder. So I failed, and finally the bull had to be slaughtered and sold for meat and we got a new one.

We had a last gay Christmas. Oddly I remember nothing of sadness or regret at the prospect of leaving Amani, although I loved the place so dearly. Finally we prepared for packing and departure. All commitments were made, ducks and chickens killed, sold, or given away, Bob Smith was to have charge of the cattle and of the Bustani and Plantations. Our Persian rugs were shampooed, dried, rolled and packed. Some books were given to the Club. Our beloved cat Dony was dead and Faith (Fanny's daughter) was given to the Smiths. The servants came in for many of our less treasured possessions.

Last Safari

In March 1960, we drove down the hill for the last time en route for Uganda, where Donald had planned an extensive safari. We travelled then in great style. Besides our Humber Hawk we had a Land Rover and a truck and we took Abdallah and another servant. Our American guest Bob Voatney was with us. We went first to Gombero to make a final blood, spleen and anopheline survey. Then to Nairobi. We were up at 6 a.m. to go to the airport and get a plane to Mwanza [to visit Sylvie]. Back in Nairobi I was asked to give a lecture on Nepal. The British High Commissioner, Mr. David, asked us to drinks. Afterwards we all dined at the Muthaiga Club.

[Heading north through Kenya, toward Uganda] we had tea with the Vennings at Eldoret and then went to the Soy Club. Next day Donald fished all afternoon in the Swan River. We went to Kitale and lunched with Doris and Taxi Lewis.

On April 18, we arrived at the Kampala Imperial Hotel [in Uganda]. We met Abdallah at the station for a safari to Masindi [in Bunyoro District] Mr. Barnley (entomologist) and Dr. Ibanda arrived. [Heading northwest] at Kitamba the next day, 700 people turned up for examination. Donald examined 500 spleens and I took 300 blood films. We then worked at Bikonzi. About 700 people showed up again. It was a lovely place to work under good shade.

Then we worked at Mbale. Oh dear, what crowds! There was a most ineffective chief with no control over his people. What a contrast was Mugalama. A splendid chief organized everything with no crowding, noise or fatigue. There was a heavy rainstorm afterwards. Dr. Greenway appeared and we all had a good camp dinner in pouring rain. We were all in tents. Mr. Barnley had brought large beach umbrellas, which were put up over the fire and the pudding!

On April 29 we came to Mubende along a twisty switchback road terribly pot-holed. But the scenery was charming. Hills and great masses of grey rounded rocks and bracken. Dr. and Mrs. Greenway live at 1,000 feet above the plain.

On Sunday, 1 May, we arrived at Kampala and went to church in the morning, then went for a drink with Dr. and Mrs. Williams. We were off again with millions of butterflies on the road. We crossed the Namatala River by the ferry [travelling to eastern Uganda]. A long crossing, we saw lots of stilts, some little ducks, and lots of lily waders. It was the funniest old paddle-wheel ferry. Along the road later we saw many little grass shelters built over tops of ant heaps to facilitate catching flying ants as they emerged. They are greedily eaten just like that.

It was a lovely drive to Moroto. I don't think we saw another car. The plains and big rocky mountains reminded one of Maasailand. We saw our first Karamojong, very black and stark naked. We stayed in a nice rest house at Moroto [in northeastern Uganda]. At breakfast a stark-naked old beggar appeared at the door of the dining room. Very off-putting at breakfast time!

We went to Kangole Dispensary [northeast Uganda] and took bloods there. Most amazing headdresses the men had. All sorts of feathers, often just one black ostrich feather and some with huge chignons. Most had large silver or what looked like alabaster ornaments thrust through the flesh beneath their lower lip. A lot of women wore only a little chain mail apron, a small modesty affair. Both men and women wore many strings of beads.

Next we travelled to Kotido, which was much like Moroto. The people here are called "Jie." We went to a cattle auction that was not an auction, really, and there was only one buyer. In the evening we visited several manyattas, all very much like Maasailand. While the Jie were at a cattle auction, Karamojong raided them and stole a number of cattle and killed three unarmed Jie. We met three Jie armed with spears who ran away from us as they are not allowed to carry spears.

Next we drove to Moruita camp in grassy wooded country at the foot of a 10,000-foot spectacular mountain. A great number of people came to Katamangole where we did a survey. Then we [travelled southwest, along the border with Kenya] via Amudat to Karita. We saw many huge spleens. Then we drove on to Kitale to stay with Doris and Taxi for a lovely tea.

May 12 we were back to Kampala again. Then off to Entebbe [on Lake Victoria] and stayed with the Haddows and stained slides in Haddow's histology lab. Then back to Mubende where we did a lot of work. At a place near Mianzi, we had the LAST blood and spleen to do. We returned to Entebbe to the Haddow's. We packed for weighing all next morning, stained thin films in the lab, and said goodbye to Abdallah.

We arrived at Kaptagat [Kenya] at 8 p.m., in time for a good dinner and wonderful wine. I loved staying at the Kaptagat Arms, which is at 8,000 feet. It has lovely lawns and flower gardens and very good food. Then to Naivasha and on to Nairobi. We did some slides and gave the Manson-Bahrs dinner at the Equator Inn. More slides, more lunches and dinners with friends. Then came to stay with the Goddens at Limuru. Donald left to take the car to Mombasa. I lunched with the Goddens and Heisches at the Norfolk, a most incompatible party. [Sylvie explains, *the Goddens were farmers. I had stayed a night with them when I came from England in 1952, during the Mau Mau Uprising. When Mr. and Mrs. Godden went to change for dinner, I was left in the sitting room with a gun! Ronald Heisch was an entomologist who had worked with my parents and at Taveta*]. We stayed the night at Karen with the Heisches. *Most* uncomfortable. Joan took us to the airport to fly home.

Chapter 10

Death, Marriage and the Emmanuels: Being Greek in Tanzania

by Peggy Lovett Wilson and Sylvie Wilson Emmanuel

We arrived back in England in the summer of 1960, visited old friends, collected the Hawk and made our way back to Spa House in August. I painted the staircase as best I could. Back in July, while getting out of the car to look at the view from Box Hill in Surrey, I slipped on wet ground, fell, got all muddy and broke my right wrist. I had my wrist X-rayed at the local hospital. It showed no fracture but it was miserably painful. In November I got Donald to strap my wrist again. I had a course of diathermy at the R. United Hospital that did no good.

Sylvie: I taught at Mwanza for a year, until June 1960. During the holidays, I met Nic in Nairobi. Then at Christmas, I came back to Moshi because my friend Bridget and I were going to climb Mount Kilimanjaro. We started, but she was sick, so we had to come back. I sang with the Moshi Singers in a concert. I went to be with my family in Amani for Christmas, then returned to Mwanza.

When I was coming near the end of my tour at Mwanza, I decided to resign. It looked as though Nic and I might get married. Before I left, I had the chance to do escort duty at the end of term with the girls who were going to Ngara, on the western boundary of Tanganyika (near Rwanda). We arrived at Biharamulo and found that there was no bus. So I got permission to take the school lorry to Ngara, a fascinating drive. The girls were safely delivered to their families. I spent the night with friends who had a leopard cub, which was very nice as it was very small.

In Mwanza we had various expeditions. One of the nice ones was going in the boat across to a little island where a family kept cows and pigs and other animals. Another time, a whole lot of us went down to Shinyanga where the diamond mines are for the wedding of one of the African staff.

When I finished in Mwanza, Nic had already gone to Greece in January because his mother had cancer. He stayed with her until she died in May 1960, a few weeks before I arrived. So I saw him in Greece, and we were a bit on-off. I wrote to my parents, "Well, it's obvious that everything's finished." Apparently, there was great joy, and then the next letter was, "No, it's not off." I went to Switzerland and stayed with the Swiss cousins for a few days, then travelled on to England.

I'd left Mwanza, left the Colonial Service, and returned to England to teach at an English finishing school, but it just seemed pathetic after teaching African girls. The finishing school girls had money and clothes were important to them. They weren't really interested in learning. They were just there to enjoy themselves. It was quite interesting to see how the other half lives. The African girls I taught had wanted to learn. Of course, most were much younger, poor, and they had no background of social education. But these finishing school girls weren't reading books or doing anything very much. They played tennis. I remember thinking, "what a waste of time." But they paid me and that was useful. It was my job for just a few months.

Nic and I wrote letters to each other and it was decided: we were going to get married. Our plan was to get married in Moshi—there was no point in considering marriage in England because of how my parents were. It had to be a quiet wedding because of Nic's mother's death just a few months before. So he said, "Right, come out. It will be nice for you to come out just after Christmas."

It was a very unhappy time because I wasn't really communicating with my parents, although we were living in the same house. When Nic and I got engaged, I put it into the Times *and asked my father if he would like to see the paper. He said "No."*

My mother realized that she would lose me if she didn't make at least an outward change. So she said, "Let's go to London, darling, and get your dress." My father didn't want to see it.

Peggy: On 6 of December, Donald and I drove to London. Sylvie and I went to the Bridal Boutique in Putney and chose her wedding dress. She was to be married to Nicos Emmanuel as soon as he was out of mourning for his mother, who had died of cancer.

Sylvie and I went to *Tosca.* We shopped at Galeries Lafayettes and Liberty's. Martin Turner came with us to *My Fair Lady.* Afterwards, we had supper at the Cafe Royal. I almond-iced Sylvie's wedding cake. On the 16th we asked the Daveys to a fondue supper. On Christmas Eve Sylvie and I went to Midnight Services at Ditteridge. Christmas day, Donald was ill with a tummy, but came with Sylvie and me to dinner at Miss Harper's, feeling grim. On Boxing Day Sylvie and I went to a party at the Skrines in Bath.

Sylvie: We had a very quiet Christmas. The day after Boxing Day my mother, Mrs. Hucker and her daughter drove me to London for my flight.

On 27 December, Mrs. Hucker, her daughter Jean, Sylvie and I drove to London to see Sylvie off by air for East Africa. The next day was a quiet, unhappy day.

Sylvie: There wasn't much talk with my father.

Peggy: On 29 December 1960, Donald died after breakfast.

Sylvie: I arrived in Nairobi. There was Nic to meet me, and we were going to stay a couple of days. It was quite funny about an engagement ring. I had always thought I'd like an aquamarine and diamond ring. We started talking about it. Then Nic had to deal with his brother's car that needed things doing. We got wedding rings, but the engagement ring was never bought. Then we drove down to Moshi and Nic's brother said, "Your mother phoned." By then it was too late to call.

The next morning, Friday, I went to phone. I was sure that Daddy had died, because when I said good-bye to him I felt I'd never see him again. I actually thought he might have committed suicide. That was my fear. But he had a heart attack and died immediately. There seemed no point in postponing the wedding as it was to be very quiet anyway. And Nic's sister Helen had come out for the wedding, as had my sister Angela.

Nic and Sylvie at their wedding, December 31, 1960.

So on New Year's Eve, we went to the Hellenic Club in Moshi. The next day we were all at my brother-in-law's house for lunch and we were given presents—or I should say, I was. Our wedding was at the Orthodox Church and I couldn't understand a word. But one doesn't have to make any promises!

Then we gave out the wedding cake that I had brought from England, as well as the traditional bag of sugared almonds. Nic, Angela and I had lunch before leaving for Nairobi for Angela's flight back to England that night. Later, Nic and I went to the sisal factory to meet the "wazee" (the old or important workers) as well as all Makonde workers who cut the sisal (and made ebony carvings in their spare time). It's a shame there was no one with a camera as I was in my wedding dress and shook hands with them all.

There was no point in my going back to England for the funeral. Later, I felt so sorry that I didn't write much to my mother, but I had such a mixture of feelings then about my father, the beloved daughter who failed him. It was extremely painful.

Uncle Ashley said, "Your father was actually depressed." He was clearly depressed. I think he was kind of ready to die. He'd had angina, which I knew nothing about. Just the year before, he talked about going to America; he was going to rent a car to drive us right across America. I thought, ooh, fantastic, great fun. Then that stopped and he was going to write about malaria, but he just wasn't feeling up to it.

Those years in Amani were not easy. There was not much malaria work, which was what he was interested in. It was just so much travelling, dealing with building and difficult people. Perhaps when you had a vision, it's really very hard. Then his beloved daughter not going into the career he had envisioned. My father died when he was 59.

Peggy: All through this account, I have said practically nothing of my feelings. Great desolation of spirit came over me after Donald's death, caused by the knowledge that if I had been more understanding, if I had fully realized the depths of his mental and spiritual disease and suffering caused largely by his refusal to accept his beloved child's right to live her own life, and partly by his steadily worsening heart condition, I could have done so much to support and comfort him. But he shut himself away from me completely, and I didn't have the courage to break down the barrier of his isolation.

I think he was so unhappy that he wanted to die. When we came back to live in Spa House, to begin with, he made little plans about how he would write the book on malariology in East Africa, how he would use one of the attics as a study, and how we would have our after dinner coffee up there. But as the autumn went on, he seemed to know that he hadn't long to live, and arranged all his papers and business communications carefully.

He had wished to be cremated after death. Angela was out in Africa with Sylvie, but the Powells came with me to the crematorium in Bristol. Mic Gillies came, which touched me very much. After some time, I took Donald's ashes to Monkton Combe and scattered them into the river where he had spent some of his happiest times when at school there.

Sylvie: Great Aunt Gwendolyn was married to a Great Uncle Wilson. She was completely deaf. She loved to come to Amani and my parents were very good to her. "Which evening dress should I wear?" she would ask. After my father died, my mother sent her the obituary and she wrote to my mother:

> *The last few paragraphs (of the obituary) were very good. I love thinking it over and how true in life it was. I often think of him, how kind hearted he was, and no wonder he had so many friends who understood him and enjoyed his conversation. He was so very special, so very different from most people. You really mustn't blame yourself too much about his obsession with Sylvie's marriage as he had heart trouble and he was really over-doing himself. He wrote to me that he could not begin his book until he got the house as he wanted it to be.*
>
> *I think it is great that you should write everything up and I am sure eventually that it will bring more peace of mind to you. To have a settled occupation always seems to have that effect, even though at times it may seem to be difficult and a heartbreaking job. It is so good to know Donald was appreciated by his friends so deeply. Even as a little boy there was always something about him that was so attractive and that only increased as he grew older. So you are the girl he met at Birmingham—his mother told me that he proposed to you.*

Peggy: Angela had done a year's nursing at the Middlesex Hospital. When she came back from Africa, she didn't want to go on with the training but wanted to come to live at home with me to keep me company. I said all I could to dissuade her but she was quite determined. I was touched by her devotion and she was a great comfort to me, but it was really against my wishes.

I was very occupied during the spring and summer in writing two papers. One, on our final observations at Gombero, was published in the *Transactions of Tropical Medicine* [Wilson and Wilson 1962], and one on the results and findings of our last Uganda safari was published in the *East African Medical Journal.* These were the first papers that I had tackled on my own.

That summer we had the annual Church Fete in Spa House garden, complete with competitions, raffles, and tea. I think it was one of the last fetes of its kind to take place here in Ditteridge. We made a lot of money and everyone enjoyed it, not least Mr. Dancey, the grand old man of Ditteridge. I first then had trouble with my back and an X-ray showed the collapse of one of my lumbar vertebrae.

A nice young man named Jasper Jewitt who was working at Corsham Court in the

Arts department lodged with me for that summer and autumn. He would come rushing in at suppertime saying, "What can I do to help? I'll do anything, just tell me." Usually I would ask him to mash the potatoes for supper. I tried to make a successful cream caramel, his favorite pudding, and after one or two failures eventually succeeded pretty well.

Angela came back in the winter from a tremendous travel in Eastern Europe and Egypt and North Africa and was wildly jealous of poor Jasper. It spoilt the relationship and he soon went to live somewhere else.

Nic Emmanuel's Family Story: Being Greek in Tanzania

Sylvie points to her copy of J.P Moffett's Handbook of Tanganyika, *and his observations of the importance of Greeks, the second largest European community, to the country.*

> When the Germans embarked on the construction of the Tanga Line in 1892 it was to Greek contractors that the actual construction of the line was entrusted. Greek contractors also built the Central Line, begun in 1905 and finished just before the outbreak of war in 1914. Greeks were pioneers in the planting of coffee in the Northern Province (Mweka Coffee Estate, Moshi, was established in the 1890s), of rubber in the Tanga, Eastern, Central and Western provinces, of cotton and sisal in many of the places where they are grown now, of tobacco near Tabora and Iringa and, of more recent years, of papain in the Northern Province" [*Moffett 1958, 303*].

Nic Emmanuel was born in Tanganyika in 1925 and brought up in Moshi. His father Gregory had come to Deutsch-Ostafrika (now Tanzania) in 1906. Nic's nephew Gregory is Nic's brother Costas's son, named, like Nic's own son Gregory, after Nic's father. With the help of Nic's brother Dimitri, nephew Gregory assembled the following information on his grandfather Gregory's journey and settlement in Tanzania.

The Emmanuel family in Tanzania are descended from seamen in the Aegean Sea. Gregory was born on the island of Tenedos and attended the Grand National Academy in Constantinople, graduating in 1894. Trading his family's Tenedian wine, he made his way to the thriving Greek community in Egypt. There he worked as a house painter, boasting to Dimitri that he had his own ladder, and on a tramp steamer ferrying Muslims from Egypt to Jeddah on their pilgrimage to Mecca. He eventually worked as an engineer for the Suez Canal Company.

In Alexandria, Gregory met Constantine Meimaridis, a good friend from Tenedos, who persuaded him that there were good prospects in East Africa, especially in railway-related construction in the Kilimanjaro area of Deutsch-Ostafrika. An abundance of cargo was being landed in Mombasa, transported by train to Voi, then hauled by ox-wagon over a rough track through thick bush to Moshi, as there was no road or railway line connecting the two towns. But the ox-wagons couldn't haul very bulky or heavy loads. Meimaridis had purchased a steam traction engine, or road locomotive, and intended to take over the heavy transport business between Voi and Moshi, a distance of about 90 miles. He offered a partnership to Gregory, who accepted.

In about 1906, Gregory Emmanuel and Constantine Meimaridis sailed from Alexandria to Mombasa where the steam engine waited. They loaded everything on the train and went from Mombasa up the line to Voi, where they assembled the large machine with the help of an Indian mechanic. The machine was named Tinga-Tinga, a phonetic Swahili nickname derived from the pinging noises the large flywheel made as it turned. But Tinga-Tinga was too heavy and cumbersome to negotiate the primitive track. It often sank through the soft sand and got stuck, or it would smash through the crude wooden bridges at stream crossings, and in the rainy season it would get thoroughly bogged down in the viscous mud.

Around 1908, the two men dissolved the partnership. As compensation, Meimaridis gave Tinga-Tinga to Gregory, who put it to good use hauling heavy freight around the Moshi area, or sometimes using it as a tractor with farmers to plough their fields.

Gregory then became a successful contractor for the Dar-es-Salaam to Kigoma (on Lake Tanganyika) railway construction project. According to Nic's brother Costas, following the German defeat in World War, German properties in the Kilimanjaro area were seized by the British and administered by the Custodian of Enemy Properties (COE), who auctioned them off. In the early 1920s Gregory returned to the Moshi area, borrowing money from another Greek from Tenedos, Nicholas Christofis, who became his silent partner, and was awarded two farms.

Gregory lived at Chombo (in Moshi, near present day KCMC) where his first house had mud walls, an earthen floor, and a grass thatched roof. The house at Lambo was built of large river stones with a corrugated metal roof. A huge bougainvillea covered the whole front of the building and part of the roof. When Gregory took possession he found a large male lion snoozing under the bougainvillea. Fortunately it ran off into the bush when it realized there were people about.

In 1920, when he was 45 years old, Gregory returned to Tenedos to marry. On that trip he wrote a postcard to a friend in East Africa, telling him how hard it was to find a bride. However, on September 9, he married Irini D. Perrou, who was 24 years old. She was a refined, cultured woman, who spoke French and played the piano and had been a teacher at the school. She had also been educated in Constantinople. She returned with Gregory to Tanganyika.

According to Nic, "Father started in sisal after he came back from Greece. He had 500 virgin acres. He originally was growing coffee. Tanganyika was the world number one producer of sisal." The next year, Gregory tore down the mud house at Chombo and built a new one of cement blocks with a metal roof. During the course of the next four years Gregory and Irini had four children: in 1922 Eleni Lekanidou, in 1923 Constantine (Costas), in 1924 Dimitrios (Dimitris), and in 1925 Nicholas (Nikos).

With the 1923 Treaty of Lausane, the Emmanuels' ancestral homelands Tenedos and the Moskhonisia were formally ceded to the newly formed, ultra-nationalistic and militant Turkish state that replaced the moribund Ottoman Empire. During the pogroms and the exchange of populations between Greece and Turkey that followed, about 1.3 million Greeks left their homes in Asia Minor and sought refuge in mainland Greece and other countries. As a result, during the 1920s the Greek population of East Africa grew dramatically. A large number of Greeks, many from Tenedos and related to Gregory or Irini, came to Tanganyika, where Greeks became the second largest expatriate European community (Germans being the largest group). In both Moshi and Arusha, thriving Greek communities needed a Greek school. A Greek school was built near Moshi. Later a much larger school was built in Arusha.

Sometime in the 1920s Gregory acquired his first car. Nic recalls, "Father was a terrible driver but never had an accident. He believed in saving fuel—he drove from the coffee farm down to Moshi 12 miles without starting the car.

The Emmanuel Children in Athens During World War II

In 1933, Irini Emmanuel took her four children, Eleni, Costas, Dimitris and Nicos, to Greece to continue their schooling. They sailed on the Deutsch-Ostafrika Linie ship S.S. Usukuma. *The customary grand celebration, complete with fancy dress and a ceremony presided over by Neptune, was held as the ship crossed the Equator and they were given certificates to commemorate the event.*

In Athens the boys were enrolled in Athens College and the family leased a house at 163 Kifisias Avenue in Ambelokipi, in Athens. Gregory came to see them for short visit in 1937 and then returned to Tanganyika.

Three years later, on October 28, 1940, war came to Greece when the Italian Army invaded through Albania. Nic remembers, "The Germans were getting closer and closer to Athens, so Mother and my older brother went to the British Embassy and explained, 'we are here, my Greek husband is in Tanganyika, which is a British protectorate.' She asked for help getting her family back to Tanganyika. They said a ship was sailing from the port of Piraeus. 'If there is space available, you can go.'

"The British authorities eventually sent a message, 'There is a ship you might go on.' We were very happy. The day came. We had arranged for a taxi to come for us and carry our luggage. We were ready, expecting the taxi, the ship was in the port of Piraeus. Just a few minutes before the taxi was supposed to arrive we heard the air raid. There was an agreement that the Germans would not bomb Athens antiquities. When the air raid came we went up to the roof to watch. We saw a stuka, a well-known dive-bomber, heading to Piraeus. Soon we heard the bombing, and then the ship was sunk in the port. Those who got there early, died. That was the last chance of getting out of Greece.

"When the Germans occupied Greece we were ordered to take radios to a particular workshop. We had the PYE [British radio] frame made of wood. The Germans locked the mechanism so it wouldn't turn to anything but the Athens station, which they controlled. So I removed the back panel that they had sealed and there was a small screw to restrict movement.

"Every evening we would take the radio to the basement, remove the screw, and listen to BBC news bulletins and share the news with the neighbors. One boy would be outside keeping guard and somebody would be downstairs listening to news, making note of it and then distributing it among the neighbors. There was one awful night when the screw dropped. We could hear some shooting outside. There was great panic until we found it and were able to set the radio back to the German radio station. One night we heard the Germans chasing someone. We heard gunfire and ran down to replace the screw."

Nic continued, "I made two bottles of wine with grapes from a local farmer to be drunk after the Germans left Greece. I was worried that it might explode so I put them in a wooden box with the end shoved against the garden wall and left them until the end of the German occupation. Then we had a big celebration with the neighbors.

"We were cut off from father during the war. Father had financed us and suddenly that was it. We had a lot of relatives in Athens who helped as best they could, but we owed £10,000 at the end of the war and had to repay that.

"What prevented starvation was the Red Cross, who were given access to imported food. It was nothing to walk on the street and see people dying of starvation. The food was second-rate—dried beans eaten through and through with insects that were kept in a tin in the cellar. One morning I saw a dead rat in the beans. Yes, we knew about hunger. Yet we were very fortunate because Athens College gave us all scholarships so that we were able to continue with our education."

Sylvie recounts: Their mother sold her jewellery, then borrowed money from relations. Nic said that you'd see people just falling down in the streets and dying of starvation. We had a Greek friend whose grandparents both died of starvation. In Athens, it was terrible, all the things they saw.

Nic recalls, "We exchanged only five letters with Father through the Red Cross during World War II. After the war, there was only one way back to Tanganyika. We left Greece and went to Egypt and stayed a month. We got a lot of assistance and were eating well. When the time came we traveled on the Nile 25 days to Kilimanjaro. During that time we had to change our transport—there were sections for the trains, sections for boats. The final section was arranged for us to sail in a proper passenger boat from one end of Lake Victoria to the other, Uganda to Kenya, Kenya to Tanganyika. By the time we arrived in Tanganyika, we had gained weight!"

Irini and her three sons were finally able to rejoin Gregory in Tanganyika in 1945, after a separation of eight years. Their daughter Eleni and her family arrived in Tanganyika the following year.

Return to Tanganyika

Nic recounts, "When I returned to Tanganyika, I wanted to get a job. There was a Greek school, built by the Moshi Hellenic community where I was taken on as a teacher of English and athletics. I had studied English at Athens College. But I left teaching because father had another estate, Lambo, 16 miles from his proper estate, Chombo." Both farms were located in the foothills of Mount Kilimanjaro, just north of Moshi. Chombo was a fairly well developed coffee estate at Uru, while Lambo had been abandoned for some years, with just a few scraggly coffee trees in it, at Machame.

At that time their father Gregory worked the coffee farm at Chombo. After the war the price of coffee was very high and Gregory was able to pay off all the debts incurred by his family during the occupation. A partnership with his nephew, Stelios, to develop the property at Lambo had just ended with the completion of agreed-upon work. So his eldest son, Costas, took over as manager at Lambo. Nic observes, "Lambo estate was 2,000 acres and only 250 were cleared. The rest was bush; you could run across a lion, or a snake. My brother Costas killed a 5.5-meter long python and when he skinned it, the skin was about 20 inches wide and there was a small gazelle in its stomach. Once we saw six elephants. You had to get a bulldozer to destroy the large anthills. We had a good deal of work until we got a chain tractor and could cut them off, bit by bit, to get the queen."

Sylvie explains that Costas and Nic expanded the estate and planted much more sisal, then started the coffee. In 1950 with the Korean War, the price of sisal absolutely skyrocketed. When we were married, Nic was managing part of the estate where most of the coffee was grown, but he and his brother Costas were also managing the sisal.

Nic continues, "When the Greek ambassador came to Tanganyika he visited Kilimanjaro and we have a photo of him with Father. Mother died in 1960 at the age of 64, and Father returned to Greece in 1961. Both of them died in Greece. Father was a man of few words. He was compos mentis to the end." Gregory Emmanuel spoke Greek, Turkish, English, Swahili, and some French. On May 24, 1977, after a fall, he died from complications due to pneumonia at the age of 102.

Sylvie: Becoming Greek in Tanganyika

Soon after I met Nic, I decided that if you marry somebody of another nationality you should certainly learn their language. If an English woman marries a Greek man, the first language of the household should be Greek.

So I started learning Greek. We saw a lot of the Greek families and I was determined to learn. I bought a book but it was ancient Greek! Nic brought me another book and said, "If you're going to learn Greek you might as well learn what we speak." When we went out in those early days of marriage, at social gatherings the men would all be together on the verandah and the women together inside the house. Many of the older women couldn't speak any English and so you would have to speak to them in Swahili; it was most peculiar.

I'm very fond of Nic's sister. I first met her in Greece a few months before we were married. I'd started learning Greek and was very nervous. She opened the door and I said, "Kalimera." She was so surprised that I greeted her in Greek. After a few glasses of wine my Greek started getting better and I, less nervous.

So I learnt Greek. I think this pleased my father-in-law, who was there at our wedding. Nic's sister had come out just for that. They were a bit concerned about Nic marrying an Englishwoman. But Greek became the language we used with each other, which sometimes made it difficult because there were a lot of words I didn't know. Yet Nic never ever teased me or made fun of me. That was one reason some of the people I know who were married to Greeks never did learn. But I felt it was important, as we were so often with a group in the big Greek community, and if you weren't able to speak Greek, you were really rather isolated.

I always got on very well with Nic's family. Nic's father was very good to me. He was only in Tanganyika for a few months after we got married because the family felt that after his wife died he should go to Greece. We saw him in Greece when we went on holiday there, and he always sent cards for the children's name days and Christmas and so on.

Nic's family in Tanzania were all very friendly. We were very fond of Nic's oldest brother Costas and his wife Ketty, who was Greek, so I saw a lot of Ketty and her children. Nic's middle brother Dimitri had an English wife; they weren't actually here for long because they went back to Greece. I was very fond of Nic's cousin Thespina. She taught me to make filo pastry.

I write a bit of Greek, though very little. I could read stories to the children, but I must admit I was lazy. I never really carried it on so that I could read a newspaper or pick up a novel and read it.

Our children are trilingual because they speak Swahili as well. Sophia was interesting; when she was about two and a half, she stopped speaking Greek. She understood it, she just wouldn't speak it. I think it was because she was a perfectionist, partly, also she didn't have other Greek-speaking children around her. That makes a huge difference. Later, she became more Greek than the Greeks. In the International Baccalaureate she earned the highest distinction in Greek and she studied Greek at university.

There were cultural differences that we had to overcome, however. For instance, the Greeks didn't bother unduly about Christmas. New Year was important. For me Christmas was important with the Christmas tree and the candles. The Orthodox Easter is often at a different time from the Roman Catholic or Anglican Easter, so I would do hot cross buns for our Easter and then do the other things for the Orthodox Easter. We'd often have a lamb done on the spit or we'd go to somebody else's house who did because that was the tradition.

Peggy: In 1962, I was treasurer at Ditteridge Church, a job I didn't like at all, but after Donald left me I decided that as far as I could, I would take on anything I was asked to do. I couldn't manage to balance the budget, but when I went away, kind Mrs. Ody took it on with complete success.

I was also Diocesan Representative on the Church Council. At a meeting in Chippenham, a Canon talked about the great need for doctors at the Mission hospitals of the Transkei. I wrote and offered my services for a limited period. I was tired of giving First Aid lectures and I thought I might as well go out to South Africa and perhaps relieve some Mission doctor for a while, even if I only took on a few clinics. I did not feel capable of doing much more and my ill-knitted right wrist was very painful. I could barely write. I had consulted a man in Birmingham, said to be an authority on old wrist fractures. He was entirely unhelpful and said that I had traumatic arthritis for which no one could do anything and he would give me a splint.

However, I went to London and saw the Mission authorities and was appointed to work at a Mission hospital in the Transkei at the magnificent salary of £1,300 a year, to be paid mostly by the Health Authorities in Pretoria. I was told that all household requirements would be provided. I decided to go first to stay with Sylvie and Nic in Moshi.

Sylvie: My mother came round completely to Nic, and was very fond of him. She came here to visit us. That was a very happy relationship. My sister also came and stayed with us. For a time, Angela and her husband were living in Nairobi because he was lecturing there and that made it easier for them to come here and us to go there.

Peggy in South Africa

I flew to East London [South Africa], spending a night in Johannesburg. It seemed a long, long, journey and we flew through a terrifying and most spectacular thunderstorm.

Then I had a long bus journey to Umtata where I was met by a nurse who worked at the Mission. It seemed quite a big hospital, quite out in the country, with hills and little streams all lined with arum lilies. I was greeted by the woman doctor superintendent who was impressive and apparently most competent, not collapsing from overwork but very happy in her job. I was given a bungalow, engaged a woman servant, and laid in some stores. The hospital was St. Barnabas and the Superintendent was a Dr. Lutwyche. The patients were Xhosa women, very poor and very primitive. Some walked for twenty miles to bring their children to the hospital.

Dr. Lutwyche drove her Land Rover for miles on shocking roads to her weekly clinics and when she returned, often late in the evening, would see and treat the in-patients and examine X-rays, mostly chest ones taken by the native assistant. It was a countryside so very different from East Africa. There were great open spaces with purple hills in the distance, small collections of native huts, and apparently no wildlife at all. Many natives had ponies and some had small herds of cattle. I went round the wards with Dr. Lutwyche on her rounds. I gave one or two anesthetics, finding my painful right wrist a terrible handicap, and I examined a class of nurses as to general fitness.

The staff of white nurses were very friendly and I thought after ten days or so I should be asked to go out on the district and see patients at the weekly clinics. But one morning Dr. Lutwyche said, "I am afraid I can't employ you. Nothing can replace general medical experience, which you have not got, and I have no time to teach you. So I want to give you this cheque for your services while you have been here. I really wanted a male surgeon."

I felt as if I had been hit on my solar plexus. I wrote to Sylvie, "I have to leave here and I'm bitterly sad and humiliated, but the truth is that my hearing is not up to it. I simply cannot hear deviations from the normal in the lungs (with the stethoscope) and since most of the work is chest TB, I just cannot do it. No amount of common sense or clinical acumen can make it work when standards are so high it just won't work."

I occupied the next day or two in making brief anopheles larval survey of the furrows and ditches near the hospital. I decided to fly back to Moshi and I got a lift to East London [South Africa] where I boarded a plane. I had a marvelous dinner at a hotel in Johannesburg with some very good local white wine. As Donald would have said, I needed something to comfort me! I stayed first in Kenya with the Vennings at Eldoret, and on New Year's Eve, went with the Vennings to a party at the Kaptagat Arms. They all said it would probably be the last time they would all gather there to see in the New Year.

General Krishna

I decided to accept the warm invitation given me by General Krishna and the Princess to visit them in Bangalore, so on the 7th January, I flew by Comet to Bombay via Aden and Karachi. General Krishna sent his courier to meet me and the next day I boarded another plane and flew to Bangalore. I was put up in a hotel in Bangalore, not a very nice one, but I didn't spend much time there.

It was splendid to see them again, both so well and enjoying life. That evening we had drinks at the Bangalore Club. Krishna drank whiskey and so did I and the Princess would have one small brandy. It reminded me very much of the Willingdon Club in Bombay. I really enjoyed seeing the Indians on their home ground, so to speak.

It was very much like the Clubs when the British were in command. Yet what struck me most was the quiet—no raised voices, no shouting and laughing, except in restrained voices. The absence of alcohol had much to do with this. To have alcoholic drinks, one had to go into the Permit Room, rather dark and depressing and I must say I missed the conviviality of the old days. All the ladies wore charming saris and talked in soft voices over tea and soft drinks on the lawn or in the lounge.

Another day we had tea with General Mohan, Krishna's eldest brother, then a white-haired old gentleman who went to live in Bangalore when he had to give up being Maharaja. We had dinner at the Jewel Box. The dining room was so dark that one couldn't see what one was eating. We went by car to Mysore and stopped at Seringapatam, a place full of eighteenth century history and ghosts of the Nawabs. We also visited the Summer Palace with wonderful floodlit gardens and fountains at Brindaban. Why did it all seem so melancholy I wonder?

A day or two later we flew to Madras in a Fokker Friendship plane and stayed in a fine hotel near the beach. Boris, who ran the main hotel in Kathmandu then, was staying there; I had always wanted to meet him. On our several expeditions we saw the five temples built in honor of the brothers who all married the same wife, and at Bahadurpura we saw the famous Shore Temple. For me there was much interest in the Fort Museum [Fort St. George] with its many relics of Clive's day [colonial figure Robert Clive, Commander-in-chief of British India] and also seeing his house and the Church he was married in [St. Mary's Church, oldest Anglican church in India].

I flew to Coimbatore to stay with the Chris Allens on the tea estate where he worked in a place called Mudis via Pollachi. Coimbatore really was a ghost town, especially the old Club where we had lunch. One could put oneself back a hundred years with great ease. The old long cane chairs, the few moldy books, the ancient bearer who served our drinks and lunch.

We set off up the hills to the estate, sadly by-passing the famous Ooty, which in the end I never saw. What a road to Mudis, 4,000 feet up and 40 hairpin bends. The ten turns on the road to Amani paled to insignificance. The Allens had a charming bungalow in the hills set in a lovely garden of green lawns and flowerbeds. This was just at the time of the little war with China and there was much talk of it and much sewing of pajamas and rolling of bandages for the troops, all unneeded, I believe. The weather was perfect, warm and sunny, and the servants were the inimitable old-fashioned types, most concerned with our comfort.

My hostess, Bobby Allen, wasn't at all well as she had sprue [coeliac disease], but she didn't let it hamper her much except that she couldn't have any alcohol. The Allens opened their one and only bottle of scotch for me which was wonderful of them as it is almost unobtainable and wickedly expensive, about £6 a bottle then. Bobby took me by car to a teak forest where we saw elephants moving and stacking huge logs on the word of command.

Back in Bangalore, the Krishnas gave a delightful dinner party with an Indian Air Vice-Marshal and his wife and also a Major Chandery and a Brigadier Divai, all charming people, relations by marriage of General Krishna. For the first time, and I expect the only time in my life, we ate off gold plates. I was terrified of damaging the soft gold with my knife and fork.

The last day of my visit we drove to the Nandi Hills. It was a very hot afternoon. The Princess had taken a tea picnic, which we had on the terrace of the building. Then next day I left and was so sad at saying goodbye. I flew to Bombay in a Fokker Friendship and then in a VC 1 via Karachi, Teheran, Cairo and Zürich.

General Krishna and the Princess near Rome.

Sylvie: My mother's visit to General Krishna helped salve the wounds of the terrible experience in South Africa, and perhaps prepare her for the adventures to come.

I met General Krishna and the Princess for the first time when I went to England in 1972 with the children. We were invited with my mother to have lunch with them at the Ritz. It was very special to meet them at last.

I had wondered what the children would eat, but the Krishnas had ordered a perfect menu for them and a different one for us. Sophia and Rena wore their smocked and embroidered dresses and everyone turned to look at the well behaved little girls as they walked through to the Ladies Room.

After lunch we went up to the Krishna's suite and the children were given a box of chocolates and a £10 note each. "Oh, oh thank you," said Gregory, so delighted that now he could buy the Scalextric he longed for.

Chapter 11

The 1960s in Tanganyika, Peggy to The Gambia and Magila

by Peggy Lovett Wilson and Sylvie Wilson Emmanuel

Angela met me at Heathrow with her car. It was a dark, foggy, snowy day. I was dead tired and slept until 10:30 a.m. In mid–February, Angela and I went to Honiton to stay with Rosie. The road was very bad with hard packed snow. The icy weather went on until the end of February. Then the thaw set in.

Sylvie: Nic had been living with his brother Costas and wife Ketty at Lambo, Machame. Then they bought the part of the estate where we are now—it included the house where we live. The Germans who started the coffee estate built the house in the 1920s. Apparently the two people didn't get on very well, so it was a rather peculiar house, because it had two entrances. In the typical way of these old German houses, the rooms were fairly small.

A year or two before it was built, the German came to my father-in-law and asked if he could borrow one of the rails they used for drying the sisal. My father-in-law lent it, and later asked to have it back. The German said, "Oh I'm sorry, but I built it into the cellar of my house." So when the Emmanuels bought that part of the estate, my father-in-law said, "Now I'll get my rail back!"

The house had been used for maize storage for some years by their neighbour Jock Taylor. Nic put it back as a house and was then living on his own. He knocked down one wall, making the sitting room and dining room all in one. When I came to live here, it was already a very nice house.

After several years Philipi came to work for us, partly as a cook but also in the garden. He has been a wonderful presence. When their children were older his wife Dafrosa also came to work for us. She is a pearl. Then I started on the garden. Nic had already brought some plants back when he visited my parents at Amani. Soon after we were married we got some roses and I gradually expanded the garden.

Before we were married, we discussed children and talked about the church because

Nic was Greek Orthodox although not practicing. I'd said I would become a member and Orthodox, but there never seemed any point because the priest seldom came to Moshi. The priest wasn't very communicative and the services were all in Greek, which I didn't understand because it wasn't modern Greek.

Our son Gregory was born on May 1, 1962. Nic asked his brothers if they would mind if he was called Gregory as their sons were both called Gregory. No problem. That was the traditional way it was done.

In January 1964, Sophia was born. Just a week later, the Tanganyika Army Mutiny was in Zanzibar and for a short time, the threat to Nyerere. I wondered what would happen if we had to leave suddenly. What should we take with us? The children, the new baby, enough nappies...

In 1968 Rena was born. Her proper name is Irini, after Nic's mother.

Before Sophia was born, Maria, our ayah, came to work for us. A great treasure for many years, she loved the children and played with them but was quite strict as well. Maria stayed in the house beyond the vegetable garden where Philipi and Dafrosa are. I remember the first time she went with us down to Jadina Hotel off the coast with the children. She enjoyed it so much.

We only went to England and Greece occasionally as it was expensive. The first time Nic and I and Gregory went was in 1963. It was summer and very hot, so we let Gregory take his shirt off in the park. The various Greek mothers or grandmothers who saw us, Gregory just with his little pants on and nothing else, said "But surely he must be cold!" I said, "Do you really think he's cold in this heat?"

When Gregory was three and a half, I started taking him to Moshi kindergarten for a couple of days a week. That first morning was the longest morning in my life. Then Sophia started. There were very good teachers at the Moshi kindergarten. Gregory's teacher when he was five was Jerene Mortensen, Greg Mortensen's (Three Cups of Tea) *mother. Then, Sophia had Jerene's lovely sister-in-law Sharin Doerring. Marilyn Walters, an American teacher whom they both had, has remained a good friend.*

They used the Scott Foresman readers. Sophia read just like that! *They'd give them papers for spelling tests and she put them in her pocket. She never bothered to look at them and always did well. She brought her reading book home one day and said, "Shall I read to you, Mummy?" I said, "Yes, please, darling." She got out her book and she said, "The tydle is..."*

I said, "What did you say?"

"The tydle is..."

I had never used the word "tydle." Of course, she had got the American usage of the word "title," which was very amusing.

After some time I was working at the kindergarten as bursar with the great salary of 199 shillings and 50 cents a month. (If it were 200 shillings, then it would have been taxable.) We decided that when the children were old enough, we would send them to the Greek school, St. Constantine, in Arusha. This was very painful because the idea of sending a six-and-a-half-year-old to boarding school did not appeal, but we wanted them to have the Greek.

Nic had already started teaching each of them Greek so that they could go into Class II rather than doing the first year there. With Sophia it was a little bit different. Nic wanted to teach her to read and write Greek, so they had a secret; they would go into the study and she would have her lessons. When she went to the Greek school she could read and write and then she had to start speaking it as well.

When they were going to school from home, both for kindergarten and secondary school, there was the daily driving them to school. Sometimes doctors' wives from Machame Hospital were taking their children and we could share, but there was a lot of driving. One time when both Gregory and Sophia were at International School in Moshi and Rena was still in Arusha, I was taking Rena back on a Monday morning. I'd arranged for somebody to pick up Gregory and Sophia but he didn't appear. Nic was away out at the beans, so Gregory saw the tractor and drove himself and Sophia to school on the tractor! When he arrived, the deputy said, "A little late I think, Gregory!" When I went to collect the children at lunchtime, I thought, "That's funny, in the car park, that looks like one of our tractors." Sure enough, it was.

Peggy: On 21 April my back began to ache and I was deadly tired. I had a long spell in bed and then Sylvie, Nic and Gregory arrived. I had a return of dysentery so took a course of entamide, which cured it in time. However I had a wretched few weeks; I was suffering crush fractures of my lumbar vertebrae, and having to get out of bed often was extremely painful. I finally asked my doctor Jim Davey to come and see me.

He was puzzled, as well he might have been, and advised me to get physiotherapy at the hospital between Corsham and Chippenham. I crept downstairs and to the garage in great pain and drove there, but it was a waste of time as I couldn't do any of the exercises advised. The pain finally got less and on Denis Powell's prescription, I was fitted with a steel and leather back support, which was a great comfort.

At home in Machame (left–right, seated) Sophia, Gregory and Rena, with Sylvie and Nic.

All through the year and indeed since I fractured my right wrist in the autumn of 1960, it was so painful that I could barely write, so as a last hope, I asked Denis Powell (Donald's cousin) if he could help me. I could see for myself that my wrist was out of alignment but until I went to see Denis, no one I consulted held out any hope. Denis was my last hope. Thank goodness, I went to him. He saw immediately what needed doing, and did it, on 17 July at High Wycombe. It was a good functional result and soon I had an almost painfree wrist. How tremendously thankful I was to Denis.

In mid–December Peter and Chris Allen, aged about 13 and 16, arrived from their boarding school for the Christmas holiday. We enjoyed their time here and so did they. I gave a punch party at enormous expense but it was terrific fun. About twenty people came. I had the drawing room much too hot and the punch was hot too. The boys, especially Chris, had lots of fun in measuring and mixing the tea, brandy, rum, spices, orange, and lemon, and it was a very potent and delicious brew. Rather hesitantly I had invited our neighbor, a duchess, but she came and I think enjoyed herself.

In 1964 I was asked by Dr. Lesley Sitwell if I would take medical charge of Magila Hospital [near Tanga, in eastern Tanganyika] during her home leave from June to November. To say that I was taken aback and dismayed is putting it mildly.

Although I had always greatly loved clinical medicine, since my Nepal days I had really had little to do with it. My work has always been with tropical medicine as concerned with microscopy, parasitology and entomology with anopheles mosquito. I really didn't know what to answer. I began by asking Lesley in my first letter whether she couldn't possibly find someone else more suitable. She replied immediately saying "There is absolutely no one who could come and do my leave." She went on to say that the African medical assistants were very good and that the hospital almost ran itself with the excellent nursing staff of nuns, that it was a nursing school for Africans, and there were about 140 beds. I was frightened of taking it on but also very tempted and not a little flattered at being asked. It helped somewhat to restore my self-confidence after the jolt given to it in South Africa. So I finally promised to do it.

Just after that I had another surprise. Our great friends the Moreaus, who had spent a bird-watching holiday in The Gambia, rang up to say that Dr. McGregor, the director of the Medical Research Council's [MRC] unit in The Gambia, wanted me to work with him and would get in touch with me. Sure enough, I was contacted from the Medical Research Council's headquarters in London by a doctor Hopwood who asked whether I would be prepared to go and work in The Gambia. I said that I had already promised to take charge of a mission hospital in Tanzania until November and presumed that closed the matter. When Dr. Hopwood had a reply from Dr. McGregor, he rang me again (most extravagant these long calls from London, I thought!). "No, the matter was not necessarily closed," he said, "for Dr. McGregor is still determined to have you!" Well, I thought, Dr. McGregor certainly knows his own mind where I am concerned.

Dr. McGregor wished to know whether I would be able to go to The Gambia from April to June to see whether I like the country enough to work there. Would I go to the head office of the Medical Research Council and meet Dr. Hopwood and talk about it. I went and was captivated by a few photos showing the visiting workers' mess, a double storied white building on a low cliff, and the Atlantic Ocean right below with a lovely sandy beach. "Yes," I said, "I will certainly go in April for two months (on approval, I thought to myself)."

"And about salary," said Dr. Hopwood. "I suppose you'll have to be on the top grade." He said this somewhat resentfully I thought.

I wrote to Sylvie in February 1964, quoting from Dr. Ian McGregor's letter of invitation. "If you find conditions to your liking the way is open for us to arrange a more long-term collaboration, my main interest is to have on the station a senior worker who is experienced in the clinical aspects of malaria. Most of my staff are short term junior medical officers and it would be advantageous for them to have a more senior person to whom they could refer for advice when I am out of the station." Dr. McGregor is the head of the Medical Research Council laboratories for Fajara, The Gambia. I am beginning to feel a stirring of excitement.

At last I have the chance to do what I have hankered after so many years.

Journey to The Gambia, April–May 1964

Dear Angela took me to Gatwick. I flew to Bathurst [now Banjul, capital of The Gambia], stopping the night at Las Palmas [Spain] where I drank two or three excellent Tio Pepes [sherry] before dinner. I was keenly interested in my first sight of West Africa—how very hot, how very flat. Dr. McGregor met me at the airport, called Yundum. All the Africans spoke English, the airport officials and the Medical Research Council African staff. Ian McGregor and Joan were most friendly and welcoming and asked me to lunch. Their garden was a blaze of flowers: phlox, zinnias, petunias and many colors of hibiscus, oleanders, frangipanis, bougainvillea. I felt quite at home.

I'm all of atremble because when I stop and think of it, I feel old and weak and inadequate for what I have been engaged to do and I'm afraid of the heat. I also want desperately to prove myself adequate. But if I'm unable to stand up to it, I shall just accept the fact and so will the MRC.

I began to teach the young doctor who is in charge of the small hospital and with whom I shared the visiting hospital mess; I have been teaching him about malaria parasites, but he also has been teaching me a great deal about clinical medicine and lending me books so I won't be at such a loss when I get to Magila and it will help me in the work there. I also have a beautiful amplified stethoscope that I can hear with; I heard from Dr. Sitwell and her leave will continue until December 9.

Do you know that I am absolutely convinced that your father has been allowed through the Almighty about arranging this part of my life? I have always wanted: A. a job no matter how humble given to me on my own merits and, B. a chance to do some clinical medicine. Both have been given to me and both have been, at this late hour, handed to me as if it were on a plate. While I hope I still have the strength to do them, at this questionably humble job, I expect I am the best-paid next to the director.

I am "on call" at the hospital, which means that I am sitting comfortably under the fan with a drink and don't fancy I will be called; I am happier than I have been since 1960. This has been such a boon to my morale as it was sadly lowered by the unfortunate South African incident, and if I can hold it down, however briefly, I find it delightful. But oh dear, my poor brain is being so stretched that I get a real headache. Dr. McGregor is so pleased to have someone that he can discuss his subjects with. He is writing a paper on some aspects of malarial immunity. He has finished the first draft, now is amplifying the second draft. It is a very stimulating paper and has convinced me of the reasons for writing it, but I have had to catch up on four years of reading in a month to be able to criticize it adequately; I wish that someone had done this for me over my Gombero paper.

I gathered that my work would be examining and staining blood films and identifying and counting malaria parasites. As this was what I had done in East Africa over so many years, I found no difficulties. Everything was made easy for me and the technicians were friendly and helpful.

I slept on the ground floor of the visiting workers' mess. This large, much altered building had been constructed by the Germans after World War I to house their Lufthansa staff between their flights to South America. With its gray metal walls inside it reminded me of a battleship; there was a large comfortless sitting room *cum* dining room. Mrs. Adah Fletcher, wife of OC vehicles, ran it and a cadaverous looking Gambian called Bryma (derived supposedly from "Abraham") cooked and cleaned. The food was mediocre and we never had anything fresh, although fish was abundant and fruit and vegetables were obtainable. Like all Gambian cooks, Bryma made great use of onions, which grew so well, and the frying pan worked overtime.

I was very cross with myself one evening. One or two of the nurses and their boyfriends were talking and laughing just outside my window, about midnight. I didn't say anything but when they stopped and I thought now I can go to sleep, the little old night watchman began to sing. Very annoyed, I called out to him to be quiet. He said, "I sorry, I no sing again."

I had a bench in a Bog Lab, which was about 400 yards from the Staff House, and I walked there at 8:30 a.m. and again at 2:30 p.m., getting back to the Staff House about 4:30 p.m. It was a very hot walk in the blazing sun. Ian McGregor, bicycling past me one day, said, "This is about as hot as it ever gets here." "Thank heavens for that," I said.

On Sunday morning I went to the church only a few yards away. It had been built as a temporary thing to serve the troops stationed there in Hitler's war. After tea I sometimes went down the steps to the beach.

At the end of the two months, I asked Ian if he wanted me to come back after I had finished with Magila Hospital. He was quite definite that he did. I flew back to England, repacked, and in ten days was off again to East Africa. I took a taxi at great expense from Tanga to Magila, about 20 miles (50 shillings).

Magila, Tanganyika, June–November 1964

Lesley Sitwell seemed delighted to see me. I was to live in her bungalow and employ her servant. She asked if I would like a bath and the old "boy" Paulo was told to bring hot water. Oh dear, the bath was a G.I. dhobi bath [washerman's tub]. As it was not so long since my spinal collapse, I found it quite impossible to curl myself into it. I thought I would have to resign myself to washing in a basin all the time I was there. However when the Reverend Mother was told, she kindly said that unless the Bishop was in residence, which he rarely was, I might use the new bathroom, which had been built for him. The poor nuns had no such luxury.

I was introduced to Miss Agnes Hayes of the Girls Education Department of the Mission, a charming woman with whom I quickly made friends. She and I were the only lay people. There were about 25 nuns including a few African nuns who lived separately from the whites.

My day began with breakfast in the nun's refectory. Miss Hayes and I sat at a table by ourselves. We kept the rule of silence at meals. When the Reverend Mother rose to say grace the nuns had to stop eating, but Miss Hayes and I had a dispensation to finish our meals after grace if we were not ready in time. Directly afterwards the Infirmary nun would ask me to see and prescribe for any sick nuns. Then I went back down the hill to my bungalow and collected my white drill coat and stethoscope. Then further down the hill to the hospital. There were three large wards, each holding about 40 beds. My first duty was to read the non-denominational prayer in Swahili in the ward in which I was going to see every patient that morning.

The great majority were women and children. There were several smaller male wards and an isolation ward. The wards were light and airy and the nuns who were trained nurses supervised the work of the male medical assistants and the female African nursing trainees. Several of the nuns could and did give anesthetics. Dr. Sitwell did all necessary surgery that was within her powers, but my surgery went no further than opening abscesses or on occasion, emptying a uterus after an incomplete abortion. All the midwifery took place in a building separated from the general medical and surgical wards. It was under the complete control of a wonderfully competent nursing obstetrician called Sister Edith Frances. There were hardly any difficult cases that she could not cope with. She was not allowed to do Cesarean sections, not being a medical specialist, but when the need was urgent she got the Indian surgeon from Muheza Government Hospital to come. I gave the anesthetics with inward trepidation as one of the surgeons who came was so extremely slow that it took ages to sew up the patient.

On occasion patients refused my care, saying that they wanted to wait until Dr. Sitwell returned from leave and be operated on by her. I remember a woman who had an ovarian cyst and whose belly increased in size week by week, about an inch a week. I was not particularly worried about her, knowing it to be a benign condition, and wait she did.

I examined and assessed and prescribed for every patient. Also I saw any new cases admitted to any ward at any time. There was no stint of drugs, which was wonderful, and if one knew a patient needed a course of the more expensive, that patient had it. Clinically I was not very often at sea. Most of the complaints were so typical and so well established that the diagnosis was easy.

The single laboratory result I laid most stress on was the white cell count. It was quite invaluable and a tremendous help in diagnosis. I had a good deal of trial and error in some cases, specially in skin diseases—never my strong point. If I could hit on some application without having to make use of the expensive cortisone drugs locally or systemically, I was very pleased. I had several cases of severe heart failure; to be able to treat them successfully and get rid of their edema using diuretics, and then stabilizing them with digoxin, was most satisfactory. There were cases of smallpox, some of them very ill indeed, much typhoid fever that I treated with chloramphenicol and mercifully had no complications, much tuberculosis, quite a number of neonatal tetanus. I had no serum but even if I had, I expect many would have died. A man brought in one evening was in almost continuous spasm. I anesthetized him and stopped the spasms, but before we could pass a food tube and catheter, to my sorrow, he died. It may have been my fault. With regard to anesthetics, one of the sisters called urgently one morning to tell me that a little child she was anaesthetizing had stopped breathing. It was the first time I had occasion to use the Kiss of Life, but to my relief it worked perfectly.

Mid-morning there was a cup of tea for me in the office and a tin labeled "Doctor's Biscuits." The nurses working in the hospital hid themselves in a sort of closet and ate most unappetizing pudding leftovers, poor dears.

One morning a magnificent Maasai elder came seeking medical advice. Also came his wife and one or two tall slim Morani, his sons to support him. There was a lot of talk about the amount of milk that they wanted the hospital to provide and how much meat could they expect! The nun Sister didn't approve of them at all, they were so very pagan. I had an animated chat about places like Lolkisale and Loitokitok, which they were delighted to hear that I had been to. They were in a side ward, which they had to themselves.

Lunch was eaten in the nuns' refectory, again in silence. One of the nuns could read aloud from some theological or missionary book. The food was quite adequate but I had the gravest doubts about the kitchen cleanliness. Judging from the severe tummy upsets I fairly often suffered, I imagine that it left much to be desired. It worried me that the nuns used the same plate for meat and pudding. I asked Miss Hayes whether I should present the community with a set of pudding bowls but she said that if I did I should be gratefully thanked and they would be put away but never used, so there seemed no point in wasting my money. My pay was 50 shillings a month, a great contrast to the salary I had in The Gambia.

Two or three afternoons each week I had to lecture to the African trainee nurses. Lesley Sitwell had typed out a complete course of lectures, but I had to set the amount of work they did and examine them on it. I was soon in despair for I could not hear a single word of their replies to my questions, they all spoke so quietly and indistinctly and my hearing was not as acute as it formerly was. At last I was driven to making them write the answers to my questions. It worked quite well and at the end of their course they all passed. Sometimes I did get comical and unexpected answers. To a question asking them to state some of the causes of headache, instead of fever, meningitis, brain tumor or whatever, I got "thinking too much," "studying too much" and such, with never a mention of the illnesses which might cause the symptoms.

They were nice girls, and so were the few male nurses, nice and intelligent. One of the latter was really very good indeed. On the suggestion of one of the Sisters, he described excellently a case of smallpox in his charge, which he cared for efficiently. It was published in the *Nursing Mirror*. I spent a good deal of time in the little laboratory teaching the very intelligent African in charge how to recognize the different species of malaria parasites and adjudication in the cross-matching of blood for transfusion. Their microscope was not very good.

Occasionally I would go to Vespers in the Chapel and then to my bungalow to bed. I found that Dr. Sitwell had no bedside lamp and neither was there one in the laboratory which could be used to throw light on the mirror of a microscope. I remedied both deficiencies on one of my rare visits to Tanga in the hospital Land Rover.

There were a few cases at Magila that I remember with shame and misery. I just could not find out what was the matter with them. A high swinging temperature was common to them and it did not come from tuberculosis, typhoid, brucellosis or anything else, so far as I could make out. It went on and on and eventually they died from sheer weakness and lack of desire for food. I longed, more than words could say, for some knowledgeable advice, but there was no one who could give it to me. But those cases were very few, perhaps three in all.

One patient, a young man, had appalling burns on his left shoulder and chest. I had never done any skin grafting so that was another case that had to await Lesley's return. By then he was absolutely ready for grafting and I understand it was a great success.

What a variety of cases I saw. One very curious case was a 3-month-old baby boy, normal in every way except for genital organs large enough for a 12-year-old. I could give the worried parents no advice except to hope that he would eventually grow to them.

One of the padres, an oldish man, was liable to severe bouts of illness, presumably cardiac weakness, and each time nearly died. He had one when I was there and he really did seem to be dying, just fading out of life. So much so that I told the Mother Superior and she called the nuns together to come to his side ward and pray for his recovery. His pulse was barely perceptible, and he lay quiet and semi-conscious, in no pain. The nuns were all gathered and ready for prayer when I felt his pulse again. To my surprise and gratification, I realized that the therapy I had prescribed had worked, for his pulse got stronger by the minute and I realized that he was not going to die. I was happy, though, that the nuns' prayers should get the credit. He made a good recovery and was soon taking services in the church again.

He asked me for a tonic to get his strength back and I prescribed some vitamin preparation. A week or two later he asked if I would give him a rather different sort of tonic. He then confided that his sexual potency was not what it had been and that his wife, who was a good deal younger than he, was not at all satisfied with him since his illness! I didn't know what the nuns would think about it, but I ordered some testosterone for him from Tanga and no more complaints.

There was the young man who brought his fiancée up for me to examine and tell him if she were a virgin, because if she were not, he was not going to marry her. I had my doubts but of course I told him she was. I hoped she would be able to fake the bleeding!

Lesley returned, having had a good leave. I presented my report and account of expenditure and was much relieved when she said that the toll of deaths was no higher than if she had been in charge. There was a little farewell party for me and many undeserved thanks. There was so much more I could have done if I had had more experience, but I had done my best.

After I left Magila there was a letter from Lesley Sitwell. She writes, "Very much thanks for your letter and wishing you a pleasant journey back to England. We often talk about the improvements you made in the work you did." (I was worried that I had made it worse.) "The pathology has so much improved and the nurses know how to take blood slides and the shrubs are doing so much better with your pruning and the garden is so much improved. We have heard about so many failures in the exams at other hospitals so it is marvelous that you got all ours through." For all their students to pass the exams was a remarkable achievement, and I was sure to attend to the gardens wherever I lived.

I didn't often leave the Mission during my five-month stay, but on at least one occasion Donald's successor at Amani, Gerry Pringle, kindly fetched me in his car and took me to Amani for the weekend. It was lovely seeing all my friends again, but it was always painful to go back. Yet I was so touched as every African I had ever known came to see me and say, "Pole, Mama." I can't begin to tell you the affection shown me by all the Africans. It was just wonderful. The extreme affection with which they speak of Donald was just amazing.

Chapter 12

Sylvie in Moshi, Peggy in The Gambia, 1964–1973

by Peggy Lovett Wilson and Sylvie Wilson Emmanuel

Sylvie: When I started married life in Moshi, there was quite a big expatriate community, mostly Greeks and a fair number of British. On Kilimanjaro, many Greeks had taken over the German estates after World War I to grow coffee. There were still quite a lot of Germans, but all the administrative people were British, and there was a hierarchy—the British were very class conscious—the administration and the medical and education workers were higher up. Further down were the public works department, sanitary inspectors, and so on. The minor government officials lived on a road in Moshi called Minors Alley, now called Bustani Alley. Then bank managers were presumably considered acceptable.

My parents were great friends with a family called Von Kalckstein, who were farming, not very successfully, but Mr. Von Kalckstein was a very good painter. I love his painting of the Pare Mountains (that hangs in our living room) and one of Kilimanjaro. Once a Greek friend who was a good painter described Von Kalckstein's painting of Kilimanjaro: "You have to look at the mountain almost like an abstract, so that it almost floats." When the war came, the Von Kalcksteins were interned, like all the Germans and Italians.

There were Italians, and a big Indian population, but everybody kept very much to themselves. The Mawenzi Secondary School was an Asian school, really. You knew them, you went to the shops, but you didn't really connect.

There were some settler types. A family my parents knew well used to rail on about the awful government people. But I don't think there were so many of those people. Tanganyika was very different from Kenya. You didn't have the lesser nobility farming people like the Happy Valley goings-on in Kenya. Kenya was a colony and that's how it developed, whereas Tanganyika was under the League of Nations. Everyone knew it was going to get its independence; that was very much the background.

Nic on Kilimanjaro with the Mountain Club.

The Greeks were very involved in sisal. Many of them didn't speak much English. Certainly the wives didn't. Nic would play tennis at the Hellenic Club. He was a good tennis player (I never was). The Moshi Club had tennis and a golf course, but we didn't actually go to it very much. Moshi had two cinemas and on Saturday evenings people would dress up for the films. The Europeans went upstairs to watch the film and the hoi polloi were down below. These were the days before television came to Moshi.

There were plenty of other entertainments. When I was still at Machame we had the Moshi Singers. Margaret Morphew conducted and we gave concerts, not very highbrow but great fun. After she left, our conductor moved on to Faure's Requiem *and* The Messiah. *We enjoyed singing and our audiences were appreciative of our efforts!*

The Kilimanjaro Mountain Club had existed since German times and Nic was very involved, first as Secretary and later several times as Chairman. When he was Secretary there were many letters to answer as all the booking was done through the Club. Someone once wrote saying that they wanted to climb the mountain and they had a nine-month-old baby and they had a nice warm backpack. What did we think? I wrote back saying, "Well, if you want to kill your baby, then do go up the mountain!"

I especially remember an expedition when we went up to the Shira plateau and camped. Nic and the serious climbers went on a long day hike, the walkers to where they could look down towards Moshi. I went with Rena to a little stream near the camp site where we enjoyed splashing around in the water and lots of little frogs.

Marangu and Kibo Hotels organised mountain trips but all the hut maintenance was up to the Club members. New huts were being built as well. There were real climbers among the members: Mike Adams did the first solo climb of the Heim glacier. Axe Nelson, a very tall American missionary, was also very involved. There were several dramatic mountain rescue expeditions when climbers were lost or hurt—or as on Mawenzi, killed when climbing. The Mountain Club had an annual meeting and dance, and we had social meetings at our house.

The Garden Club flourished. During my second year at Machame the Garden Club was also involved in an Agricultural Show in Moshi. There was a class for jam making and one for flowers. I made marmalade (for the first time) and to my surprise, I got first prize! Then there was flower arranging. Again I wasn't sure what the competition would be but I took down an arrangement, prepared to hide it if it looked awful. But when I looked round I thought that mine was worth submitting. I had taken my copper kettle and filled it with gold roses and yellow nasturtiums. I won first prize for that too!

We had monthly meetings of the Garden Club with speakers when an interesting one was available. My collection of ferns started from a man who spoke for nearly an hour on ferns; it was fascinating. We had a Rose Show and a Children's Show and in September the big flower show with many classes: vegetables, tuberous plants, Barberton daisies, and many other varieties, also for flower arranging, flowers of one colour and so on. One year I had picked 47 wild gladioli growing in the sisal for the Borissow Cup for the best exhibit of an indigenous plant or flower. I was very disappointed not to get the prize—the judges thought the gladioli were from my garden. The last big flower show was in September 1973, just before nationalisation.

The Moshi Gun Club was also very active then. There was a range at our neighbour's for clay pigeon shooting but the club also had rights on the plains between Meru and Kilimanjaro during the open shooting season. This was for bird shooting and we went on weekend camping trips that were great fun. I remember Nic's horror (like my uncle Dicky's) when some Italians were shooting birds on the ground!

Nic's brother Costa enjoyed shooting animals, different kinds of buck. One of our friends shot a leopard once and came back proudly. I said disdainfully, "Why didn't you just shoot a cat instead?" After all, they had put out bait and I thought this was hardly sporting anymore than it was when my mother shot her lion!

The Motor Sports Club organised rallies and hill climbs and later there was a Go Kart track. Nic raced in them all and sometimes came back with prizes.

Moshi Shops

In those days we were able to buy most of what we needed in Moshi. Not like years later when Rena said, "Aren't we lucky, Mama, to live somewhere where you are happy all day because you were able to buy a kilo of salt?" Some of the shops in Moshi were owned by Indians who had been here for several generations. A letter from my father to my mother in 1940 asked her to buy him more khaki shirts from Moledina, a very good Indian shop, that sold fabric and clothes.

Litos was the Greek baker. A Tanzanian friend told me how her father would buy her bread from there if she had been to the doctor. She said she sometimes pretended that she had a sore throat so that her father would take her to Litos!

Our children enjoyed going to the Moshi library, which had quite a few children's books. The Twiga Bookshop, run by a rather peculiar English couple, had Dinky cars, so that was popular with Gregory. You could also get Poole China there.

The Emslies, friends of my parents, had a grocer's shop (later it became a travel agency, owned by an Indian family but still called Emslies) and my mother would order her Christmas turkey from there. Then there was Moolji's, the main grocer's shop. And a Goan lady (originally from Goa) would bring fish up twice a week from Tanga.

When it came to birthdays, I would take the children to the Post Office as it was fun opening the post box to see what had come. Letters and parcels came quickly. At the news agent, we even had the Sunday Observer *from England on Monday morning. That was service!*

When I was at Machame, Nic and I sometimes had dinner at the Piccadilly Hotel, then owned by an Italian. Very good it was too! It was conveniently on the road up from the station so many people went there. The Lion Cub Hotel is now the Lutheran Center. It was given to them.

The Radio Specialist sold records, and there was Bata, a shoe shop, and the European dress shop. Jinja cotton from Uganda was available at a fabric shop and I made all the children's clothes with that or material I bought when we went to England. Now you can buy clothes at the secondhand market where a lot of the clothes are not even secondhand, but new.

Churches

Initially, Anglican church services in Moshi were held above the railway station. Then, the first church was the chapel of St. John the Divine. The building is still there. That is where my grandmother's funeral service was held before she was buried up at Old Moshi. Once when I was about two, a chaplain was conducting the service, my father was reading the lesson, and my mother was playing the little harmonium. The congregation consisted of me on one side and one other man on the other. There are church records of services and of a chaplain in Arusha who would sometimes come to conduct them. Church records indicate that on occasion the priest conducted services with "myself and the Holy Spirit."

A few years ago, we were going through some of the old papers in the office and there was a drawing labeled, "Moshi Mission, Kilimanjaro, 1896." I looked at it, and thought, "If it's Lutheran, why is it here?" I took this picture home. In one of those incredible coincidences, I happened to open a book that had been my grandfather's about the Anglican Church in East Africa. It said that in 1886 the Anglicans had come to Tanganyika but they had difficulties with the Wachagga, the major tribe in the Kilimanjaro region. They handed their mission over to the Lutheran Mission, and so that was what had been up at old Moshi. Then after World War I, a chaplain came and that was the beginning of an Anglican presence in Moshi.

In 1955 money was raised in Moshi for a church for the English-speaking congregation. There already was one for the Swahili services in another part of Moshi—the new church was called Saint Margaret's because there were many Margarets in the congregation. After I was married, I would go for an eight o'clock communion service and then the morning service. Various people came, not only Anglicans but other denominations as well.

I always took the children to the Anglican Church but they were baptized in the Orthodox Church. There was Gregory, then Sophia. Then, when it came to Rena, we'd been to another baptism and the baby was dunked right under. I thought, "Uh-uh." After the service, when I'd had a few drinks, I went to the priest and said, "I would like my baby to be baptized. But she chokes a lot, so please, could you not put her right under?" I knew Gregory and Sophia hadn't been right under. I discovered that Nic had been to him as well because he didn't like the idea of Rena being dunked. We came to have the baptism service, and once he dipped, twice, and the third time he put her right under. I was mad. But she didn't suffer.

We attended the occasional Orthodox services. When there were still many Greeks in Moshi, the church at Easter would be so full there would be people standing outside.

On the mountain, the Christians were more Lutherans or Roman Catholics. Up our valley there were more Lutherans because of the older German Lutheran presence. Around Mount Kilimanjaro, the valleys were significant because there was little communication between them and the dialects are quite distinct; when a Chagga from Machame marries a Chagga from Marangu they won't be able to understand most of the language and will communicate in Swahili. I talk to Themi Marealle every so often and encourage him to record these dialects. The children are not going to learn these tribal languages and their importance will be forgotten.

Nic and the Choir

A shop in Moshi sells agricultural materials—Nic was there often. One of the owners there was actually called Gregory; they were very nice people who lived near West Kilimanjaro. One day they asked Nic if he would make a donation to buy instruments for their choir, and Nic contributed. About or year or so later we got a message that the choir wanted to come and say "thank you."

I'm afraid I thought, "What a nuisance. I don't want to have company. Can't they just say 'thank you'?" Then "If they're coming, I'd better prepare," so I made biscuits and we got sodas, somewhat resentfully. Then the bus came up that they'd had to hire, and they got out, the ladies all in their nice choir dresses, and they had brought sodas as well, and a live goat that was a present for us! They also brought their sound system with amplifiers in case we didn't have any electricity. They sang and their priest was with us and prayed, and by then I was trying not to cry too much because I was feeling so ashamed of myself. They were so gracious. So we had cookies and sodas and various ladies were happy to come around the garden and I gave them plants. It was a very special occasion.

Climbing Ol Doinyo Lengai ["Mountain of God" in Maasai language, an active volcano, elevation 9,718 feet.]

October 3, 1975 [letter from Sylvie to Peggy]. Life continues to be busy. I had the ladies coffee morning here and there were 20 of us. Then in the evening I had asked someone to supper and Nic had the Gun Club committee here for a meeting, so there were 10 of us.

But the most interesting news is our trip last weekend to Ol Doinyo Lengai with the Mountain Club. Di Bannister was able to keep Rena, and Sophia went to friends in Moshi, so I could go. Gregory came with us. We left here early on Saturday morning. Then from Arusha three Land Rovers set out. We went to Mto wa mbu and then to Engaruka along the Rift wall. At Engaruka we were able to pick up a Maasai guide we'd been told about; he was very good both at showing us the way, which you couldn't find without a guide, and on the mountain itself.

We were able to get quite high up, to 4,500 feet, to camp on volcanic sand with a few patches of grass here and there. Nic woke everyone up at 5 a.m. and we were off, all 19 of us, by 6:20. The first bit was all right, but after several hours we got to something that looked very steep and I said I didn't want to go on. Nic said I couldn't stay alone, which I would've done quite happily. I wasn't sure if anyone else would've stayed with me (in fact they would) so on I went. It was terrifying going up and I said I would never be able to get down. We got up to the crater rim at 1:00 and had an hour's rest, except for those, including Gregory, who raced off around to the very top and from there they could see the active inner crater.

Then we had to come down. The dentist's wife and I said we would really prefer to just die up there rather than face trying the descent. As it was, we did all make it safely to the bottom but I prayed a lot. Nic was a wonderful leader. He put a strong man beside each of us women who were scared, and he was in front of me and we came down most of the way on our bottoms. It was so steep and most of the way we were on a knife edge so that the ground fell away on every side and if you would slip, that would have been the end. It mostly wasn't loose scree that you could dig your heels into easily like on Kilimanjaro.

Gregory was way in front and not bothered by it at all. At the end I asked had he been a bit frightened? He looked at me in amazement, and said, "What of?" I was happier when I couldn't actually see him. When we were most of the way down three people went on ahead to make tea. Luckily they did, as they found most of the tents blown down, including ours, which was also ripped, so they put them up and came back with torches and had a rope to help pull us up a steep karongo [cliff]. Nic also had a torch, luckily, as it was 7:30 p.m. before we were back in camp, a 13-hour day. Never again!

Perhaps it's good for one to go to the extremes of fear. The Mountain Club literature only says it's a "hard slog." I suppose it was if you don't mind the sight of those awful slopes; up near the top there were some flowers but lower down very little is growing since the last eruption in 1966—I remember my mother telling me about an eruption when we lived at Monduli. She said you could see the smoke and ash come over on the wind.

On Monday morning we left at 8 a.m. and stopped to look at another crater along the way, no climbing involved. What a lot of craters there are around there! We could count 10 from the camp, including Empakai, which we looked up towards. The trip back was uneventful and we were home by 5:30 p.m., in bed by 8 p.m. Gregory was feeling very tired. So was Nic, who had felt the responsibility for the whole trip. On the way back when a Land Rover got behind, he was the one who had to go look for it.

I'm sorry my writing is so bad today. I didn't think my arms were so stiff. Luckily it wasn't very sunny on Lengai so we didn't burn. I had made smoked sausage sandwiches and when I tried them, I said to Nic and Gregory, "Don't eat them." They tasted sour and I made them throw them away. When we got down to the bottom and had some, the sausage tasted perfectly all right. Isn't there something about the sour taste of fear? I've never been so frightened in all my life! I won't be climbing any more mountains. To add to this, as we were up there on the mountain we could see the smoke curling around, and I certainly did wonder if I would ever see Sophia and Rena again. A terrible fire up on the mountain must've burned thousands of acres.

Peggy: Return to The Gambia: 1964

Towards the end of my time at Magila, Angela stayed with me for a few days. She hired a car and was able to take Abdallah, who was pretty ill, to the hospital in Tanga. Although I have never known for certain what was the matter with him, I am pretty sure he had syphilis. His stay in the hospital worked wonders, or rather the drugs did. I hadn't liked to investigate his illness, thinking it would be embarrassing for both of us.

Angela drove me to Moshi to stay with Sylvie until I flew back to England. Back in England, I was very busy, with Mrs. Hucker's invaluable help, sorting, choosing, and finally packing into wooden cases my belongings to send off to The Gambia. I had to have china, linen, curtains, cutlery, bedding, so many things that we had brought home from East Africa in 1960 and which I had never thought to need again. I had learned a good deal from Donald about packing, but even with all the care I was capable of, a few good china articles got broken on the journey.

Angela saw me off from Gatwick, as she was to do on so many subsequent occasions. Again I spent the night in the hotel at Las Palmas, the only hotel I ever stayed in with a loo, a bidet, and a bath that ran only tepid water. I enjoyed the coach drive from the airport to the town generally in twilight, and the return trip just after breakfast. The hills were high and on the whole bare, and made me think of the brave Guanche women who sooner than give in to the Spanish, French, and Portuguese invaders, would try and push them over the cliffs to die on the rocks below. The beaches were very stony.

It was a short morning flight to The Gambia. The airport is at Yundum, a very countrified airport with sandy paths, many flowering shrubs, and tables out of doors where one could have drinks when meeting and seeing off friends. Besides the superbly dressed Gambian ladies, mostly of the Wolof tribe, there would often be others from further down the coast just as exotically dressed in long closely-fitted dresses with turbans often of the same material, symphonies in pinks, mauves, oranges, greens. The young ones usually had marvelous figures, and many had lovely faces with large eyes and good features, gold earrings and necklaces, faces well made up, and painted finger and toenails. The effect was rather spoilt by the piece of stick that many of them perpetually chewed. It was a kind of tooth cleaner.

The other two principal tribes in The Gambia are the Mandinka and the Fula. The Mandinkas trace their history back to the old empires of Mali. Away from the coast they are more numerous than the Wolofs or the Fulas. The latter are small and lighter skinned and are good with animals. There are several other tribes but these are the main ones and each has its own language. Those who live near the coast or in the towns can speak English. Fairly recently the currency was changed to the old dalasi worth 25p and the butut which is 100 to the pound.

To begin with, I lived again as a lodger in the Staff House, but Dr. and Mrs. McGregor soon asked whether I would like to have one of the two-story all-electric flats. I gratefully accepted and occupied it all the time I was in The Gambia. It was so near to the sea one could have driven a golf ball into it. To begin with I had a most unsatisfactory cook-steward but later, due to Angela on her first visit to me, I had a very nice lad indeed, and I had him for seven years, named Sainey Javara, otherwise known as Jatta. I had an excellent part-time washwoman, Marie, and after several failures, a really excellent garden boy called Yaya. He was Fula and knew no English. He used to work stripped to the waist and wearing some cast-off big straw hat and very short shorts. He was dishonest but delightful.

The laboratory I worked in was only 300 yards from the Staff House building, a mere nothing, but I found it too much on a hot afternoon so I asked to be allocated a bicycle. I had not ridden one for about 40 years, but it was the perfect answer. The bicycle tired me so little compared with walking. Later I bought an old car, and in 1970 when on leave in England, I bought a new Austin Morris that I still had in 1979.

What drove me to do things of discomfort? I was constrained to be re-learning the principles of basic organic chemistry so I could explain how antimalarial drugs are synthesized. I fear I most often seem very egotistical and I think I shoot a line, but it's because often I try to measure up to what I feel is expected of me.

Work and Social Life in The Gambia, 1967

In January all the great and the good used to come out, as they used to do in Amani, because it was winter in England, in Europe. I had the Hensworths to lunch and they went out of their way to tell me that Ian McGregor had said I was such a help to him. That was the very thing that had been wearing on me since I came to The Gambia, that I wasn't really worth employing. Sir Harold said, "You can put that out of your head at once." That from him who is the kingpin of the whole MRC setup in the world.

In March I went to a party and as usual, I came back feeling ashamed of this ridiculous charm that, in spite of myself, I seem to put out. Oh well, we are as we are made.

I also had a dinner party for ten and made moussaka, which was taking a very long time. Luckily the guests were late, so there was a time for a whiskey and soda to revive me before they came. In May, I realized I was a lot happier since I had regular medical

Peggy in The Gambia with three medical assistants.

work to do. Like the other doctors, I would be on call some of the time for the hospital. I feel of real use and I get again the thrill I used to get at Magila when patients smile brightly and tell me that they are much better. I get up to 50 people at the outpatient clinics.

A few days ago I had an incredibly heavily infected human placenta with malaria parasites, 900,000 cubic centimeters. We chopped it up and minced it and washed it and filtered it and centrifuged the filtrate until we had only leukocytes and parasites left in the filtrate. That was then freeze-dried and sealed into little tubes and will be a lovely present for Ian upon his return!

July 21, my 70th birthday. I wasn't really going to tell anybody about it but they found out. Miss Gibbons sent me a cable, "Greetings Mamazo," but then ever so many people sent me cards and lots were members of the staff here. I was given armfuls of roses—I was overwhelmed and hard put to dispose of them in vases and jars. In the middle of the morning Barry Laing, the acting director, asked me to go to a staff meeting in the library. Everyone assembled and then to my astonishment, he made a speech of good wishes to me and I was presented with a wonderful electric frying pan. I have no idea how anyone knew it was my birthday here, let alone my 70th.

I decided that as my three score years and ten had come I must have a little party. There was a lot to do to get ready for the party in the evening and my nice hairdo, which I had done on Thursday, was rather spoiled, as I was dripping with sweat. Mrs. Laing was a wonderful help and finally all was ready. I bathed and changed and was receiving guests at 6:30, having had a good stiff whiskey to fortify myself. About 45 came but there should've been 10 more. However, it seemed a nice lot. Various people arrived by ship that evening, including Tony Wilkes, who used to work at Amani. He was thrilled to come in for a big party directly he got here. It really went with a swing.

I'd asked people for 6:30 to 8:45 but the last guest went at 9:50. There was enough to eat and plenty to drink. I got smoked salmon and caviar and asparagus and pate and the usual sausage rolls and anchovies, etc. When everyone had gone, Jatta, my servant said, what would I have for supper? I said, "Nothing at all," and went straight to bed. I'd been standing for nearly 3½ hours!

Work in The Gambia, 1968

Going again up to Keneba on the boat; we stayed there for two days to stain and examine 200 slides a day. Dr. McGregor was against my going because it would interfere with the placenta examination I was working on.

I have no idea how many blood films I examined during the eight years I was there, but it must have run into many millions. I was always as careful and as accurate as it was possible to be. The populations of four villages were examined every year and malaria parasites noted and counted. I made up most of the stains I used and I always stained all the thin films myself using Giemsa. I noted the numbers of the species present and recorded the numbers separately. Later I took over the making of blood films from the placentas that were collected both from the Royal Victoria Hospital in Bathurst, later called Banjul, and from several out-stations. I weighed each placenta, made and stained thick and thin blood films from each one, and identified and counted the parasites present and the presence of malarial pigment that sometimes, in a heavy infection, occurred in great blocks or chunks. Later I was asked to record the numbers of the different stages of parasites present. The findings were to be compared with the amount of malarial antigen recovered from each placenta.

From time to time I had some clinical work because if the regular medical officer was away or ill, I would take over the outpatients while Barry Laing covered the inpatients. I enjoyed those times very much and proved to myself that I was still a pretty fair clinician.

In December 1968 just before Christmas, I wrote to Sylvie that I felt lonely on these holidays and wish I had someone to do something with. It was lovely having my friend Joan Baldock stay for some time. But then I wrote to Sylvie (December 31, 1968) that in fact I had not been alone for Christmas and had a lovely time, as I had 38 of all ages here for a party. There were curry puffs, sausage rolls, crab pâté and sandwiches, champagne punch, fruit wine punch for the younger set and Sprite and Fanta for the very young.

And now my news, which makes me very cock-a-hoop! Ian McGregor has asked me to be co-author with him and David Row, a well-known immunologist, on a major paper on the relation of malaria parasitemia to the immunoglobulins of 1,100 people. I have done all the blood examinations for it and I'm really thrilled and honored to be brought in on it [McGregor et al. 1970; 1983]. At long last I become a fellow of the Society of Tropical Medicine in my own right. I left it a bit late to join, haven't I?

Luncheon for Peggy in The Gambia with the High Commissioner and his wife and other guests.

Sylvie wrote to Peggy in 1968, in response to Sylvie's description of sewing a dress: "Don't have an inferiority complex about dressmaking. When I am 70 I shan't be doing a paid research job. I wish I could be as good an example of unselfishness and loving and not complaining to my children as you have been."

Angela's Wedding, 1969

My sister Rosie and Angela came to stay with me. It was Rosie's first visit to the tropics and she was enchanted by the flowers and fruit and the seashore. She thought pawpaws were the most delicious fruit in the world. Also in 1969 Angela decided to marry Mike Gardner, so I flew home for the wedding. Before coming to The Gambia with Rosie, Angela had made her wedding dress and her wedding cake, and planned her wedding for Easter Monday. Forte's very obligingly agreed to bring out everything [to Spa House] for a luncheon for about 40 people. Mike hadn't wanted a party or to be married in Church, but Angela said no wedding in Church, no wedding at all. So he had to agree and Ashley Turner agreed to come and marry them. Everything went splendidly, and they were a very good-looking couple.

In two days I returned to The Gambia. Not long after, to my great dismay, I developed hepatitis and came home to go into the Tropical Diseases Hospital. Nobody could imagine that I had straightforward hepatitis; they felt sure it must be cancer of the liver. I was kept in hospital for about a month and made a complete recovery! So back to The Gambia.

About a year later I slipped and fell heavily on the tiled floor in my flat. I was wearing sandals with rather unsteady heels. I went down in an awful crash. X-rays next day showed that I had an impacted fracture of my left humerus. Again I was invalided home and did not return to The Gambia for four months.

Writing in 1971 to Sylvie: Hey I'm forgetting to tell you about my medal! The Royal African Society is going to present me with an engraved bronze medal which says "Dedicated Service to Africa" and my name and letters after it and I'm to be an honorary life member of the Society and also to get a money present. They present five annually so it's not a very common honor. Occasionally for very exceptional service they give a gold one. It's nice. There's no award I would rather have and until the letter came I had no idea of the existence of such a thing. I wonder who proposed me for it?

I must say I wish there hadn't been so much to do about that medal. Every single African refers to it. If I had, say, a CBE, they wouldn't have taken the least notice.

I haven't told you my main bit of personal news yet: now my microscope and my chair are all so arranged that I can sit back in my chair and have the eyepieces so I can look into them without bending forward. Someone here took the trouble to arrange this, which, if I hadn't been such a dimwit, I could have done myself.

I went to the top of the steps which go down to the beach and sat there for a bit, watching a girl lying in the sun who burned herself dark brown and watching a Gambian fishing for prawns. He came up to the flat with a big washbasin full. I must try the Greek recipe for braised prawns. I've been sitting up on the balcony in a lounge chair reading, writing, and watching the sea. The beach is just not attractive at present; the sand is so black.

Peggy with the Africa medal, 1971.

December 1971: Yesterday I had one or two people to lunch and one was—you'll never guess—Thomas Marealle, late Paramount Chief of the Wachagga. When the chiefs had their jobs taken from them, he could have had a job of some sort, but when he was asked if he'd like to work for the United Nations, he accepted and was here in that capacity. He said he knew Nic very well, and he claimed to have come to your [Sylvie and Nic's] wedding, which of course he didn't, but he was a very nice person. He brought a lot of photographs, starting with his grandfather who was chief in 1912 and fought for the Germans. He brought his son and invited Dr. Florence Mahoney, presumably a Gambian as well, and her 10-year-old son. Such dear little boys. Florence comes, I imagine, from slave forebears. Marealle said, "It's very rude, but can I ask how old you are?" and I said, "Yes, it's very rude, but I'll tell you."

Christmas day I went to Communion at 10:00 and then to the McGregor's annual drinks get-together. It is really very noble; they asked people for any time between 10:30 and 1:00. I went to sleep later in the afternoon and in the evening, I put on the lovely gold and scarlet gown Angela had sent me and went out to Christmas dinner. A superb dinner it was, with friends. We toasted my darling children and grandchildren.

I have been organizing the service of nine Lessons and Carols. Sometimes I wish someone else would do the flowers. It is very noisy this evening with church bells ringing, I suppose from the Methodist Church in Daca, drums beating, things rattling and jingling.

January 1972: I was writing another paper on my own concerning the breakdown of malaria immunity in pregnant women. I have lots of figures over six years to show that in a hyper-epidemic where no active malarias are taken, that there is a breakdown, especially in first pregnancies. April: The slide I sent to England to demonstrate at the laboratory meeting on the 16th of March has created great interest, even the name I gave it, *Cannibalistic Large Mononucleus*. Joe Shute says no one had ever seen or heard of such things before. I have finished the first draft and when I finally get to publishing, it should create a lot of interest.

I'm quite done with too much partying. I do wish no one would ask me again for months. Last night we were eight here, with considerable strain, as I had invited the Bishop and his wife. He talks non-stop for hours all about his plans, hopes, and dreams for a school and a technical college and lord knows what. One cannot help but admire his enthusiasm for the Christian cause and to get the Anglicans on their feet spurred on by the competition from the Catholics and Methodists. But oh, how wearing! The other guests put up with it nobly, but they ate so much: cucumber soup made with yoghurt, a trifle sour for my taste but they liked it. Then smoked fish and rice, two helpings each, leg of lamb done with rosemary and marjoram, endive stewed with butter, and a truly delicious mint sauce I made, all gone! Lemon mousse all gone, and three bottles of wine. We forced the Bishop off his monologue part of the time, though it was hard to do.

I enjoyed my work in The Gambia. The work, monotonous as it would have seemed to many, was never so to me and I always hoped to come across something out of the common run. There was the unusual slide from the placenta with containing many more than usual tremendously enlarged mononuclear leukocytes, and a very interesting slide from finger prick blood showed that the red cells containing parasites were enlarged and thinned and in many cases had simply withdrawn from their contained parasites leaving the parasites free and unenclosed. Another interesting slide of finger prick blood showed the large mononuclear having become totally cannibalistic and having ingested numbers of granulocytes.

No one took much interest in these unique phenomena. I sent some of them to London and requested their return but P.G. Shute was bad about returning slides and I was shocked that he had missed the point altogether. I took an immensity of trouble in working out parasite rates and percentages but they were of no interest to anyone. It was all done by the MRC Secretary [a very high position in the MRC].

After tea I often went to the beach and walked along the shore. Occasionally I had a very cautious bathe but I was always afraid of going out of my depth as I was not strong enough to swim. There was often a strong undertow. The McGregors were incredibly good to me, taking me for beach picnics and asking me to innumerable lunch and dinner parties, and generally seeing that I wasn't left out of any fun. All the members of the staff, too, were extremely friendly.

For quite a time I had the Senior Sister Marguerite Hurst living in the other top flat and we were good friends. When I had my fall she was kindness and helpfulness itself, and I was intensely grateful to her. On the whole I liked the climate, but it was too hot at times. I disliked the wind and got the full force from the sea. Sometimes I would thoughtlessly leave in the big mosquito gauze screen looking on to the balcony. Having gone to sleep in perfect calm I would wake to all hell let loose—rain pouring into the sitting room and a gale force wind. My nightgown was drenched through immediately and then I would have an awful struggle to take out the heavy wooden frame gauze door and get it onto the balcony where I would let it fall onto the rail with a crash. However, it didn't happen often. I tried to remember to get Jatta to remove it before he left.

When we were supplied with air conditioning in bedrooms, it was a great boon, and it was wonderful when we got air conditioning in the labs. Before it happened I sometimes felt quite sick and peculiar trying to concentrate on my work with the temperature about 90F in spite of having the ceiling fan full on.

Peggy and Angela when Peggy was awarded the OBE, 1973.

In 1973 Dr. McGregor gave up his post as Director of the unit, which he had held for over 25 years. However, he intended to make an annual visit to Keneba to collect venous samples from cases that were especially interesting. He said, and I fully agreed, that he would not advise me to put in for work under the new arrangement.

My dear Angela met me as always on my return, and I was very glad to live and settle at Spa House, looked after in every possible way by Mr. and Mrs. Hucker, my most wonderful friends. Sadly, Mr. Hucker died from heart trouble in June 1978.

August 6, 1973, letter to Sylvie,

"You are going to have a surprise! Or perhaps you have had it already—me getting an OBE in the Birthday Honors. But isn't that nice? We all know that the British Empire is no more but I shall take the honour *in memoriam*. And how nice for Angela that she will be able to go with me to get it. Unless they make a muddle and give it to me out here. It is Ian's parting gift to me. He really has done me proud, one way and another." In the autumn of 1973 I was honored by receiving the OBE from Her Majesty the Queen in recognition of my work with malaria in Africa.

"Saturday, late afternoon, but just back from the Commonwealth Society luncheon. I was called the Chairman and sat between the acting President and the Minister of Finance and oh goodness me, I was *overwhelmed*; the clapping my few words brought, the compliments and congratulations and references to my years in Africa, and at the very end of the speeches the whole company roared out 'For she's a jolly good fellow.' The British High Commissioner and the Vice President were nowhere, I assure you, in comparison. If it hadn't been that they were all so affectionately friendly, I should have felt most uncomfortable, so much in the limelight and when someone said 'Whom the Queen delighteth to honor'—well!

Sylvie: On my mother's last visit to Tanzania, she said, "I want to go out to where the European Hospital was." We went there and she said, "To think that my little baby daughter was born here and just buried."

My mother came out to visit us several times after she retired from The Gambia. We took her to Pangani and she would sit on a chair on the beach in the shade and watch the children playing. We went for an expedition to Mount Meru on her last visit at Christmas 1978. When the rest of the family went ahead I said, "Let us go on as far as you want, slowly." Going up a hill (we were at about 6,000 feet) she was puffing and said, "It wasn't like this forty years ago in the Himalayas!"

Peggy and Sylvie on Mount Meru.

The last evening of her visit we had dinner on the verandah in the moonlight. Very memorable as it was, though we didn't know it at the time, for it was her last visit here. Flying here from England was too tiring for her.

After that I used to go and visit her at Spa House in the winter. Angela went every fortnight for two nights and of course Mrs. Hucker kept looking after her.

Chapter 13

Independence and Nationalization, 1961–1983; Sylvie's Garden

by Sylvie Wilson Emmanuel

We were all aware that Independence was coming in Tanganyika. After the First World War, Tanganyika was taken away from Germany and given as a trust territory, not a colony, to Britain, under the League of Nations. The aim was that Tanganyika would eventually become independent, sometime far in the future. But because of Tanganyika's culture and Julius Nyerere's leadership, it all happened much earlier.

Tanganyika was very different from Kenya. It didn't have the settler problems, the Mau Mau, or significant problems between tribes. One of Nyerere's great innovations was fostering the use of Swahili and that brought the country together. The Chagga never had a radio station, as there could well have been. In Kenya, the Kikuyu and the Luo had their own radio stations. If you are having some friction, the radio is a very good way of building up hostilities, as happened in Rwanda.

Yet there were differences in Tanganyika between parts of the country. Perhaps I'm biased because of living there and liking the people, but the Chagga at Kilimanjaro were intelligent and prosperous, perhaps in part because of living in a better climate and being healthier. My father was very aware that many people's problems come from ill health and malnutrition. When people are healthier, school is always easier. The earliest good school for boys was at Tabora. Then there were the mission schools. When I came to teach in 1957, there weren't many girls' schools. The Tabora Girls' School, like the boys' school, was the top one. Machame Girls' School was moving up, and Mwanza, and other schools as well. It helped in Tanganyika that there were few British settlers; there was not the same agitation by them as in Kenya. The Greeks had less interest in politics and were more interested in making money out of their sisal or coffee estates. The others, for instance, the Afrikaners, really weren't involved in politics at all.

There was obviously a colour bar, but it wasn't official. I was very aware of it at Moshi kindergarten in the 1950s when the District Supervisor's wife was from the West Indies and their little boy was "not quite white." Problems over him going to the kindergarten were resolved and he did attend. The primary school in Moshi was for white children. There was an African hospital and a European hospital. Only later the European hospital became Kibo Hospital until it was closed, and that was for people who could pay, obviously more Europeans.

In November 1961, we were up at Marangu. Nic was asked to lunch, as Nyerere [then Prime Minister] was going to give the Tanganyika flag to the person who was to raise it at 12 p.m. on December 8 on top of Kibo, the highest peak of Kilimanjaro. I had to go into Moshi for a meeting of the Tanganyika Council of Women to ask for volunteers to help with Flag Day.

With the agitation by Nyerere, who would become President, and TANU [Tanganyika African National Union], independence was granted in December 1961. We were all very happy about it and I can still remember that evening. We had gone to dinner with Gilead Shangali, who was one of the sons of Chief Abdul Shangali up at Machame, and several other people, including Danish friends. Afterwards we went down to Moshi and were outside the Boma when the Tanganyika flag was raised. It went off very happily and peacefully. Everyone was very quiet during "God Save the Queen," but when the Tanganyika flag went up and the Tanganyika anthem was played, there was so much cheering and shouting you couldn't hear it. Afterwards there were fireworks. It was a bit cloudy so no one could see the fireworks set off from Uhuru Peak, the top of Kilimanjaro. However we managed to go where we saw a glow in the sky and for the last few moments, a wonderful light lit up the ice. It was wonderful being there, seeing it. The name of the highest peak on the mountain was changed from Kaiser-Wilhelm-Spitze to Uhuru Peak, as it should have been. Uhuru [Swahili for "freedom"]. It was the greeting of the weekend.

On Saturday morning Nic rushed in to get the new stamps and then we had a flag raising on the estate. Costas said proudly, "It must be the best flag pole in the district." He had used one of the new three-inch pipes from the irrigation system. Quite a lot of activities were organized for the workers. Angela wondered why they weren't all getting presents, but as they were getting three days' pay, it wasn't a cheap holiday for the estate.

On Saturday afternoon a prize was given to the best decorated camp. The workers spent Friday decorating, then the ngomas were most interesting. On Monday Nic and I went up to a baptism at Machame, the child of a Chagga who owns part of KNCU [Kilimanjaro Native Co-Operative Union]. After the service there was a huge party at his house with pombe [home brewed beer] and every other European drink. They produced goat and rice about 2:30 p.m. The KNCU band played, and luckily we were told they were to play the national anthem as the arrangement was quite unrecognizable. I wasn't very keen and we tried to slink away. We were caught and had to go back so it was 3:15 p.m. before we left.

We got back home for some lunch. Then it was time to go down to the estate again, where there had been a bicycle race in the morning and in the afternoon a football match with a cup, a baby show, and Nic did some magic that was enormously entertaining.

Initially life didn't seem to change. It was gradual. For instance, when we heard that freehold land was to be converted into leasehold, we thought, "There's not much difference between freehold and having a 99-year lease." But slowly things began to change.

Nyerere had been influenced by his visits to China and to Israel and the kibbutz. That's when he developed his idea of Ujamaa villages where people would live together and farm together.

Not everybody wanted to do this, to give up their little houses. In quite a few cases they were forced, even at gunpoint, and some people were hurt or worse. I can still remember a Norwegian friend who went back to Norway; he had been teaching in Tanzania, and he wrote to the Norwegian government saying he didn't think it was right that Norway was giving money to Tanzania when people were being forced into Ujamaa villages. He was told that obviously he had stayed too long and become "infected by colonialism."

Ujamaa did not work well on Kilimanjaro among the Wachagga who are basically capitalists at heart. Many Chaggas were well educated and they did not get on so well with Nyerere. Nsilo Swai was sent off to be Tanzania representative to the United Nations [July–December 1962] to get him out of the way.

Gradually other things changed. Nationalization of houses in towns and cities affected Asians considerably. If they had more than one house, the second house was taken. They weren't given compensation and were told that if they'd had it for more than ten years, they obviously didn't need the money. This was hard on many of them. Small shops closed, many up on the mountain [Kilimanjaro]. Shops run by Asian traders up there were closed. There was an unsuccessful attempt to nationalize butcheries.

Then larger scale plans were implemented. In 1967 sisal estates were nationalized, except for the ones owned by Karimjee [a South Asian family-based trading company in East Africa] and some of the Swiss estates, because of Switzerland's connection to the World Bank. Gradually there were causes for concern, but always you thought, "Oh well, if that happens, it'll be all right." How did it not click what was happening and what was planned?

There was a meeting at West Kilimanjaro. When Lord Lothian was here he told Nic, in an interpretation of Nyerere's policies, that he didn't think there would be wholesale annexation of farms. You can imagine going around the house and trying to decide what to take if you had 24-hours notice and told to take one suitcase. This was after two farmers from West Kilimanjaro had been deported from their farms. It really shook the community around there. There was also word that the Ujamaa villages were to distribute and market everything. I wrote to my mother, "They haven't explained this in detail and no one can see how that they could, for instance, market the entire coffee crop. This is one way of forcing everyone into the Ujamaa villages. But the KNCU doesn't like being branded as middle men as that would mean that they have no future."

In December Nic had a visit from the Minister of Lands. They wanted to take our land for a Ujamaa village. It would have been different if we still had all sisal, but there was so much arable land now. He was very nice about it; he didn't want to turn us out completely so he might let us keep the coffee. He didn't know when it would be, or any details.

Nic's brother Costas was in favor of not doing any ploughing, but Nic said we must do it. You can imagine how desperately uncertain we were feeling. It wasn't just money, but it was Nic's life and somewhere we love. So we couldn't look forward to 1972 as obviously there would be many changes.

In June 1972, Nyerere was again in West Kilimanjaro and saying that for everyone who wanted to abide by the Arusha Declaration [1967], there was a future, but not for big (or small) estates and private farms. Everything must be large state farms, cooperatives, or Ujamaa villages. In the Acquisition of Buildings Act of April 1971, he did say that for those dispossessed of their lands, there should be compensation for landowners who wanted to move to other countries. Although relations with England had not been good because of arms deals to South Africa and Rhodesia, things were better and Nyerere was prepared to ask the UK if they were ready to buy out the expatriates' farms if they so wished, as the country of Tanzania didn't have the money to do it. He gave no time limit but said that once there were enough Africans to run them, the farms would be taken for them.

When Nyerere was at Kilimanjaro, it was perfectly obvious what was going to happen, but again, we put it out of our minds. So it was a huge shock when, on October 23, 1973, all of the coffee estates on Kilimanjaro were nationalized. Only on Kilimanjaro were coffee estates nationalized, not Arusha, not Mbeya in the southwest. We thought, "What have we done wrong so that this happened?" Greeks were a nobody country in the middle of the Junta's rule and therefore a nobody country to Nyerere.

We heard a touching story about one of the Greeks whose farm was nationalized in 1973. His father died in Nairobi in December and all the people who had worked for him on the coffee farm that had been nationalized paid for an air ticket for one of them to go to Nairobi where the old man died, to the funeral. They picked a huge bunch of lilies from the old people's gardens to be put on the grave.

I was teaching history at the International School in Moshi when we were nationalized. The head of the school saw how upset I was and said, "Do just go home today." I enjoyed my teaching that year. It was African history and one of the students wrote to me later, "I, who was never interested in history, passed the International Baccalaureate. A miracle. You were the only one who ever pushed us in our lessons."

In 1974 the British government paid farmers in West Kilimanjaro for their farms, but these were British owned. When the land had been allocated for farming after World War II, the district commissioner at Moshi, Millard, who had been in the RAF, made sure it all went to ex–RAF pilots. No Greeks who applied for land were given any.

On Kilimanjaro everyone was told there would be "full and fair compensation" for the coffee estates. Well, some compensation was paid after some years but by then the money had been devalued and it certainly wasn't full and it wasn't fair compensation. Most of the estates were Greek-owned and many of the people were old so they just left. People were told they could go and get land in other parts of the country. But if you've been nationalized once, you're not very likely to go and look for something else.

Just before nationalization in 1973, in September, Nic took Gregory to Athens College where Nic had been a student. Sophia was in Arusha at the Greek school as a boarder and Rena was at the kindergarten in Moshi. Then came this bolt out of the blue. The owners of the estates on Kilimanjaro were summoned to a meeting. Costas went and they were told that from the next day, the estates were nationalized. Bank accounts were frozen. This was a huge shock.

The next day people started coming to our home. The Regional Commissioner came up and in my best British way, I went over and shook his hand, to his surprise—he was a horrible little man. He said, "Where are all the tractors?" I said, "This is one estate."

They gave the sisal part to one cooperative and the coffee part, actually under a separate title, to another cooperative. As it is run as one estate, a lot of the tractors were down at the sisal factory.

Then the regional police commander came, because all our guns were to be taken away. They said that was so no one would commit suicide, ha! The man who came knew Nic well because they had done rescue trips on the mountain together. I could see that he was embarrassed, and after a bit of a chat, I finally said, "I know you've come to get the guns, haven't you?" He said, "Yes, yes, I'm so sorry." I was actually sorry for him as well, because he didn't know how to ask it of me. So they took away the guns. (We were given them back some years later.)

Our bank accounts were frozen. Many friends came up to be encouraging. The Baptist minister and his wife came up and he said, "You'll go through all the processes of grieving," and that is how it was. A dear Scottish lady from Marangu Hotel came and I said to her, "Oh Marjorie, look at all I have to pack up. Look at all the children's toys, what a job to do." She said, "My dear, I come from the western isles of Scotland. I have second sight. You'll be here long after the children have grown out of their toys." I didn't quite believe her but sure enough, she was right. I'm afraid our Anglican pastor didn't come because he felt it might compromise his position. Not a very good decision.

We kept trying to phone Nic in Greece. I went down again and again to try. I think they blocked the phones, but I finally did get through. Then Nic came back. I assumed we'd pack up and go, but he said, "No, no, no. If we leave, we will never get any compensation." Most other people were busy packing up.

Later the Cooperative came and said they needed our house for the manager. Nic said, "There are five houses on this estate and I don't think you really need this one." There was the manager's house and the assistant manager. There was a house that Costas had lived in and another house built by the people who originally had our estate. After a while they said, "We need rent," and Nic said, "After I get compensation, we'll start paying rent," and we did eventually. It wasn't a lot, but we paid.

Some people were wonderful. Our own gardener's wife brought us a chicken because she was so sorry for us. Several of our Tanzanian friends said they'd avoided us because they didn't know what to say. People varied. One of the most unfeeling was a Finnish-Swede missionary. They were interested in possibly buying or taking over the Greek Church and I was saying something about our situation, and he said, "You've had the estate for a long time. How many years? Haven't you?" I thought, if someone came to take over your home in Sweden, what would you think? But most people weren't like that.

Christmas that year Gregory came from Greece for the holidays. It was a very traumatic time in Greece because on November 17 there'd been the uprising of the students at the Polytechnic against the Junta [in power from the coup d'état April 21, 1967] when a lot of students were killed. Our nephew, Costas's son, was among those who had been in the Polytechnic. He managed to escape when the tanks came. But after a short time the police and army people came to the house and took him off to prison where they beat him. They wanted him to be an informer; that he wouldn't do. They let him out and mercifully, he was able to come out at Christmas; he stayed away from Greece until the Junta was kicked out the following year [July 24, 1974].

I didn't know what to say to Sophia when she came home that weekend. Only recently she told us about the horrible teacher who had told children from Moshi, "Your farms have been nationalised. They have been taken away from your families. You will have to go away." What a thing to say to a child, causing so much distress that we never knew about. Rena was only five and a half and I tried to pretend as if nothing important was happening. Years and years later, she was on a church retreat and the counselor asked her, "When you were very young did you lose something that you were very fond of?" Everything came out about knowing that our house was to be taken way from us. Even our dog went up to the neighbour's for a while.

It got so that every time that I heard another Land Rover coming up the drive I started trembling. But there was no violence. You just didn't know what would happen next.

My mother also came out at Christmas as did Gregory from school in Athens. She said "Darling, you are so bitter." It was difficult not to be. At the New Year celebration at the Hellenic Club my mother said it was like a funeral; everyone was so gloomy. But it was the end of an epoch for so many, especially for the old people who had lived here so long and now had nothing.

At the end of his first year, Gregory had come back from Greece and said, "I don't want to go back to that school." It suited us because I hadn't been all that happy with him there, but I didn't want Nic to feel any regrets. By then, we didn't have the money to pay the fees, so he went to the International School in Moshi. Later Sophia and Rena went there as well. The school was adding extra classes and then offered the International Baccalaureate. We were very fortunate. If we hadn't had a good school, we would have had to leave.

Nic said, "We have to do something," so he went to Royal Sluis, the Dutch company. He had grown seed beans for them and they agreed to put up all the finance for new tractors and money for current use, provided Nic found land to farm. He found land he could rent near Kilimanjaro airport where he could grow beans. So in the spring of 1974 he grew seed beans. They were very successful that year, until we suddenly had rain one night in July and the next morning Nic said, "That's £10,000 gone." We managed to live with the beans for quite some years. Royal Sluis was incredibly honorable and helpful to us.

Nic farmed near the airport for several years. In those days animals were still on the Sanya plains and he did shoot the odd Thomson's gazelle among the beans. One night a whole herd of elephants walked through. They didn't actually do much damage but it was obviously one of their paths.

After several years when the lease expired Nic went well beyond Arusha for two years and after that he was way down in the bush, near Tarangire. So he bought an old caravan and when it was time to go planting he would take the caravan and live there during the week and come back for weekends. I was left at Machame. By then Gregory and Sophia were at the International School and Rena was at the Greek school, coming home for weekends,

We would pack food for Nic, but when there was a cholera outbreak, they weren't allowed to take food in or out of the area. One year, during the rains at Easter, when Gregory had a motorbike and had gone with him, I was expecting them to come back for lunch on Easter Sunday. They didn't return so I thought, oh, perhaps something's come up. When they weren't there the next day I thought, they'll be here for lunch. I heard there's been so much rain they couldn't get across one of the bridges. Early evening Gregory appeared on his motorbike. There was one place where he could get across. Sometime later Nic appeared as well. We had no mobile phones in those days and we just had to wait till someone appeared.

There were good years and bad years. There was the year the rats came at the time when the beans were drying up. The rats weren't so much eating the beans as biting the pods, but once the pods hit the ground you couldn't harvest the beans. I went out with Sophia, Rena, and Gregory and a couple of friends. I was in the caravan with Rena and I could hear shrieks and bangs, then shrieks and bangs. The children had all gone down into the storeroom and were busy killing rats!

The whole Greek community in Moshi left, as everyone lost their livelihood. There was a community meeting to decide the fate of the Greek Orthodox Church and the Hellenic Club with its tennis court. Each town had its own Hellenic society; Arusha had one; Moshi had one; Tanga had one, and each one managed its own business. There were no Greeks to look after the church, and the bishop in Nairobi said they weren't willing to pay for it to be looked after, so they looked around for a buyer. The Baptists bought the church plus the clubhouse where the tennis courts were. The money was to be used for children's scholarships at the Greek school or Greek children at the International School in Moshi until the money was used up.

Costas stayed for a short time. Then he left. He worked for a time in Greece, then got a job as manager of a very large sisal estate, Kibwezi in Kenya with Brooke Bond. He did a wonderful job there, increasing their production. When he was older, he retired to the family's lovely place in Crete.

We stayed on. You never knew. There was always the uncertainty, rumors about this and that. Would they chuck us out? The part of the garden where we had been growing strawberries was taken over.

They took all the cars, the brand new Land Rover that had just been bought for the estate, and they took a Renault 4 I had been driving but that was in the name of the company. Luckily, our VW Kombi was in my name and mercifully Nic's Porsche was in his name, so they didn't take those. The manager came with our little Renault up the drive to be washed in our garden!

Everything had been very open, but we planted a hedge. That's how we started putting up fences. It was sad to see the farms going down because they didn't have the managerial experience or the finance. They came and would ask Nic's advice. He'd say, "Well, no. I can't give you any advice." Because if something went wrong then they could come back and say...

They were gradually getting rid of the sisal altogether. The coffee was slowly looked after less. They were interested in growing maize and cabbages. The local people were getting very little. There was no longer a lot of casual work like picking coffee.

Nineteen eighty-two was a bad year for the beans. In April, Nic went off to the shamba. I wrote to my mother, "If it has not rained by tomorrow he will lose 400 acres of beans, and in the next 4 days, he will lose 500 acres of beans." The final straw was that year. Nic planted because there was some rain, the beans came up nicely, and then there was no more rain and he didn't harvest one kilo of beans, zero.

The shops were almost empty, with none of the basics, just tea, bicarbonate of soda, Vaseline, and onions, a few garments, but no kangas, no fat, no oil, no rice, no soap, no flour, no sugar. I asked friends to bring beer kits from England, and then I started making wine from plums, pears, parsley.

By the middle of June, I wrote, "There are now five tractors back here. It is so discouraging seeing them come up the drive. Usually it is wonderful to see them come at the end of the harvest, but they have not harvested one single kilo of beans from Lolera. We are hoping to go up to West Kilimanjaro because there has been rain there for short rain beans. We have had some rain here but cannot use this land." Farming, and life in general had just become too difficult. You couldn't get diesel, you couldn't get spare parts. You couldn't get this and that and the other thing.

In April 1983 we had been invited up to a Remembrance Service early in the morning for Mr. Aikaeli's wife. We used to buy milk there from her. Her husband had been very close to Nyerere. The Remembrance Service was to start at 8 a.m. but when we arrived, Mr. Aikaeli was still in his dressing gown. We were offered whiskey, brandy and even champagne, to which we said, "No thank you." It was a beautiful service, all in Swahili, and after the service we were served breakfast. There was to be a baptism, and lunch was offered, but we said that since it was Easter we would go to our own church.

Even as we had this lovely Service of Remembrance, in the same month the anti-corruption drive was in full force and shops were raided to discover who had hoarded. One man in Arusha reported to the police that he had thrown away a case with 1,000,000 Tsh [Tanzanian shilling; in 2020 $1 is 2,314 Tsh] and they found it. Dafrosa said that she met a woman who had been given too much soap from a person with too much soap. "They are not tried but put in detention." I must say I was very worried because we had been able to buy a whole case of toilet paper and I wondered if I should throw it away.

We had a very funny story when we went to Pangani. Between Tanga and Pangani we saw someone who looked as if he was carrying a bottle of Teachers whiskey. Further on somebody else was carrying a bottle of Teachers, and then a third one. We stopped and asked what was going on. They said that somebody had a case of Teachers and had been so afraid of being found with it that he had thrown it into a pool of rainwater and it had been fished out. They said, "You can buy one!" But we were worried it wasn't good, so they said, "Just try it." It was obviously good, so we bought one bottle, but did not buy another because we were worried that on the way back to Moshi we might be caught with two bottles of whiskey.

In May, we had quite a severe earthquake. Philippi and I were in the kitchen one evening and at first I said, "Oh they must be bush babies," and then I said, "They must be baby elephants." I shouted for Rena who was shaking with fear as her desk was shaking. We went outside and it all went on a bit longer, similar to the one when Sophia was a baby. Nic had been driving back from West Kilimanjaro and with the bumpy road, he wasn't even aware of it.

In June 1983, Nic lent a planter to Arusha Chini, where the huge sugar plantation is, and asked that he be paid in kind. "Now we have enough sugar to make pear wine. We've just started drinking the beer kit beer, which is all right."

In June, "I'll take this opportunity of sending a letter that can be posted in England.

Most Air Tanzania planes are grounded due to lack of fuel, so I don't know when you will be getting another letter. The incoming flights are bringing enough fuel to take them out, so I'm hoping that Sophia will make it in to Kilimanjaro Airport on Sunday.

"Nic's barley looks quite good—the barley is from West Kilimanjaro. He was growing it for the breweries. The 450 acres of beans that were lower down on West Kilimanjaro are hopeless as there were only 4.5 inches of rain. Some of those at slightly higher altitude aren't too bad but there is a losing battle with weeds. Really, if we cannot even grow anything, anywhere, I don't know what we are doing here trying to farm."

In July I describe problems of getting petrol. "One day we did manage to get some petrol but it took two hours and people are being very aggressive in the queue. Someone bashed our Porsche with their Land Rover. So now we sit round at home. Sometimes I think that there is nothing worse than not being able to get petrol. Some crude is going to Dar es Salaam to be refined, but there is no diesel to bring it up country."

Nic went again to get a permit for diesel and was given 50 liters. Lots of the mills milling maize flour cannot run and one place charges 40 Tsh to mill a "debi" [20 litre tin]. Down in southern Tanzania were 8,000 tons of coffee to be transported to Dar es Salaam to be exported to get the foreign exchange to get more diesel, but there was no diesel for the lorries.

"It is a shame for Sophia and Rena because we cannot go anywhere or do anything. We were sending Philipi on Sophia's bicycle to get some milk. Unfortunately it had a puncture and we cannot get the puncture kit to repair it. Luckily, we have friends who will probably give us one today. I'm sorry for this long catalogue of moans, but it is difficult not to feel a bit dominated by everything going on here. I cannot even go to church and ask forgiveness for one's grumbles.

"In July, Nic and I went down to Moshi with the Porsche and Land Rover to queue for petrol and we waited 3 hours and the petrol station ran out of petrol. On Wednesday I waited 6 hours and Nic 7.5 hours and it ran out. On Thursday we waited 3 hours and it ran out, and we went to a long queue at another petrol station but it was hopeless. Today we went down at 5:30 a.m. and there were 25 cars ahead of us, but like yesterday, there was no petrol at all in Moshi. We hope some friends are bringing a little for us today or otherwise we are completely stuck.

"Sophia's bicycle was mended and Philippi went off to get milk. Otherwise you would have to pay 25 Tsh to go by bus from here to Machame. I don't know how long people will take it. The criticism in the petrol station is devastating.

Nic grew beans for a long time. Eventually, when that got too difficult, he tried one or two other jobs. One was work with the CDC (Commonwealth Development Cooperation) on an appraisal of the sisal estates near Tanga and one on coffee. Farming was just too difficult. You couldn't get diesel or spare parts. You couldn't get this and that and the other thing.

Early December 1983. "Rena has been with the school on an expedition, on Kilimanjaro. She came back this afternoon quite triumphant as she had completed the circuit of the mountain. They walked about 200 km. and one night they had to bivouac because they didn't reach the next hut. This was at about 14,000 feet. On the 4th day she had pain in her knee. The next day she had so much pain that she cried but she didn't give up. This is quite something for a young person of not quite 14. She was really high when she came down from the mountain, better that than getting high on drugs! It took her two or three days to catch up on her sleep."

In January 1984, we went to those lovely Kikuletwa Hot Springs [near Boma N'Gombe] for Sophia's birthday and Nic had tied a rope so everyone could swing into the water. It is very shady under the great tall fig trees and everyone can swim in the very clear water. There are lots of lovely water plants as well.

A rather exciting development. Nic will now be working directly this year [1984] for Sluis, the bean company, and they are taking over his machinery. That means he will no longer be having to deal with the diesel, etc. He will be working at Lolkisale, an area not far from Arusha, not as far as when he was planting beans at Lolera. There will be a small house that he can stay in, so I will be able to join him sometimes. I don't know how it will all work out and hope it won't be too exhausting.

In the midst of all this we have other exciting news. The borders are finally open again and we can go to Kenya. We are now waiting for the Sunday driving permit. For some time no driving was allowed between 2 p.m. on Sunday and Monday morning to save fuel.

"Last weekend was lovely. We left very early on Friday morning and had no problems with the border, though we had an hour's wait on the Kenyan side trying to get insurance for the car. Then we had our breakfast picnic and on to Nairobi. What a lot of memories that road has: seeing elephants at Namanga when I was about 8 years old, taking puppies with my parents to friends in Moshi, and places we fed Gregory when we were coming home from Nairobi after he had been born. We got to Nairobi and saw friends who were staying at the Norfolk Hotel where we had a magnificent lunch. What fun to have a meal in a hotel—and such a good one."

I didn't do much shopping, just essentials like bicycle tyres and margarine, sugar, and shoe cream. Then we left for Kibwezi where Nic's brother Costas was working, arriving in the early evening. What a lovely time we had! It is a beautiful place with lots of sisal growing among baobab trees, lots of bush with animals, and a great many lovely birds, too. There used to be 90 acres under irrigation and black net to keep cool the asparagus fern and chrysanthemum cuttings for export; that was lit by 6,000 light bulbs. Then the fashion changed and no one wanted ferns and the chrysanthemums got a disease. They found two rhinos in the sisal while we were there. Because they were afraid that they would be poached, they were moved. One rhino was not very fierce and you could feed it sugar cane. Imagine feeding sugar cane to a rhino!

When we got back Nic went back to Lolkisale. As he said, starting to work for someone else after 37 years of independent work was going to be quite different and difficult. I hope he doesn't get too exhausted with the driving. I'd hoped that we could get him a servant, and in fact we did.

"Nic came back rather more cheerful on Thursday. He's been given the Sluis Land Rover to use, and he won't live in the little house in Lolkisale unless they do something about it. It would get very cold with no fireplace. We managed to paint the house and improve it. There was a refrigerator. I tried to plant a few things that never did very well. But there was a birdbath and every day birds came there at mid-day—yesterday there were 12 cordon bleus and little red cardinals fighting over who got the next bath."

In November we had an expedition with the Mountain Club to Lake Chala, the crater lake not far from Moshi, half in Kenya and half in Tanzania. Lots of ISM school children were there. It is a very steep walk down to the lake, a very deep lake. People wanted to swim, and Nic said, "Well, do be careful of the crocodiles." You could see people looking at one another and shaking their heads at this silly old man. We all swam and we had a picnic lunch. Then friends arrived and started to fish, and after a while Arne said, "Oh, I saw a crocodile there!" The moment that was said, you could see how fast people rushed out of the water. We did swim a little more, but very close by. Everything was very green and pretty and they are now talking about building a hotel there.

Return to Coffee

In about 1995, the government concluded that the majority of the coffee estates on Kilimanjaro were being badly run. There was no profit, and they wanted investors to come in on a shareholding basis. Nic thought about it, but feared that if you put money in, then when everything was going well, they can turn around and say, "Right, bye bye." He said "No." He leased. He was actually the first person to do it. (We probably paid more than we should have.) It was not the whole estate, only the part that had been given to the nearest cooperative society and they kept a bit of land for themselves. It was nearly 400 acres. They have since taken other bits of it off for this and that. It's now about 370 acres.

It's just not easy. All of the Kilimanjaro estates had their water supply allocated by the Germans. After the Germans had their farms expropriated, the British accepted the German distribution, so whoever had the estate had the water. Now the African population is increasing and everybody wants water for their own use and for irrigating bananas and coffee and it's more and more difficult to get. We built a large earthen dam and that is enough to support the farm for two weeks. It is 21 miles for water to come to our farms through Chagga land. Coffee prices went up and down and everything costs more. Several big companies have come in, invested in some, and put several of the other old estates together. They say that you really don't make money. Nic doesn't believe this.

On the mountain, so many of the Chaggas keep taking out their coffee trees because they reckon you don't make money. On the terms of the lease, we're meant to be planting a certain amount of coffee. It was supposed to be increasing every year. Initially, you paid more for the coffee land than for the arable land. So it suited them to have more coffee. The arable land is where you're growing maize, cash crops. Year to year. Coffee is a permanent crop.

Visiting Pangani

Pangani was a historic trading center on the Tanganyika coast, especially known for the slave trade, with sugar and coconut plantations nearby. Remnants of lovely old Arab buildings were in abundance, as well as German and British colonial sites. There was even a cinema in this little village. It is an interesting place.

My parents first went to Pangani in 1932. My mother wrote, "Donald made a campfire with dried palm fronds and there was a bright moon. Pangani was such a charming place,

I wish we were to live there. Such a wonderful shore fringed with huge palms backed by avenues of tall feathery casuarina trees and such delightful Arab houses." My father really didn't care for the coast, preferring mountain streams and lakes for holidays. My mother took us on the 25-mile drive from Muheza to Pangani, where we slept on camp beds under mosquito nets hung from the trees. Later, my mother would go with my sister and stay.

When the West Kilimanjaro farmers were bought out in 1974 by the British government, most of the British people left. Some Pangani houses were owned by them. The International School bought a house for teachers and for school trips. Next to it we took over another little house once owned by one of the British who left. Built in the 1950s, it was very basic. The nice thing is it's so simple so if people break in, there's really nothing to steal. Except for one time when we had a couple of young chaps working there, very good Christians, Assembly of God, who wouldn't wash our glasses if we had been drinking beer, but felt it was perfectly acceptable to steal the boat engine.

Before we had beds, we had mattresses on the floor and of course mosquito nets. Once there was a terrible smell and we looked and looked and finally under the mattresses we found a dead rat; obviously Bushka, the cat, had chased it under there and it died. That was the year of the rats, and in general, rats were everywhere.

That year I managed to get margarine and cooking oil—great excitement! Sometimes we would find things like that in Pangani. Much later, I was looking through bits of material and I saw a silk sari that dear Mr. Raja's wife was selling. I took it home and made my dress for Sophia's wedding. The other bits I framed and my Indian friend said this is Kashmiri silk. You mustn't wash it. It must be dry-cleaned; it was quite beautiful. I paid the equivalent of £5 for it.

We eventually had beds, a dining room table, and chairs. I put up some Greek posters. We have a little two-burner gas stove and added a charcoal grill outside. It's not actually on a great big sandy beach, which is nice in some ways. Our house is up on the cliff and you go down steep steps to the bay with mangrove trees. If you do it right you can swim across the little bay and then swim right through the mangroves. You can see kingfishers and occasionally look up and see monkeys. When we first went there, walking on that headland we'd see bushbuck and quite a few wild pigs. Then the wretched pythons killed several of the dogs kept by various people working for us. Along the way, a Swahili Arab person found out the way to catch a python. You kill a goat, or if you don't kill it you tied it up, and when the python comes and eats the goat, it gets caught by the horns coming up through, and you can get your python!

In September 1983, we had a lovely expedition to Pangani. Hiring a big boat and using our little engine, we went up the Pangani River. It was a magical day, as if we were in quite a different country. After the mangroves, there were coconut and betel nut palms and huge clumps of red and white striped pyjama lilies. We went up to the house of a relation of Ali Choba whom we knew from Pangani. He had unfortunately gone down to Pangani, but his lovely young fourth wife was there and prepared delicious food for us. We had not expected food and we had already had a picnic. There were puppies outside and chickens and the funniest thing was watching the chickens pick ticks off the puppies.

We sometimes had Christmas at Pangani. In 1983, Sophia and Rena said that we were going to have our Christmas dinner in Machame before we went down, and insisted that they would open their presents in Machame. We decorated a sisal tree and had a

Nic with Timoteo (left) and Abdallah (right) fishing at Pangani.

lovely time. We arrived in Pangani on Christmas Eve and had friends for a marvelous dinner of grilled barracuda and kingfish. Christmas morning Sophia, Rena and I went to the Catholic Church at 10 a.m. It was a very long sermon, finally over at 12:45 p.m. But it was a pretty church and a very reverent service after we moved (I was sitting next to someone who had had rather a lot to drink the night before).

We had a burglary in the house in Pangani. Among the things stolen were the little engine that we were able to recover in time, all our saucepans, kettles, teapot, gas lamp and Dietz lamp. But we had a lovely time swimming and fishing.

Nic got a windsurfer when they first came out, a big heavy one. Then there was a dinghy, and later a bigger boat. In 1988 when Sophia and Thanasi came out at the start of their marriage, somebody woke up one morning—no boat in the bay. It had been stolen! Luckily it had actually not been taken very far; it was found and it wasn't badly damaged. The thieves had taken away the big engine that we got back after a few days' search and they hadn't noticed a small spare engine inside. The boat theft meant we had to put a watchman on the boat, depending on the tides when you can take them in and out.

Nic and the Thief

A thief had stolen two chairs off the front veranda. Nic was going to go back to the beans and he left me with his revolver. One night I heard a noise. I looked out and could see this thief walking across the front lawn carrying a chair! I got the revolver but I couldn't remember how to fire it! When Nic came back he said I was too frightened to use it, but I was just too confused.

Nic heard Freya our dog barking on a Sunday night at 2:20 a.m. So Nic rushed out with his shotgun and there, near the fence by the back gate, was someone creeping along, so Nic shot him in the leg. The next day Robert, our gardener, was asked to make inquiries. Sure enough, a well-known thief was reported to have gone to hospital. He said the police had shot him. Now the police are going to make a case against him for libel. They say if it had been a police rifle his leg would have been broken and this was birdshot. The locals say Nic shouldn't have shown so much mercy and should have killed him, as it would have been good riddance.

The next bit of the story was that Joachim, Philippi's son, saw two of our stolen chairs at a little shop and he told Philippi. So Nic went up to the CCM office—that's the local party office—and he and the local party official were given a search warrant. Unfortunately the woman who had the shop had obviously got suspicious as they only found one chair and she said it was hers. Nic said it was his, so they went to the local court the next morning. Nic had managed to get his mark on the stolen chair because the woman had gone in to get dressed up and while she was doing that Nic had put an N on the stolen chair and the one he'd brought from the veranda at home to show they were the same. The court agreed the chair was Nic's as he turned it upside down and said, "Look." The court fined the woman four hundred shillings for the two stolen chairs that we didn't get back, and a hundred shillings for telling a lie. Nic was praised for not asking for too much compensation and for agreeing to have the case tried at the little local court. So I don't think we'll be so bothered with that thief anymore!

Nic and the Lutheran Church at Machame

The Lutheran church nearby wanted to build a new church and they came and asked Nic for donations. He said, "Well, I'll pay for the roof when you've done all the walls." We paid a lot of money for the roof.

On a Sunday in December 1994, we were invited to the Hosiana Church for the service there, although the church was not finished. It started at 10 a.m. and finished at 2 p.m. There were baptisms, three weddings, and 140 confirmed. The priest congratulated the congregation on the way they all came so promptly to church but said of course, with the old building, it was so they could get a seat inside. He hoped they would continue the practice in the new church. Then there were thanks to all who helped in the building. They came to us and thanked Nic. When the priest came to me I said he should thank God as he caused Nic to do it, and he announced that to everyone. Then they called Nic up and he was presented with a magnificent walking stick—he pretended to hobble as he came down from the altar. [To give a cane is an expression of gratitude and honor.]

Then they called me, to my surprise, and gave me some lovely cloth that the deaconesses opened up and draped around me. It was very touching.

Just after that the rain came down and minister Swai said how thankful they were that the new church had its roof. There were lots of collections; everyone filed past, giving not only money but also chickens and sugar cane. We were invited to lunch and it finished with a goat on the spit. It was very well cooked as Robert our gardener had done it! He was used to cooking our lamb on the spit at Easter.

Nic knew a lot of the women because they used to come to pick coffee. When he came back into the shamba, one of the headmen had been there for years after we leased the land back. When he died, he was buried in the shamba. Nic spoke at the funeral and said, "There were two grandfathers here. Now I am the only one left because Robert has died." Afterwards one of the local people came up to Nic and said, "You know we're different on top but inside we're all the same."

So we've stayed and stayed and stayed. I don't know how long it will all go on. It's an uncertainty, but thank you God that we've been here so long and had what we've had.

Peggy's Final Years

Some years after my father died, my mother reflected on how she wished my father had praised her work. After he died, she had the chance to return to Africa and do important work on her own without being dependent on my father. She was able to do work that was recognized for its own value.

In 1981, after a great doctor friend here died, I wrote to my mother and she replied, "Darling, you were not lacking in sympathy and love for me when your father died. My main sorrow was the grief in knowing that I had failed in understanding the kind of mental stress and problems he was suffering when he died and I couldn't help him. But these problems are best put behind us, as I wish he could see the lovely family and children and marriage that you have."

She also wrote, "I went to a tropical medicine meeting where Ian McGregor and Leonard Brucequat told me rather excitedly that my work on malaria and placentas had brought something to light, something quite new in the immunological world. I'm very excited and I'm to be fully informed shortly. Except for my donkeywork, it took Ian and Leonard to see the wood for the trees, and to see a new immunological cycle. "There is a new antimalarial that has been around for 1,000 years that is connected with wormwood."

When I visited my mother in 1983, she was having breakfast in bed and reading John Morris's autobiography, Hired to Kill *(1960). She said, "Now I know why he wouldn't marry me!" John Morris was an English adventurer, British soldier, and mountaineer who was in the Everest expedition in 1953, and head of the BBC's Far East Service in the 1950s. My mother met him in Nepal and became friendly with him. He came to visit her and my father in Tanga in 1933. They took him to Amani and Tanga, and they had a wonderful four days full of lively conversation. In his autobiography he revealed that he was a homosexual.*

Letters to My Mother, 1985

April 1985: I went to church on Good Friday. I did the flowers on Saturday and Rena came with me on Easter Sunday. Much of the sermon was a repeat of Good Friday. I listened to Trevor Huddleston on BBC yesterday and some of the reflections were that

Jesus came to give his life more abundantly and not only in the most spiritual way. He managed to say more on his five-minute talks than our priest in Moshi.

I had just left my mother and I wrote, "It was horrible leaving you as the time goes by so quickly. As we never say it, we always think that it might be the last time we meet on this earth. It must be so horrible to have no belief in life after death so that partings are so final. Anyway God bless you and look after you until I come back next year, and since this is April already, next January is not so long."

In December 1985, Gregory rang up to say that my mother had had a stroke. She had put the cheese biscuits on the dining room table and poured herself a drink but obviously felt peculiar and managed to sit down. That is where Mrs. Hucker found her the next morning. Mummy wasn't cold as she spent Sunday night in the dining room; although there was no fire, the central heating had been on.

On Wednesday she had times when she was completely conscious. She once asked, "Gregory, when will I talk to him?" Angela and Mrs. Hucker stayed with her the whole time, talking to her continuously and reading to her, and didn't let her slip away. She had no pain, only brief difficulty breathing the day before. Mummy died on Thursday at 4 a.m. She died most peacefully.

Before I knew of her death, Nic was driving me up to Nairobi to fly to England. We were listening to the Faure Requiem, *that lovely piece of music, and I had a great feeling of peace. Later, when I was in England, I was telling my sister Angela about that peace. It turned out that at that particular time, the priest was there with Mummy, praying, and she was basically unconscious.*

I flew to England but she had died just before I got there. I phoned from the airport and heard the news. The British Airways people were so kind and collected my baggage when they saw how upset I was. Angela collected me from the coach. Mummy looked just asleep as I expected her to.

I wrote to Sophia, Rena, and Nic. "There was so much to do, phoning many people who would expect to attend the funeral on Monday. The hymns will be "Jesus Lives," the Easter one, "Oh Love that will not let me go," that Mummy had at Daddy's funeral, and "Hark the Herald Angels Sing." It is rather suitable when you read the words and it is Christmas. Angela said that Mummy used to sing it all the time and nearly drove Daddy batty because he said she rarely sang on key. Then there was the cremation. I had taken some lilies and azaleas from here that were originally from my mother's garden at Amani. My mother, Margaret Wilson, died December 19, 1985, at the age of 88, at home in Spa House.

Angela was three years younger than me and we were very different. We saw very little of each other as we were growing up. She went to boarding school when she was five and we didn't go to the same secondary school, and when she was twelve years old, I was at school in England. But she was such a huge support to our mother after Mummy retired. Most of her children's school holidays were spent at Spa house.

Angela died far too young, in February 1994, when she was only 55 years old.

Sylvie's Garden, 2019

We are still in our house at Machame, on a slope of Mount Kilimanjaro. From the veranda we watch the mountain go pink in the sunset. The mountain has changed much over the years, as have we. Yet even as the glaciers melt, sometimes the mountain is covered in snow. If it is covered in clouds for several days, I feel uneasy, as though something is missing.

The trees and shrubs and flowers that surround the house reflect our history here. The Germans planted quite a few lovely trees, the Nandi flame trees, a huge eucalyptus, a frangipani. The birds and monkeys enjoy fruit of the enormous wild fig. Growing up this very old fig tree is the huge pepper vine that keeps us and friends in pepper. I brought it from our neighbour's house, Jock Taylor, when he died and his wife moved away. An ancient mringa tree flowers in July and the petals come down like snowflakes.

Sylvie at home in Machame.

My mother gave Nic the araucaria tree from her garden in Amani. It is now so tall that it dominates the garden. A bougainvillea named Lady Wilson is also from my mother's garden; it is a lovely rust color that I've never seen anywhere else. The white azaleas and a lovely purple allamanda were also gifts from Amani.

Soon after I was married, I thought it would be quite fun to have a little pond. My mother said you must be sure that the water flows in and out or you'll have a wonderful breeding ground for mosquitoes. Luckily, the main irrigation pipe was exactly where I wanted my pond, so with a small hole in it we could have a fountain. When Gregory was four he helped Robert, our gardener, build a little mud house near the pond. A large mango tree nearby provides plenty of shade for all the heliconias and gingers, balsams and begonias and ferns.

A few years ago one of our grandsons who was five went to Kew Gardens during the Festival of Tropical Plants. "Oh," he said. "This is just like Gran's garden!"

Some plants recall family holidays or expeditions. I collected wild gladioli that grew in the sisal. At Lake Duluti we picked up big oval seeds from the Oncoba Routledgei that I brought home and sprayed gold for the Christmas tree. One day our ayah Maria said, "Oh look, Mama, there's a little plant," and it's a big tree now. It has a flower like a white rose with yellow stamens, very pretty and lightly scented, but it only lasts a day. I have a feeding table for the bush babies in its branches where I give them bananas or avocados. I call them every evening at dusk and two or more come down from the high branches; some I can even stroke. They are wild and very shy of strangers, but they still come to see what is for supper.

Once when we were at Mombasa near the ferry there were Cassia fistula trees with yellow flowers. Again it was Maria who said, "Oh Mama, look, there are some seeds." We planted it, Indian laburnum, and it flowers in January or February, In the right year it's a mass of gold—if you're inside the house, it's almost like a great light glowing. There were one or two tangerine trees and now there are more because the children and I used to walk in the garden, spitting out tangerine pips and they grew up.

Before nationalization I started growing strawberries to sell—I even bought little boxes. We used to have so many that the children would say "Oh, not strawberries again!" But when we were nationalized they took that bit of land. Then later, we leased that land back and I made it into a rose garden; in those days you could order roses from Nairobi. A few roses came from friends at Rasha Rasha where my mother would be summoned when someone was ill or injured. We also had floribunda and China roses from friends. But finally all the tree roots came in and I gave up on a rose garden. But there is a lovely Mussaenda that people think is a poinsettia. And growing on the trees there are several indigenous orchids that I found near Pangani; they are sweetly scented at night. There is also an orchid from Thailand given by our Baptist friends in Moshi who were so kind when we were nationalized. The leaves gave good ground cover and after thirty years we finally had some flowers! There is also a vanilla orchid with pretty flowers but unfortunately it is not the spice variety.

Near the frangipani the cats' graves are carefully looked after. Most of the dogs were buried among the banana plants. The huge bougainvillea near there used to be a home for white tailed mongooses that we occasionally saw at night. On occasion we would see a duiker.

There are many other flowers in the big herbaceous border. We were fortunate that Robert worked in the garden for many years. Now I consult with Philipi over so much to do with the garden, though I think he enjoys the vegetable garden more than the flowers.

We now have strawberries again. Like my mother, I have a big patch of wineberries. We enjoy the wineberries during the cool weather—they grow wild higher up on the mountain. The grandchildren love them and they make a lovely sorbet and nice jam.

In the vegetable garden we grow lettuces, leeks, carrots, beet root (some exciting varieties from America), tomatoes, sometimes successful and sometimes not, as diseases, insects, and birds hamper tomatoes. We have a lot of lima beans. We grow herbs: thyme, rosemary, marjoram, tarragon, basil, and my big bay tree is very popular with Danish friends. Near there is the avocado tree that is not so good and several that are better. We fight with all the various insects and diseases, let alone monkeys and squirrels! How does the monkey know that at 2 p.m. there will be no one in the vegetable garden so he can help himself to maize or pawpaws or avocados? And the lovely passion fruit—the monkeys take some and the squirrels take some. Great rats come for the pumpkins.

One year we had a lovely long visit with our children and grandchildren. We took them camping for the first time at Mkomazi National Park, then spent two nights at Tarangire National Park, though they were disappointed not to see any lions. They spent a few days swimming at Pangani, and Nic took them fishing for barracuda. The children loved the picnics in the garden here at Machame, the tractors, and eating lots of bananas and passion fruit. Nic gave a lovely speech about his history and family, and I must say, we were all astounded to hear him speak so openly about all we had been through and how we had been sustained and loved.

My mother was happy to retire to England after her many years in Africa but we should hate to leave here. Our grandson said miserably before he left, "It's not just you and Papou. You'll come to Greece to see us. This is Africa!"

Bibliography

Behar, Ruth, and Deborah Gordon, eds. 1995. *Women Writing Culture.* Berkeley: University of California Press.

Brittain, Vera. 1978. *Testament of Youth.* New York, London: Penguin (First Published 1933).

Campbell, G. 1852. *Modern India: A Sketch of the System of Civil Government: To Which Is Prefixed, Some Account of the Natives and Native Institutions.* London (cited in Miele 2017).

Crozier, Anna. 2007. *Practicing Colonial Medicine. The Colonial Medical Service in British East Africa.* London, New York: I.B. Tauris.

Dale, Ivan, and P.J. Greenway. 1961. *Kenya Trees and Shrubs.* Nairobi: Buchanan's Kenya Estate Ltd.

Dias, Clarence. 1970. "Tanzanian Nationalizations: 1967–1970." *Cornell International Law Journal* 4 (1, Article 4): 59–79.

Dobson, M.J., M. Malowany and R.W. Snow, 2000. "Malaria Control in East Africa: The Kampala Conference and the Pare-Taveta Scheme: A Meeting of Common and High Ground." *Parasitologia* 42: 149–66" (cited in Packard 2007, 288).

Fanon, Frantz. 1963. *The Wretched of the Earth.* New York: Grove Press.

_____. 1967. *A Dying Colonialism.* New York: Grove Press.

Feierman, Steven. 1974. *The Shambaa Kingdom: A History.* Madison: University of Wisconsin Press.

_____. 1985. "Struggles for Control: The Social Roots of Health and Healing in Modern Africa." *African Studies Review* 28 (2/3): 73–147.

Ford, John. 1971. *The Role of Trypanosomiases in African Ecology: A Study of the Tsetse Fly Problem.* Oxford: Clarendon Press.

Frankopan, Peter. 2015. *The Silk Roads: A New History of the World.* New York: Vintage.

Geissler, Paul Wenzel, and Ann Kelly. 2016. "Field Station as Stage: Re-enacting Scientific Work and Life in Amani, Tanzania." *Social Studies of Science* 46 (6): 912–937.

_____. 2017. "Ethnography as Re enactment: Performing Temporality in an East African Place of Science." *Senri Ethnological Reports* 143: 187–210.

Ghyselen, Astrid, Paul Wenzel Geissler, Johan Lague and Peter E. Mangesho. 2017. "Scenes of Amani, Tanzania: Biography of a Postcolonial Landscape." *Journal of Landscape architecture* 12 (1): 6–17.

Grayzel, Susan R. 2002. *Women in the First World War.* Great Britain: Pearson education, Ltd.

Hartwig, Charlotte. 1972. "Music in Kerebe Culture." *Anthropos* 67: 449–64.

Hartwig, Gerald W. 1969. "The Historical and Social Role of Kerebe Music." *Tanzania Notes and Records* 70: 41–56.

Ibhawoh, Bonny, and Jeremiah I. Dibua. 2003. "Deconstructing Ujamaa: The Legacy of Julius Nyerere in the Quest for Social and Economic Development in Africa." *African Journal of Political Science* 8 (1): 59–83.

Iliffe, John. 1979. *A Modern History of Tanganyika.* Cambridge: Cambridge University Press.

Lee, Jennifer. 2002. *Call the Midwife: A True Story of the East End in the 1950s.* UK: Merton.

Lee-Warner, W. 1910. *The Native States of India.* London (cited in Miele 2017).

Malowany, Maureen. 2000. "Unfinished Agendas: Writing the History of Medicine in Africa." *African Affairs* 99: 342.

Marks, Shula. 1997. "What Is Colonial about Colonial Medicine? And What Has Happened to Imperialism and Health?" *The Social History of Medicine* 10 (2): 205–219.

McGregor, Ian A., David S. Rowe, Margaret E. Wilson, W.Z. Billewicz. 1970. "Plasma Globulin Concentrations in an African (Gambian) Community in Relation to Season, Malaria, and Other Infections and Pregnancy." *Clinical Experimental Immunol*ogy 7(1): 51–74.

McGregor, Ian A., M.E. Wilson and W.Z. Billewicz. 1983. "Malaria Infection of the Placenta in the Gambia, West Africa: Its Incidence and Relationship to Stillbirth, Birthweight and Placenta Weight." *Transactions of the Royal Society of Tropical Medicine and Hygiene* 77 (2): 232–44.

McLeod, Roy, and Milton Lewis, eds. 1989. *Disease, Medicine and Empire.* UK: Routledge.

Miele, Matteo. 2017. "British Diplomatic Views on Nepal and the Final State of the Ch'ing empire (1919–1911)." *Prague Papers on the History of International Relations* 1.

Milne, A.A. 1924. *When We Were Very Young.* London: Methuen.

Moffett, J.P., ed. 1958. *Handbook of Tanganyika.* Dar es Salaam, Government of Tanganyika.

Nyerere, Julius K. 1967. *Socialism and Rural Development.* Dar es Salaam, Tanzania Government Printers.

Packard, Randall M. 2007. *The Making of a Tropical Disease: A Short History of Malaria.* Baltimore: Johns Hopkins University Press.

Parker, John. 2005. *The Gurkhas: The Inside Story of the World's Most Feared Soldiers.* London: Headline Book Publishing.

Pedersen, Rasmus Hundsbæk, Thabit Jacob, Faustin Maganga and Opportuna Kweka. 2016. "Rights to Land and Extractive Resources in Tanzania (1/2): The History." *DIIS Working Paper* 2016 (11). Copenhagen: Danish Institute for International Studies.

Said, Edward. 1978. *Orientalism.* New York: Pantheon.

Scott, James. 1998. *Seeing Like a State.* New Haven, CT: Yale University Press.

Smith, Bonnie. 1989. *Changing Lives: Women in European History Since 1700.* Lexington, MA: D.C. Heath.

Solomon, Barbara Miller. 1985. *In the Company of Educated Women.* New Haven, CT: Yale University Press.

Somerville, John. 1924. *Isaac and Rachel Wilson, Quakers, of Kendal, 1714–85.* London: Swarthmore Press, Ltd.

Tilley, Helen. 2011. *Africa as a Living Laboratory.* Chicago: University of Chicago Press.

Tucker, Shelby. 2010. *The Last Banana: Dancing with the Watu.* London: Stacey International.

Turshen, Meredith. 1984. *The Political Ecology of Disease in Tanzania.* New Brunswick, NJ: Rutgers University Press.

Tusher, Pauline. 2005. *My Journey In and Out of Africa.* Incline, Nev.: Stillwater Cove Press.

Vaughan, Megan. 1991. *Curing Their Ills: Colonial Power and African Illness.* Stanford, CA: Stanford University Press.

Wilson, D. Bagster. 1936. "Rural Hyper-endemic Malaria in Tanganyika Territory." *Transactions of the Royal Society of Tropical Medicine and Hygiene.*

Wilson, D. Bagster, and Margaret E. Wilson. 1939–40. "Control of A. gambiae on Coffee Estates." *East African Medical Journal* 16 (11): 405–415.

_____, and _____. 1962. "Rural hyperendemic malaria in Tanganyika territory: Part II." *Transactions of The Royal Society of Tropical Medicine and Hygiene* 56 (4): 287–293.

Wilson, R.J., Ian A. McGregor and Margaret E. Wilson. 1973. "The Stability and Fractionation of Malarial Antigens from the Blood of Africans Infected with Plasmodium Falciparum." *International Journal of Parasitology* 3(4): 11–20.

Wolf, Eric. 1982. *Europe and the People Without History.* Berkeley: University of California Press.

Index

Numbers in ***bold italics*** indicate pages with illustrations